W9-BMJ-324

BY MARZIEH GAIL

Avignon in Flower

Persia and the Victorians

The Sheltering Branch

BX 1301
G25

THE
THREE
POPES

AN ACCOUNT OF THE GREAT SCHISM—
WHEN RIVAL POPES
IN ROME, AVIGNON AND PISA
VIED FOR THE RULE OF CHRISTENDOM

BY

MARZIEH GAIL

SIMON AND SCHUSTER
NEW YORK

JUL 20 1970

152583

*All rights reserved
including the right of reproduction
in whole or in part in any form*
Copyright © 1969 by Marzieh Gail
Published by Simon and Schuster
Rockefeller Center, 630 Fifth Avenue
New York, New York 10020

First printing

SBN 671-20174-3
Library of Congress Catalog Card Number: 79-75861
Designed by Edith Fowler
Manufactured in the United States of America
Printed by Mahony & Roese, New York

For Harold, again

CONTENTS

ILLUSTRATIONS

POPES AT AVIGNON PRIOR TO
THE GREAT SCHISM OF THE WEST

POPE	REIGN	
CLEMENT V	1305–1314	*Moved Papal Court to Avignon, 1309*

Vacancy of the Holy See

POPE	REIGN	
JOHN XXII	1316–1334	
BENEDICT XII	1334–1342	
CLEMENT VI	1342–1352	
INNOCENT VI	1352–1362	
URBAN V	1362–1370	
GREGORY XI	1370–1378	*Died in Rome March 27, 1378*

(The above period is described by the author in Avignon in Flower.)

POPES DURING
THE GREAT SCHISM OF THE WEST

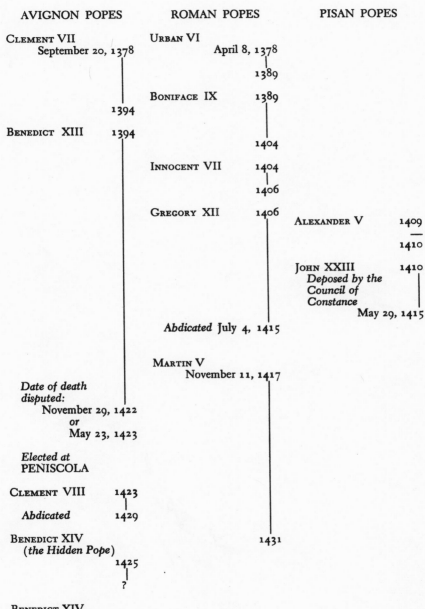

AVIGNON POPES   ROMAN POPES   PISAN POPES

CLEMENT VII   URBAN VI
  September 20, 1378   April 8, 1378

             1389

        BONIFACE IX 1389

      1394

BENEDICT XIII 1394

             1404

        INNOCENT VII 1404

             1406

        GREGORY XII 1406

                ALEXANDER V 1409

                       1410

                JOHN XXIII   1410
                Deposed by the
                Council of
                Constance
                  May 29, 1415

      Abdicated July 4, 1415

        MARTIN V
        November 11, 1417

*Date of death
disputed:*
  November 29, 1422
    or
  May 23, 1423

Elected at
PENISCOLA

CLEMENT VIII 1423

Abdicated 1429

BENEDICT XIV   1431
(*the Hidden Pope*)
    1425

    ?

BENEDICT XIV
 (*the Second*)
 *Died in prison
 without successor.*

PROLOGUE

THE WAY BACK

THE POPES were Frenchmen all, rooted to home. Seven long decades before—hardly anyone could remember the details now—they had exchanged the Tiber for the Rhône.

Dimly, people knew that Clement V had taken the Papacy away from Rome and had himself crowned in the Church of Saint-Just at Lyons. This was long gone, in 1305, and men said Clement had sold his tiara to France's King Philip the Fair. Four years after his crowning, Clement had wandered to Avignon, a town unwalled, forlorn, just across from French territory, on the left bank of the river. In those days the place did not belong to the Holy See. It was distinct from the ancient region called the Comtat Venaissin which lay about it, and had come to the Popes in 1274.

Thereafter Clement's successors raised up the splendid Palace of the Popes, to prove that Avignon, not Rome, would be the center of the Western world. They built themselves the "loveliest and vastest house on earth." Then—memories served better here—young Prince Andrew was murdered down by Naples, and many thought it was the work of Joanna, his wife, the heiress to this place. No proven murderer was ever found, however, and Pope Clement VI, sitting in this very House, had said she was innocent. And directly after that Joanna's city of Avignon had a new owner, Pope Clement. He may or may not have paid the Queen a trifling sum.

So it was that Frenchmen sat on the papal throne, enriched the city with lapping Christian gold, chose most of their Cardinals from among their kinsmen, or at least among their race—and let the Vatican and the Lateran crumble away.

Yet Christ, said the scholars, quoting Thomas Aquinas, had "ordained that the Head of His Church should be in Rome itself, the capital of the world . . ." This twinning of the Catholic Church and Rome derived in part from the "Donation of Constantine"—a forgery dating probably from the late eighth century and which would not be exposed till the fifteenth—according to which a grateful Constantine, cured of leprosy and baptized, had given Italy and the Western Provinces to the Pope of Rome. Included in the hoary fabrication was the Roman Pontiff's spiritual supremacy over all the other patriarchs. Although the Gospels do not report that Jesus ever mentioned Italy or Rome, and Acts 23:11 refers to a time after the Crucifixion, this tradition was to continue down the centuries. In modern times Pius XII would speak of Italy as the "heart" of the Church, telling a vast audience: "Italy, designed and willed by God to be a land in which the center of His Church has its seat, was the object of . . . His special love."

Even so, the years flowed by, as the river flowed under Bénézet's bridge—the one the angel made him build, when people·said the Rhône at this point could not be spanned. And the French Popes did not return. From their aerial palace gardens they gazed down over plains and rounded hills, silver and green with olive trees. They watched the January snows on Mount Ventoux, and the planted fields walled with black cypresses and yellow cane against the wind. They could not leave. Their delights were all summed up in the wine of Beaune, which did not travel well. Petrarch says that the Cardinals, urged Romeward, would answer: "But Beaune is not there."

In 1367 Urban V actually went back. When he said goodbye to southern France, a number of his Cardinals, who had dreaded the whole thing—the voyage, the turbu- lent Romans, the climate of Italy, the sirocco instead of the mistral—turned too sick to leave. Others of them, on that May 19, as the anchors were raised, gave out with hideous cries, hurling insults at the Pontiff: "Evil Pope . . . impious Father, where are you taking your children?" They wailed, wrote Petrarch, as if they were being carried off by the Saracens in chains.

Cautiously preceded by two thousand men-at-arms, Urban entered Rome in October, and found ruins. The Lateran Palace was full of bats and owls, and its walls flowering. France exerted a mighty pull. After three anxious years, Avignon drew him home again.

In 1370, delicate French Pope Gregory XI sat on the throne. Mostly, the world beyond France did not want him at Avignon. That world was still a feudal jigsaw, unlikely bits and pieces, the heaped remains of royal weddings, conquests, fiefs granted for forgotten reasons, confusing legacies. England, for instance, had a huge fief in southern France, and the King of Naples was also Count of Provence. There was a potpourri of rulers: king- and queenlets, Dukes, Prince-Bishops, Margraves, knightly Orders—and a variety of states: Papal States, city-states, appanages, duchies, principalities, countries like England and France. Then there was a confederated hodgepodge of rulers in Germany (which area looked eastward now, rather than south or west); and over Germany stood the Holy Roman Emperor. The Emperors and the Popes had been partners once, each with a say in the other's election, but they had turned enemies and seesawed back and forth for generations. Whereas Charlemagne had been the first Emperor of the West, crowned by the Pope in 800, in 1452 Frederick III would be the last; that is, in less than a century from now, the old Holy Roman Empire would in effect come to an end.

Gregory's view of the power structure was the same as that expressed by Pope Boniface VIII in his Bull *Unam sanctam* (1302): quite simply, the Pope was top man. "We are taught by the Gospels that there are two swords," Boniface had written, "the one to be wielded by the Church, the other for the Church; the one by priests, the other by kings and soldiers, but by the will and permission of the priest. . . . But the one sword must be under the other." Then in 1356 the Emperor, second sword Charles IV (the one still there during Gregory's reign) countered with his own "Golden Bull," which declared he was to be elected by seven princes, only three of them ecclesiastical, and he said nothing about the Pope's confirming it.

To Gregory, such notions of a layman's sovereignty were merely one man's heresies, the man being Marsilius of Padua who, not long back (1324), in his *Defensor Pacis*, had declared that the lay power, the Emperor, was above the Pope. Marsilius reminded his readers that Jesus had acknowledged Pilate's power over Himself as "given . . . from above." It was only, said Marsilius, because the Roman Bishops were misled by the Devil that they had gone after "secular rule." Marsilius and his co-author had already been taken care of by Avignon—finished off with such papal epithets as "pestiferous wretches," "beasts from the abyss." To this day the Pope still calls himself "ruler of the world."

Gregory could hardly know that a wind of change was blowing; that individual, differentiated man was on the way; that the nation, the parliament and council, the national church, the "simple layman armed with Scripture" would soon enough be placing themselves higher than Rome. Meanwhile, he must go back there, to the chief seat

of his power. More than most, he had his own conscience
to reckon with, besides all the outside pressure to make him
stay or make him go. Scholars, orators, envoys, had long
been presenting their arguments, pro and con. France, her
rivals thought, was getting too strong—she should not be
allowed to keep the Papacy too. The gold-hungry Italians
wanted him back, although the city-states dreaded his en-
croachments and his Legates' misrule. The Republic of
Florence made war against him and invaded his Papal
States, and some eighty cities and towns leagued themselves
with Florence. His own Cardinals were fastened here in
Avignon, clinging to the Rock of the Lords. To put it
scripturally, the carcass was here, and here the eagles
gathered. Not that his Curia was united otherwise. One
bloc was the Limousins, such princes of the Church as
came from the southwest region, around Limoges; a powerful grouping who had elected three out of the last four
Avignon Popes. Against these was another pro-French
bloc, and there were four Italians. Then there were all the
women relatives, noble "Ladies of the Pope's Household,"
their opinions and doings no less important for being unre-
corded. In the end it was a woman who uprooted them all.

Her name was Catherine, and unlike the ladies about the
Curia, she was lowborn, of no rank, only the still-young
daughter of a dyer of Siena. But she had a magic which was
not of this world, and with it she addressed as intimates and
subordinates the Popes and Princes of her day. (Her letters
are still available, some four hundred of them, also her
prayers and a book of doctrine. She would be canonized
later on, in 1461, by a Renaissance Pope.) Chosen as their
ambassador to the Holy See by embattled Florence—the
Florentines still being at war with the Pontiff—Catherine
reached Avignon in 1376, and during her interviews at the
Palace goaded the timorous and ailing Gregory to give up
Avignon for Rome.

He left at what would prove a terrible hour, left though the brother of the King of France had knelt before him and begged him to stay.

"If you should die there, which is likely," Louis of Anjou cried, "the Romans will make themselves masters of the Cardinals' persons, and preventing the Papal Court from returning to Avignon, they will force them with daggers at their throats to elect a Pope perhaps fatal to the Church."

Then, that last day, as Gregory quitted his Palace on the Rock, the Pope's mother stood in his doorway, flung herself down on the floor, tore open her robe to bare the breasts that had nursed him and sobbed, "I shall never see you again!" And after that, at the Palace steps, his horse had fought against him and when at last he was on its back the animal refused to move from its place.

If the omen had prevailed, instead of Catherine's urgings, it would have altered the whole course of Western life. No need to repeat the Avignon story here; enough to say that for their own good, they should not have come, but having come, the Pontiffs should have stayed; that soon two rival Popes—and later three—would fight for the tiara, even in battle sometimes, each army with its flag showing the twin keys; that Luther, far from being a beginning, was instead a culmination—and that, in medieval language, the bark of Peter split in Avignon on the Rock of the Lords.

A diary which was kept of the return voyage, a long versified account, shows why, quite aside from reasons of piety and politics, the way back was unpopular with both Pope and Curia.

Leading off with the sobs of abandoned Avignon, the diarist, who was the somewhat gastronomical Bishop of Senigallia, dates his first entry from the departure on September 13, 1376. They spent the night at Orgon, "an inconvenient nesting place," he says, dry and rocky, along the

Durance River. If only the Pearl of Pontiffs, he cries, would
turn backward to the golden pinnacles of his palace by the
Rhône! On Wednesday they reached Aix, before sundown.
Here was beauty and a splendid mansion, streets strewn
with flowers and decked out with brilliant silken hangings.
A rich table was provided, set with the choicest wines and
foods. On Friday they crossed over wild mountains and ate
a sumptuous dinner at Trets, "for this little town abounds
in all sorts of victuals." Saturday they made for Auriol, pic-
turesque, fertile, but with smoke-blackened houses.

In Marseilles a huge crowd received them, with flaming
torches, "musics and symphonies" and pious chants, but the
press of people augmented the southern heat and Pope and
court were close to suffocation. Twelve days, Gregory remained at the noble Abbey of Saint-Victor, waiting for the
north wind. "O glorious and noble city," apostrophizes the
poet, "was it not enough for thee to have thy fame, the
splendor of thy edifices, the abundance of thy holy relics,
the lively beauty of thy men and women, and the unnumbered vessels that hasten to thy harbor from all the climates
of the world—that thou must also join thereto the signal
favor of possessing, twelve whole days, the Roman Pontiff
and his servants?"

French Pope Gregory left Marseilles in tears. He embarked on a splendid galley specially built for him and offered by the people of Ancona, while the rest of the court
set sail in thirty galleys supplied by other Italian seaports.
They all dined in Saint-Nazaire. Later a tempest blew up,
and they disembarked "on a deserted shore." Then they
had a good wind to Toulon; then a worse tempest opposite
Fréjus, when even the boatmen turned pale. The passengers
groaned aloud and made vows to Saint Cyriac, and somehow they reached Saint-Tropez, passed the Abbey of Saint-
Honorat and at night made Antibes. Thursday at nine they
went by Nice and, "with incredible transports of joy," en-

tered the harbor of Villefranche. "We fell avidly, like starvelings, first on the dinner, then on the supper, the one and the other copiously served up . . ."

Friday, in spite of a rough sea, they sailed on. They reached Monaco Point and had to turn back to Villefranche. For this, the author blames Saint Francis, "lover of poverty" and therefore inimical, envious of the Church's wealth. He takes occasion to remind Saint Francis that some years previously, the roof of the Great Chapel at the Avignon Palace "was reduced to ashes on your feast day," and now, more of the same, "on this day of your octave, you prevent the Papal Court from peaceful navigation. . . . See, then, the poop is shattered, the sails are torn, the cables break, the servants lift up the costly furniture and put it over the side in little boats . . . one hears no more but loud and harrowing cries."

Saint Francis hindered, but Saint Calixtus helped. The sea quietened, the sun shone, and they spent the night at Savona. The poet does not forget to chide the Mediterranean for its treatment of Pope Gregory: "O sea, why dost thou leap and bound with such great fury? Dost thou not know the power and mildness of the one thou bearest?"

Genoa was rich, dazzlingly luxurious, but dry and rocky. The inhabitants were proud. Pope and Cardinals spent twelve days here. (We learn elsewhere that they reached Genoa October 18, and that Gregory visited Saint Catherine of Siena in the night, she restoring his courage, and he obtaining her promise to pray for him every day.) On the twenty-ninth of October they left Genoa, and the following day visited the Monastery of Saint Jerome, Gregory climbing the steep paths on foot. The place was wild and beautiful. They gave rich presents to the monks, who certainly could use them. Stopping briefly at Porto Venere, they had a poor dinner, but excellent wine. That night they reached Leghorn. On the sixth of November they were at

Porto Pisano; here some envoys brought costly gifts; but

why, the author asks, had the people not defended the
Pope in his war against the Florentines?

On the sixteenth of November, before dawn, the party
left Piombino, and that evening had a good dinner at Port'
Ercole, contrary winds then blowing them to Elba. Here
the Pope walked in an olive wood and it was too arid a
place to pitch the tents. The sea had carried away the
Cardinal Lagier's treasures and furniture, but he himself, on
the shoulders of a rustic, rode safely ashore. The tempest
was frightful; several galleys were sucked down with their
treasure.

On the twenty-first of November Cardinal de La Jugie
died.

At last they got out of Portoferraio and came back to
Piombino. The people, says the author, were joyful to see
the Pope safe, "but this joy was barren, since they brought
us no presents. . . ."

The next day, harried by the sea, they made Orbetello.

*The Apostolic Subdeacon who was carrying the Cross in
front of the Pontiff almost got drowned. . . . What a
desolate beach! Alas! My poor companions, nourished up
to now in delights, here you must dine on pork flesh or, for
a treat, one of those unclean, deafening frogs. Since, however, we are bereft of fine wheat, of choice wine, and cream
off the milk, since we are eaten away by the tainted air, let
us feed our eyes and our minds on the presence of the
Pearl of Pontiffs that, even as manna from Heaven, the
Lord has sent down to us!*

"We left the sick at Orbetello," he adds, "and hastened
out of that accursed land, where we all would have per-
ished." On foot, leaning on his stick, torches before him,
Pope Gregory walked to his galley.

Corneto came. High towers, beautiful wide streets, a fertile plain. The population received them with transports: bells ringing, trumpets, cries of welcome. The "Gem of Pontiffs," deigning to overlook their past offenses, remained in their city five weeks, quitting it Tuesday, January 13. "I begin to believe," the diarist hopefully writes, "that the diviners, the haruspices, the astrologers, and the physicians gave out with lying prophecies when they foresaw a bitter end to our voyage; they read the constellations wrong . . ."

On a quiet sea, in the moonlight, they sailed all night with the north wind, and the next morning reached the mouth of the Tiber. After a good meal they entered Ostia, "a city encircled by handsome ramparts, but sad and deserted." The Romans had dispatched to meet them certain venerable, bald and decrepit envoys, with torches lit in welcome, who began clapping their hands, and to the din of trumpets danced stiffly in the streets.

Early Friday morning, the Pope had a trumpet sounded to awaken the fleet. Slowly, they rowed up the Tiber, all very depressed because the invalid Gregory was suffering, presumably from the stone. They came to the Basilica of Saint Paul, where a multitude crowded the shores, weeping and shouting. Magnificent horses in embroidered housings and silvery bells had been readied. "The Lords Banneret [so named for their banners, these were the district chiefs who ruled Rome] and the standard-bearers, blowing the horn, ran here and there like maniacs and stamped their feet." There was a prodigious number of torches. Everybody was shouting: "*Evviva il Santo Padre! Evviva nostro Signore Gregorio!*"

That night the Pope remained on board his galley. On Saturday, January 17, 1377, "in the Church of the Healer of Nations," he knelt down on a carpet of gold and heard two Masses, the second of which was said by none other than the Bishop of Senigallia. He then visited the Palace

of Saint Paul and after that came the formal procession:
there were "players, performing astonishing wonders"; an
infinite multitude of dancers, drunk with joy; a corps of
trumpeters; the army with flying banners; a *corps d'élite*,
the young nobility, advancing as one man. When the Pope
left the Palace of Saint Paul, "A thousand players, dressed
all in white, clapping their hands in rhythm, executed, as
they passed along, admirable dance figures, to the sound of
sweet music." The Church's flag flew, and at Rome's gates,
the Pope received the keys.

Music; bells; the great in their silks; everywhere dazzle
and beauty. Women crowding the rooftops to see better,
throwing down sugarplums and winter flowers. The ailing
Pope exhausted by his long ride on horseback.

"As for us," ends the diarist, "we were worn out, voice-
less, and perishing of hunger; for we had been shouting ourselves hoarse all day, singing the praises of the Lord. . . .
Therefore with what delight did we restore our debilitated
frames by means of a succulent supper, abundantly served!
Glory then to Jesus Christ and to His Holy Mother!"

The diarist of Senigallia knew more about the menus
than the motivations of the Curia. Why had Gregory spent
those five long weeks at Corneto? The truth was that, egged
on by rebellious Florence, the Romans were planning yet
another revolt. They could not help seeing the difference
between themselves and flourishing Florence; between
their shabby present and their glorious past. Perhaps
Florence, battling the Holy See, was right after all. And so
they kept the Pope waiting five weeks at their front door.

The day he entered Rome, Gregory may have had a
moment of hope: the Lords Banneret came before him and
spread out at his feet a flag of liberty, sent them by Florence
as a warning that if they received the Pontiff, they would
lose their freedom. But at once, these chiefs lifted up their

flag and took it back, as a symbol of their own authority, and he watched his dream of bringing stability and order fade away. Rome's pledge of peace was only words, the Italian cities would never submit.

There was, Gregory saw as the days went by, at least one man on whom he could lean. He had done well, in 1375, after Pedro de Luna had served him as counselor and confidant at Avignon for seven years, to make him Cardinal. Unlike the French who pined for home, unlike the Italians who now were at home and accordingly had subtly changed —this Aragonese stood firmly at his side.

De Luna now proceeded to acquire the Apollinaire Palace near the Torre Sanguinea, and had it restored. To show that he meant to stay, he even selected his burial place at Saint Lawrence Outside the Walls. He did not, of course, guess that it would be a long, long time before he would stretch out in his tomb, nor visualize the faraway place where they would lay him down: "neither knoweth any soul in what land it shall die."

Soon after Gregory's arrival there were riots in Cesena, brought on by acts of papal troops under Robert of Geneva. Robert first prevailed on the inhabitants to surrender their weapons, and pile them at his feet, after which his mercenaries streamed out of the citadel in a torrent and fell upon the unweaponed town. Mothers were cut down with children in their arms, babies' heads were splashed against stone walls, young girls and the youngest matrons only briefly escaped death. Winning that day his sobriquet, "Butcher of Cesena," the Cardinal Legate himself ran among his murdering troops like a madman, shouting, "I want blood! Blood! Blood! Kill them all!"

One bears in mind that this followed in less than a year the slaughter by still another Cardinal Legate of four thousand inhabitants of Faenza: there, five hundred leading

citizens had been hanged in chains, the town sacked, and
men, women and children chopped down.

Apparently the mild and timid Gregory preferred com-
manders who were his opposites. Perhaps his judicial mind
admired balance; personal mildness could best be compensated by ruthless servants. The timid, besides, are fearful,
and the fearful are more inclined to murder than the brave.

Increasingly, Gregory gave himself over to melancholia,
and busied himself with the internal affairs of the Church.
About this time (May, 1377), he issued five Bulls against
John Wycliffe. That Englishman had gotten out of hand—
he was placing kings ahead of the Pope: England's Parliament, Wycliffe had said, was right to forbid the drain of
gold to Rome. Besides, Wycliffe had put the Vulgate into
the common tongue and had gone about preaching that
the Church meant only the righteous. And he attacked the
very cornerstone of Church supremacy: the priest-wrought
Miracle of the Mass.

By now, the Pope had less than a year to live. One disap-
pointment followed another. Catherine of Siena had been
wrong, he reflected; France's Duke of Anjou, foretelling
disaster should Gregory leave Avignon, had proved the
better prophet.

It is true that the alliance between his Papal States and
rebellious Florence began to break up in 1377, providing
one hopeful glimmer in a dark year. Prospects for peace
brightened, for the war was costing everyone too much.
Florence's bill alone was already three million florins, plus
the incalculable losses sustained by her citizens abroad,
excommunicated and therefore no longer having any rights
at all. Meanwhile the Pope's own treasure had been so
gutted that he was forced to borrow ninety thousand florins.

Too ill to bear the summer heat, Gregory left for Anagni

at the end of May, and he stayed there till November. During this time his moral courage never failed him, though he had kidney stones as well as other ailments, and he went on working to improve things at Rome and win the peace. Beginnings were made; when he returned from Anagni the people welcomed him with joy.

Then rumors spread in Rome that the Pope planned to go back to Avignon, and the Bannerets assembled to take preventive action. There was no need. Gregory was too sick even to begin the long voyage home, nor was he the man to throw aside a chance for peace by leaving before an agreement could be reached. He intended to leave Italy at a later date if his health could be built up. And on January 19, 1378, he directed the Cardinals, seemingly as an emergency measure, to proceed with the election of a new Pope should the need arise before September: "If I should die before September," he wrote, "the Cardinals in Rome at the time of my death must elect forthwith, not waiting for those absent, and even, if need be, not entering into Conclave—by this means to deprive the factions of time to accomplish their maneuvers—that one whom they will deem most worthy to occupy the Holy See." Thus the dying sometimes prophesy. Gregory was dreading a schism in the Church: he had made the gravest of mistakes in coming back to Rome, he saw that now.

For some reason September stayed in his mind. He must have hoped he could recover by that month; hoped they could get him back then to his shining palace by the Rhône, with its strong, embracing walls; back where it would be safe, when his time came, to hold the Conclave in the usual fashion, free from Roman mobs. Southern France would be turning all white and gold in September, and the grapes would be ripening on the hillsides.

Then it was March, and Gregory knew that his hours were sifting away. He had them bring in to his bedside

Pierre Gandelin, chief of Castel Sant' Angelo, the strongest
point in the city; and, between feverish mutterings, and
sighs at having abandoned his Avignon Palace for Rome, he
enjoined upon this man, bowing at the foot of the bed, to
surrender his keys to no one, except at the command of
those Cardinals who were still in Avignon. A few days more
Pope Gregory wrestled with his torment, and on the twenty-
seventh of March he lost, and they buried him in a church
in the Forum, where he lies yet.

The Catholic Church as men had known it was now
gone forever. Already split three hundred years before into
West and East, the Church would now be riven again by
the West's Great Schism. Beyond in the future, brought on
by coming struggles of rival Popes, rival Christian Kings,
rival Colleges of Cardinals, rival clergies and universities,
saints and scholars, Protestant Christianity was waiting. A
different world was born when Gregory died, that day in
Rome.

PART ONE

ROME

1 THE FATEFUL CONCLAVE

E VEN THE HEAVENS had sent a warning of disaster.
At the moment the Conclave was to open, a bolt of lightning struck the Vatican. Furniture cracked and burned.

More explicit than Heaven, the Lords Banneret had
threatened to chop off the Cardinals' heads: "Take heed,"
they cried, "take heed, give us a Roman Pope, or we will
turn your heads as red as your hats!" The Cardinals had
not so much gathered in the Conclave, they had been
trapped there. The Bannerets stationed a people's guard at
sensitive points throughout the city, blocked every issue,
handed out weapons to the mob, and beyond in the coun-
tryside dammed up a waiting torrent of thousands of angry
peasants, each equipped with farm tools honed into im-
plements of vicious death.

In vain the Cardinals shouted at the Bannerets that a
Pope elected under threats of force would be no Pope at
all. Such a man would be only an intruder, they repeated:
"*Ille non esset papa, sed intrusus.*" In vain they reminded
the officials of their oath to abide by provisions set forth by
Gregory X in his Constitution *Ubi periculum*, at the Council of Lyons in 1274, which bound the civil authorities to
protect the Conclave from pressure and force. Indeed, to
preclude outside influence, the electing Cardinals were to
be locked away *cum clave* and to receive their food through
a window. (Not for nothing had that Gregory made his
Constitution. For two years, nine months and two days
before they elected him, the Cardinals had sat in Conclave 33

refusing to vote, until finally the people put them on a diet of bread and water and tore the roof off their palace.)

For days the Bridge of Sant' Angelo had been crowded with porters, carrying off to safety bales of the Cardinals' possessions. If only, the owners thought, they too could be huddled off. For days, whenever the rabble had glimpsed a prince of the Church, they had taken up their chant: "Give us a Roman or an Italian Pope!"

Cardinal Robert of Geneva put on armor under his robes. Cardinal Pedro de Luna dictated his will. . . .

"France has gorged herself on Roman gold. We mean to feast on French gold for a change!" the rabble sang. Camping in the streets, they had kept up a din with their hoarse cries, their trumpets, fifes and drums, already in anticipation plunging their arms to the elbow as they looted—it was old tradition—the palace of whoever should be chosen Pope. "Rome has been a widow seventy-three years," they cried. "Give us an Italian Pope!"

To gain time, or because of the lightning bolt, the Cardinals did not enter their Conclave on April 6, as had been planned, but delayed it one more day.

Toward evening, on Wednesday, April 7, 1378, a watcher from Castel Sant' Angelo saw a number of Cardinals cross over the bridge hard by. He noted, too, a great many Romans going over, and following these "an infinity" of mountaineers, men who were subjects of the Romans. Some had hurling devices, others had lances, others swords. They were bounding along in disorderly fashion after the Romans, heading for Saint Peter's Square, that wide space across which the Cardinals had to pass to enter the Conclave.

"More than twenty thousand were there," it was later testified, "such a mob of men and women that Saint Peter's with its galleries and its outside steps and the ledges on the square before it and the roofs roundabout were teeming."

In vain the Cardinals had cried to the Bannerets that any man elected under violence would be no Pope at àll. It was clear that the civil authorities, though bound to protect the Conclave and lock the electors away, had some plan of their own.

"At the moment of our entry," a Cardinal said afterward, "Saint Peter's Square was black with people . . . mostly armed. As we Cardinals came up, the crowd gave out with horrible shrieks, the mob crying in its own tongue for a Roman or an Italian Pope. Many were there who threatened and vilified the princes of the Church."

Another Cardinal said he had had considerable trouble getting through the armed men, and that the Romans were shouting: "By God nailed to the Cross, we will have the Pope!" (Those shouts in the street: forgotten voices of never-to-be-identified men, filtering up some way after six hundred years from ocean depths of time.)

In the press of people, some of the Romans tore the rings from the Cardinals' fingers, seeing which, Robert of Geneva slipped off his rings and passed them to a companion. The Bishop of Marseilles, chief guard of the Conclave, had his keys ripped from his hand. He tried to claw them back, but panicked and ran off, so that for hours the Conclave—held on the second floor and consisting of two chapels, a vestibule and cells—was open to the four winds. On the excuse that armed soldiery were hidden upstairs, the Romans streamed in and posted their own guards about the palace. Only one door, the one onto the courtyard, had been sealed up with bricks. "At last," said the Bishop of Marseilles afterward, "I went and closed up the Conclave with another key and two great beams."

The Romans in effect had taken over the Vatican and many stayed throughout the night. Gangs broke in and roared down the halls. They sacked pantries and grabbed up food, battered their way into cellars, staved in barrels; they guzzled the wine imported from Beaune, and let it lap out on the floor. At intervals they kept up their chant: "*Romano o Italiano lo volemo!*" Others pushed into Saint Peter's, started pulling on the bells and screaming, "If they don't give us a Roman we'll kill them all!" The shrill brass trumpetings, unrelenting drumbeats, raggedly pealing bells, the drunken cries, drew an ever-swelling crowd, latecomers adding their own hoarse voices to the rest: "We want him Roman!"

About eight o'clock in the evening, the sixteen Cardinals had gathered in the chapel, prior to entering their cells. Suddenly an armed delegation from the Roman people appeared before them. Humbly enough at first the leaders sank to their knees; their message, however, reduced itself to a naked threat: "Elect us a Roman or at least an Italian, or die!"

For the Conclave, Cardinal d'Aigrefeuille answered them reasonably enough: "With all this pressure and force you will accomplish one thing only: you will but void the election. Any man so elected would be only an intruder and no Pope at all. *Ille non esset papa, sed intrusus.*"

At this moment young Cardinal Orsini advanced on the delegation and cried: "Get out, you Roman pigs! Go back to your people and call them off, or I will drive you back with a club!"

The massed crowds heard of it, out in the square, almost at once. They thrust up their speaker, a bold Trasteverino with an unearthly voice, who bellowed to the Vatican walls: "By the bowels of God, you shall make an Italian or a Roman Pope, or else you shall die!"

As the hours wore on, the people ran in with bundles of sticks, dry branches, straw, any inflammables they could find, and started a huge bonfire against the chill—directly

beneath the Cardinals, locked in on the second floor. It was
a poor night for sleep.

Early the next morning Thomas degli Ammanati was riding through the streets of Rome, heading for Saint Peter's.
The sun had just risen. Before he reached the Vatican, he
came upon a noble of his acquaintance, named Malatesta.

"Where are you going, my lord Thomas?" Malatesta
cried.

"To attend Mass at Saint Peter's, with the rest of the
prelates," Thomas answered.

"What!" Malatesta said, "can't you hear the hammering
on the bells of Saint Peter's, calling out the people to mis-
chief and arms? Can't you hear the Capitol bell?"

*I listened, [Thomas said later] and sure enough, they
were hammering on the bells. People were running up,
brandishing their arms.*

"What does this mean?" I asked Malatesta.

*"I come from Saint Peter's," he said. "I saw the mob
streaming into the palace, I heard them shrieking at the
Conclave. Today will see pillage and death, I tell you. The
Cardinals will be the first to fall."*

*I rode on. When I got to the door that led to the stairway
of the Conclave, I saw so much wine spilled out that had I
set my feet down they would have been completely sub-
merged. Somebody had thrown down planks and stepping-
stones across it so you could reach the door.*

Thomas turned his horse about, its pace quickening as they
headed for its stable.

As the sun came up, testified another witness—the Superior General of the Franciscans—he too heard the rapid,
clanging bell notes, distinct from the usual ringing, and
used only to warn of dire events. It was, he said, "as if the

heathen or the infidels had surrounded Rome."

The Cardinals themselves were attending Mass. They were on their knees when the Romans, who had slept a little toward dawn, burst through the door to the bell tower and started hammering on the bells. "We are lost!" the electors cried. "What is it? What can this portend?"

One said, "It is the exorcisms. They are beating on the bells to cast the devils out." But another told the prelates at either side of him, "I know better what this means. I fear we are about to have a right evil exorcism now." As he spoke, a hail of stones rained down from the bell tower.

The quavering Bishop of Marseilles peered in at the windowlike aperture to the Conclave. Beckoning to Cardinal d'Aigrefeuille he implored him, "Now or never. If you want to escape whole, elect a Roman or an Italian, and do it now!"

The Conclave hastily decided to send a deputation to the inner window, and call out to the massed crowds, promising them either a Roman or an Italian Pope. The mission was perilous. There were no volunteers.

"This would contravene our freedom," the Cardinal of Florence, the dean of the Cardinals, objected. "And if we broke our promise, they would kill us." But d'Aigrefeuille and young Orsini seized his hands and half dragged him to the window.

Here Orsini could no longer contain himself. "Oh cursed men!" he shouted. "Do you imagine thus to get you a Pope? You are starting a fire in Rome this day that will burn the city to ash!" The extorted promise was then flung down but it no longer satisfied the people at all. They growled that the matter was dragging out too long.

Withdrawing from the window, d'Aigrefeuille took hold of Orsini by his cope and told him, "Come, come, my lord, let alone an Italian or a Roman, better I say to elect the Devil himself than die!"

The electors stared at one another, rejecting face after face. Nothing but panic could seat an Italian on the throne: there were only four Italian votes. The Limousin faction, strong because there had been a succession of Popes from that region, commanded seven. Against them, adamant, stood the anti-Limousins, including Pedro de Luna and Robert of Geneva. They had five votes. As for the Holy Ghost, supposedly guiding the Conclave, it was so little in evidence that someone proposed to elect the next Pope by drawing lots.

There were cries downstairs of "Set them afire! Burn them up!" The Cardinals knew that in the streets, Frenchmen that day were being manhandled and robbed, and one was stretched out dead. They finally determined to summon a number of prelates, one of whom was Bartolomeo Prignano, Archbishop of Bari. Another was Thomas degli Ammanati; he told afterward how, reluctantly, he mounted his horse again and rode to the Vatican, but was unable to reach the entrance to the stairs. "The guard did what he could against the straining people to get me through, but in all that noise I couldn't even hear what he said. . . . Drunken, screaming, they were taking axes and hammers to smash in the bricked-up door."

Bari, however, duly appeared. His presence there is the one hard, causal fact to which all that happened afterward can be traced back. Exactly what transpired between him and the Cardinals may never come to light. But there was an arrangement—that is obvious—and it could not have been impromptu; at least some of the voters must have considered it before. "It was something conditional," Pedro de Luna said later on. "In case we were to be savaged by the Romans." When asked, however, if there had been talk among the electors as to choosing Bari, de Luna proved vague: he could not tell, or he had forgotten. Other witnesses remembered that Bari had not sat idle before the election came up. There had been various pre-Conclave meetings that the Romans held, to assure the naming of a Roman or an Italian Pope. Bari, they said, had been seen at those meetings. He had bought himself a tract of land, they said, which made him a citizen of Rome, and eligible to attend. Still others affirmed that Bari had paid Nardus, one of the Bannerets, an unexplained three hundred florins in gold. At all events, he came.

At midday, during a lull, but with armed mobs still hemming them in, the Cardinals ate. Most likely, in the circumstances, instead of bringing in dishes freshly prepared in the various palaces, the servants made do with what provisions they had on hand. As the Cardinals' food was being passed through the window to the Conclave, the Romans importuned the attendants with cries of "Who's the Pope?" Some of the servitors murmured a single word: "Bari." The Romans thought they meant the well-known John of Baro, a Limousin, a man from beyond the mountains. This rumor running from mouth to mouth further increased the turmoil. At the moment when the Cardinals, having lunched, were rinsing their fingers preparatory to leaving table, each ordered his familiars to secrete the silver washbowls as best they could among their various bundles or in their girdles.

The exact sequence of events becomes confused and only a kind of montage can show some of the things that then took place. In one of the apartments, a conclavist discovered an opening in the floor. Using a ladder, several Cardinals, including Robert, erstwhile Butcher of Cesena, slipped through the hole. One said, "It came my turn and down I went, but the thing was perilous, for the ladder was too short to reach the floor and rested only on a piece of furniture, a sideboard." The runaways, however, were caught by enraged Romans who asked them: "Why are you not at the

voting?" Robert answered that he had cast his vote. The
Romans thereupon dragged them back through crowds that
were screaming, "To the Tiber with them! Into the Tiber!"
Robert had been struck on the head with a sword handle.
Back in the Conclave, weeping, he seized Brother John of
Besseria by his hand and cried, "Hear my confession, for I
see we are lost!" Not only the tearful Butcher of Cesena
but others as well turned to their confessors, not wanting to
pass into the next life unhousel'd, disappointed, unanel'd.

The tears of the Cardinal of Ostia have also come down
to us: someone had stolen a box containing all his jewels.
As for Pedro de Luna, he calmly took his stand in the
chapel, telling the rest: "If die I must, this is where I choose
to fall."

Useless now to address the mobs. Useless to assure them
that an Italian would be Pope. They were pounding on the
walls and on the downstairs ceiling, and shrieking for a
Roman now. "Not for a kingdom's wealth," said a witness
later, "would I have gone among them and shouted, 'We
want an *Italian!*' They would have cut me down on the
spot."

The rioters were smashing and looting, searching for fugitive Cardinals under beds and even in the privies. They
hacked holes in the Conclave walls and were staring
through. Finally they burst in and exploded the Conclave.

"I saw them," one witness said afterward. "Their swords
were out of the scabbard, their armor was on them, in they
streamed."

Greenish in their scarlet robes, the Cardinals stared about
them. And there in the midst of them, noticed as if for the
first time, was old Tibaldeschi, the Cardinal of Saint Peter's.
Old Tibaldeschi, so far gone in ailments and years that day
before yesterday he had been carried in. A Roman, old Tibaldeschi, and all down the decades his face well known to
the people of Rome. The same thought struck most of them

at once: old Tibaldeschi was their only way out. They "elected" him Pope.

They crowded around him, except for Pedro de Luna, who stood aside.

"How can I say I am Pope?" the old man cried.

Under the Cardinals' feet, the ground floor was piled with firewood, ready for the torch. The animal sounds of the mob filled the hall. The maddened people were pouring in.

"I ran up with my companion to the Cardinal of Saint Peter's," a witness testified afterward, "and I bowed deeply before him and said, 'For the love of God, save us: tell them you are Pope. Save us from perishing!' We lifted him and carried him into the chapel."

They sat him down in the papal chair. When he tried to rise, a nephew pushed him in the chest. Someone bundled a red silk cope over his bowed shoulders, someone else set a white miter on his trembling head. He wobbled his headgear off; it was put on again; a Cardinal kept it steady with one hand, propped the sagging old back with the other. They rang the "Pope's bell," intoned the *Te Deum*, and proclaimed the election to the mobs: "Here is your Roman Pope!"

Shouting for joy, bands of Romans hurried in, crammed to suffocating in the narrow chapel. The old man screamed when they pressed and kissed his gouty hands, crowded around his throne and "adored" him. With a cloth, they wiped the sweat from his face. Some hoisted him to the altar, begging for his blessing. Instead, with what breath was still in him, he cursed them, calling again, jolted out of his nightmare, "This is farce! How can I say I am Pope?" And when those near enough to catch the words, shouted, "Who then is Pope?" He cried, his old voice cracking, "My lord of Bari."

After holding him up before the crowds and exhibiting

him as Pope, they at last carried him away to the papal
bedchamber, and stretched him, almost dying, on the bed.

Meanwhile, out in the city, other Romans battered their
way through his doors, and smashed and trampled as they
looted his palace.

THAT NIGHT AND
THE MORNING AFTER

Thrust out to the Roman mob as a sacrifice, old
Tibaldeschi had, willy-nilly, saved the day. The Cardinals
lost no time in disappearing, many through breaks in the
walls and floor. The contrived respite, the Heaven-sent ruse,
in addition to Bari's rumored election, had bought time.
The murder lust of the crowds veered elsewhere.

For a while the second (or first?) of the Cardinals' two
electees also vanished. Prignano of Bari was nowhere to be
seen. The Bishop of Todi finally discovered him in one of
the Vatican's downstairs apartments and proposed that the
two of them go up to the papal bedchamber and see old
Tibaldeschi. Bari accepted, but they found a cousin of
Todi's at the door who told them: "Don't go up. The
chamber is packed." They waited. Todi again proposed that
they go up. As they passed through the room of the para-
ments, the vestments and church hangings, a brother of
Todi's named Anthony stopped them again.

"The old Cardinal of Saint Peter's is not the Pope,"
Anthony said. "I heard it from his own lips."

And as the rumor ran that Bari was Pope, the Romans
took up their cry: *"Non lo volemo!"*

By now Bari and the Bishop of Todi were in a corner of
the loggia. The Bannerets and other city officials came after
them and led Todi aside.

"Our lord of Todi," one of them half whispered, so that
Bari could not hear, "it is essential that the Archbishop of

Bari come away with us, and that he renounce his papacy

before the people. For the mobs are on their way, and they are out to destroy him."

I began to see [*the Bishop of Todi said later*] *what they were after; I pretended to know nothing of Bari's having been elected.*

Then I asked them: "*Why, my Lords, do you want him to renounce? Do you know for certain that he has been chosen?*"

"*We know only one thing,*" *they answered,* "*the people say he was, and Saint Peter's says he himself is not Pope.*"

"*What are you up to, my Lords?*" *I said, or something like it, not without irony.* "*You don't know for sure that Bari is Pope, yet you ask him to renounce what he does not possess? You mock him, gentlemen. You mock an Archbishop, a notable of Naples . . . Think of what you are doing, in the Lord God's name! Why pile trouble on trouble, mistake on mistake! When you find out for certain what is going on, then my lord of Bari can decide for himself.*"

The Romans withdrew, and Bari, informed at once of their intent, cried out: "They don't know me. Though I saw pointed at this throat of mine a thousand naked swords, still I would not renounce."

We could now hear shrieks from the mob. I said to our lord, "*No question. They're on their way back to finish us.*" *My brother was by us—the Cardinal of Geneva had sent him to help—and I told him:* "*Go, look and see whether there isn't some exit through which my lord can escape from the palace. He can leave Rome through the gate by the bridge. He is Pope now. Save him we must.*"

My brother . . . came back. There was no possible exit, he said, no way we could leave without being taken. So I told our lord: "Let us go into the secret chamber and hide, for they are on their way to kill us."

Todi then drew the visibly terrified Prignano into the secret room.

Meanwhile the Romans kept clamoring that they would murder Prignano if they caught him and he refused to renounce. If, however, he renounced, they said they would ask old Tibaldeschi to award him a scarlet hat.

Uneasily, the Vatican slept, holding within its walls what amounted to two simultaneous Popes. To the watching Prignano, the pictures of Saints Peter and Paul shed tears. Afterward, as he received a visitor one day, Prignano indicated those pictures and said: "How do their expressions look to you? Would you not say they are laughing? . . . When I entered the palace, I saw them shedding their tears."

There was more robbing and looting, people were beaten, locked up. One man was left on the public way, stripped to his bare skin. Prelates, merchants, clerks, officers, artists, who had been attached to the Papal Court fled Rome. One Poncius Beraldi stocked his apartments with food, stones and weapons, and walled up the door.

It was not the Cardinals who hid and rescued Prignano. They were not there. Some fled the city in disguise, some crept as refugees into Castel Sant' Angelo, a very few returned to their palaces. Thomas degli Ammanati saw them, said an official letter afterward, wandering here and there, unhonored, frozen with fear, some with no cope, some even with no head covering, not so much as a monk's pointed hood.

Pedro de Luna rode out, alone except for members of his household, went home to his palace, and barricaded himself in.

Those Cardinals who, disguised as simple clerks or lay-men, or in tattered pilgrim's dress, had taken refuge in Castel Sant' Angelo, gathered in the apartments of Pierre Gandelin and spoke of what had passed. One of them, re-called a Bishop afterward, "set his hand on a missal and told me, 'My lord Bishop, by these holy Evangels, Bar-tolomeo Prignano is no more Pope than you yourself.'"

A certain Abbot John became a liaison between the sup-posed electee and Cardinals Orsini and Saint-Eustache, now out of Rome at the Orsini Castle of Vicovaro. John was ordered by them, in the night, to "seek out your Archbishop of Bari, and carry with you, hidden under your clothes, the habit of a Franciscan monk. Greet him, and tell him from us that in view of what is happening we request him, to obviate a schism, to come to us now." Prignano's answer was: "Abbot John, I am doing very well where I am, and could not leave if I wanted to. Ask my lords to state in writing why they wish me there."

"They gave me," John later reported, "a folded paper. What was inside I know not, but on it was written: 'To the Reverend Father in Jesus Christ, our very dear friend Lord Bartolomeo, Archbishop of Bari.' I said to the Car-dinals: 'You write him as to an Archbishop and he con-siders himself Pope.' They answered, 'He is as much the Pope as we are.'"

People who arrived at the Vatican the next morning testified afterward to the débris and breakage. "You would have thought an enemy army had come through," said one. "The Conclave—doors, partitions, floor, everything—was in ruins."

Bari sat inside, wearing the robe normally reserved for his bedchamber. There was a great coming and going, and some asking others whether he was Pope. Not one Car-dinal appeared. Runners arrived and departed. After a while the Bannerets showed up, with excuses: they had been quieting the populace, still not settled down. Bari said the people were doubtless angered because they had confused him with John of Baro. The Bannerets were up and down, genuflecting and bowing. Bari's hands gestured at them, "No!" and he ordered in the common tongue, "Get up, get up: nothing is settled so long as the Cardinals don't come."

Silent, the Bannerets filed out. They went to the palace of the Cardinal of Marmoutier and harangued him, their message being essentially this: If he and his colleagues knew what was in their own interest, they should come over to the Vatican and finish up the work they had begun. For they, the Romans, had been listening as people talked among themselves in the streets, and could not be answerable for events which would surely follow if the Cardinals did not complete their business of the day before.

Emissaries appeared at Pedro de Luna's Apollinaire Palace. He called the Bishop of Assisi into his chamber and told him to put the visitors off.

"I am ill," de Luna told him, "and as you see I am still in bed. You will make my excuses and say I cannot see them now."

But de Luna must come to the Palace, the Romans said. He whom the Archbishop of Bari considered most his friend and the one most worthy of trust, he, de Luna, should with the other Cardinals set Bari on the throne.

De Luna continued to repeat that he was indisposed. More˙ envoys arrived, these with a strong retinue in their wake. Again Pedro de Luna said, "I cannot come," beginning this day, perhaps, his long lifetime of saying No. (Regrets at having yielded in this fateful hour may well have reinforced those many noes of future years.)

"You will have to come, my lord," the envoys told him. "Our orders are not to quit you till you stand in the Palace."

"What say you of force?" de Luna cried. "Not you and

not all the Romans together have the strength to force me there!" What if, at this moment, he had stuck by his No? His story would doubtless have ended there, as he paced his room in that hostile city.

The Bishop of Assisi drew him aside: "You are exposing yourself to death, my lord, and exposing us all, who serve you. Far better to go and finish badly what was so badly begun. Or keep these Romans by you, and have the bells rung for the saddling of the horses. I will take me to Castel Sant' Angelo and see how the others fare."

The other Cardinals, it developed, were being subjected to the same kind of pressure as Pedro de Luna. Arriving not alone and elbowing his way in, the Abbé de Sistre had blustered to Gandelin: "Commandant, I promise you, you'll soon be a greater lord than you ever have been before, because we've got the Pope we wanted."

"Who is this Pope?" asked Gandelin.

"The Archbishop of Bari," de Sistre said.

"How could he have been elected in all that uproar and confusion?" the Commandant asked. "He'll have to be re-elected, for sure."

"No need," said de Sistre, "he's the true Pope, and if these Cardinals don't get themselves over immediately and set him on his throne, they'll learn what trouble means."

Gandelin said he was there to protect them and that it didn't seem right that a Pope should be made in this fashion. Nevertheless he went up from the lower courtyard and delivered Bari's message.

"Get along with you!" the Cardinal of Brittany exploded. "How does Bari expect to be Pope? He is not now and never will be Pope, by any vote of mine!"

Purple at having been kept waiting so long, de Sistre was finally let in to confront the six beleaguered Cardinals. He made free with his language, said that Bari would be Pope whether the Cardinals liked it or not, and in general vilified and threatened: if they did not go, Bari would remove, he implied, not only their scarlet hats, but their heads as well. "He will make you to disappear forever from the gaze of men."

In the end they prepared a writing and sealed it with their seals. The instrument was an authorization to the three Cardinals by now at the Vatican to proceed as they saw fit.

"Once he got his hands on this paper," Gandelin said, "the Abbé told me he now had something from the Cardinals that they couldn't back out of. He was jubilant. He said the Cardinals could all go to the Devil if they wanted to. It was nothing to him any more. Also that what they had now done, they had done in spite of themselves."

Bari, waiting with three Cardinals at the Vatican, refused the document. He sent out yet another embassy to Castel Sant' Angelo. After a time, the delegation was back at the palace. Its chief reported to Bari and the very small group about him: "I bring bad news. The Cardinals at the Castle, and also, in particular, the Commandant, maintain that you are not the Pope."

"It is false what you say there," Bari blurted. "Never let it pass your lips again. Go out and find the Bannerets and tell them, unless they oblige the Cardinals at Castel Sant' Angelo to come here and throne me, they have accomplished nothing at all."

They were sitting there, the four of them—Bari and three Cardinals—[Nicolas Eymeric would afterward testify] not saying anything. In came my lord of Marmoutier and said to Bari: "My Lords are unable to come."

"And why not?" asked Bari.

"Because—they have no copes."

"Let them come in their surplices," said Bari. "But come they must."

Then Bari called to a knot of clerics, who were watching from an angle of the promenoir. They approached him, and he seized the first one's cope. And he stripped it off, and flung it down. "Good enough for a Cardinal!" he cried, raking the prelates with his eyes. And he stripped off the copes of five others besides.

Then turning to one of the Bannerets he gestured at the pile. "You there!" he ordered. "Go. Take them these copes! Come they must! Come they must!"

Suddenly, he and those about him were in two separated worlds. Behind him, they exchanged secret looks. But who knows? His mental alienation may have added the push which made his will and no other's prevail that day.

They at Castel Sant' Angelo wanted no part in this enthronement, but Bari had obviously exploited the events of the Conclave. They dared not now reject him. What if the others should crown him after all? They might as well go the rest of the way, rather than brave the fury of a Pontiff (just how furious he could become, they as yet had no idea) and risk rejection by their colleagues as well.

They were of several minds, the determined Archbishop of Bari was of one. The Romans knelt down before them and wept and tore at their own faces with their nails and begged them to go. More eloquently, the Romans threatened death, and said they would throw up a wall of sharpened stakes around the refuge—which was empty of provisions and arms. The upshot of it all was that to save their lives, to end the great public uproar in Rome, perhaps too out of sheer exhaustion which bent them the sooner— in short, to end everything, after a hundred refusals, the six Cardinals issued forth from Castel Sant' Angelo.

Even Bari himself never maintained there was a reelection that Friday. He said merely that the Cardinals "confirmed *ad cautelam*—as a precaution—the already-completed election of his person."

They dressed him in his scarlet cope and other papal vestments, sat him in the papal chair, flung wide the chapel doors and exhibited him, flanked by Cardinals, to the Roman people. He kissed the Cardinals' faces and hands. To many, his kiss must have been as welcome as that other most famous kiss that history has brought down to us.

"For my part," summed up one from the Conclave, "I subscribe most willingly to this choice, for I would rather be of those who suffer for the Faith than of those who die for it."

3 WHO, THEN, IS POPE?

O
VER IN PERSIA a hundred years before all this,
the poet Sa'dí (thereby misdirecting a whole nation) had
written:

> *Better a lie with wise intent,*
> *Than a truth which mischief would foment.*

These lines contravened his Holy Scripture, the Qur'án,
which reads: "We will hurl the truth at falsehood, and it
shall smite it, and lo! it shall vanish . . . verily, falsehood
is a thing that perisheth." (21:18; 17:83) During the century following this Conclave, Machiavelli would expatiate
on the importance of being both a lion and a fox, and say:
"Those who rely simply on the lion do not understand what
they are about . . . and he who has known best how to
employ the fox has succeeded best. . . . Be a great pre-
tender and dissembler . . . men are so simple . . . that he
who seeks to deceive will always find someone who will allow himself to be deceived." He would then point to Pope
Alexander VI as a successful example.

Thus Machiavelli also went against his Holy Scripture,
where Jesus says, in the face of death: "To this end was I
born, and for this cause came I into the world, that I should
bear witness unto the truth." (John 18:37)

So what, hewing to Scripture, was the truth of that day?
People swore to anything, and at this distance we can only
feel our way. The Roman viewpoint was simply that Bari,

53

who became Pope Urban VI, owed his crowning not to threats and violence but to the regional split in the Sacred College: it had been, then, the men of Limoges against the other French and the rest. Not one of the Conclave, however, with the possible exception of Tibaldeschi, the old Cardinal of Saint Peter's seems actively to have stood for Urban VI.

Contrary to popular belief, one does not as a rule reach and hold high office without ability. Pedro de Luna was wily as well as stubborn, and when later on he was minutely questioned about the Conclave by the ambassadors of Aragon and Castile, he walked on eggs.

The Archbishop of Bari, he said, was indeed among those mentioned beforehand. Because this Archbishop was a good organizer, and de Luna knew him better than some others, de Luna said if things should come to that, Bari was in his judgment more *"papabile"* (popable) than the other Italians. Speaking for himself, however, he, de Luna, had not entered the Conclave with his mind made up. As to his fellow Cardinals, "After reading their subsequent depositions, and remembering the situation they were in, I concluded," de Luna said, "that it was really as they affirmed, the mortal danger alone which caused them to elect the Archbishop."

What actually happened seems to be that Bari's pre-Conclave electioneering had provided him with three or four *pis-aller* votes among the Cardinals; and when, in the mounting chaos, these three or four brought up Bari's name, de Luna believed they were not improvising but had settled on it beforehand. All the electors, however, would have far preferred a member of the Sacred College.

It was fear of the Romans that determined the choice. . . . When the Cardinals assumed their seats to proceed with the election, the Cardinal of Florence [who as dean of the College had to deliver the allocution] began as follows: "Words fail me." He went on to tell us that he could not deliver his prepared address, because of the peril in which he found us all. At this point the Cardinals began talking among themselves . . . and they said that no election ought to take place because it would bring about a schism in the Church; that it was better to expose ourselves to danger than to commit such an evil act.

The Cardinal de Saint-Eustache said that on the contrary, exposing ourselves to danger would not obviate a schism, simply because the Romans would kill whom they chose, and would force the rest to elect whom they wished, and that nobody would be left to tell what had happened. Further, he said those Cardinals who had remained in Avignon, understanding this well, would elect another Pope, and thus the schism would only be the wider. No, he said, on the contrary it was better for the Conclave to carry on with an election conforming to the desires of the populace; and later, following what the chronicles related of other times, we could come together in a place of safety and hold the election over again.

The Cardinals . . . rose from their seats and began to pace up and down in the chapel. Several said it was better to please the people and elect a Roman or an Italian rather than to court death. . . . . .

This from de Luna was corroborated by the Cardinal of Sant' Angelo, who quoted some of the College as saying: "We don't want to die shut up in this place, let each get out as best he can, let us satisfy them, later when we are free we will do as has already been done in other days, as the chronicles relate."

There were, among the electors, four Italian Cardinals. Why was not one of these deemed popable? When old Tibaldeschi was proposed, Limoges objected: "He is infirm, and he is a Roman; the people are demanding a Roman, and thus the election would be void. The Cardinal of Florence . . . comes from a people at war with the Church. Nor can the Archbishop of Milan be Pope—he comes from a land of tyrants. Finally, Orsini cannot be Pope, either, because he is a Roman. Besides, he is too young. . . .

"My lord Jacopo," Limoges told Orsini to his face, "You are truly too young, and too much on one side, it is certain that you cannot be Pope."

At the end, they balloted and elected Bari. Several protested at the very moment of voting that they attached little meaning to their act. But de Luna told the investigators that speaking for himself, in giving his vote to Prignano of Bari he gave it with the intent that, should Bari be elected, he, de Luna, would be satisfied.

There is also, among the dossiers of the Schism, the report of Rodrigo Bernard, one of the investigators of Castile. He said that with his colleagues he had interviewed separately and under oath nine Cardinals (the nine: Limoges, Saint-Eustache, Ostia; Viviers, Sant' Angelo, Brittany; de Vernhio, Marmoutier and de Luna). All nine deposed that before entering the Conclave, not one intended to elect Bari—they simply intended to vote for a member of the College. More, the majority inclined toward Viviers. The only reason they finally named Bari was to obviate the peril of sudden death. Ostia (later Glandève) had actually gone to a notary public prior to the Conclave, and protested before witnesses that should he give his vote to a Roman or an Italian he would do it only through fear of being murdered. Unfortunately the notarized document was later on lost in a fire. In Paris, when attending the King of France, Bernard further interviewed d'Aigrefeuille and Poitiers. All these eleven Cardinals affirmed on their soul and conscience that this was the reason for their vote: the total absence of freedom to choose. All said, moreover, that although they

had crowned Prignano of Bari, although they had paid him
the usual honors, not one of them in his own mind considered Prignano to have been canonically elected, nor to be
Pope.

By 1380 there were two Italian Cardinals of that fateful
day still living: Florence and Milan. That one who had
been moribund (Tibaldeschi, the Cardinal of Saint Peter's),
and that one who had been "too young to be Pope" (Orsini), had vanished. The remaining two, hoping to lighten
their inner spiritual burden, sent envoys to Avignon to question the six of the Conclave still present there. These six assured the envoys that they had voted as they did only in
the terror of imminent death.

The Urbanists, of course, related afterward that there
had been no terrors. They never denied a certain tumult,
but it was, they said, nothing to be frightened about. The
Cardinals could have elected a Frenchman and still not
have been killed. They would not on that account have
been either tortured or butchered and there had really been
nothing for men so brave as the Cardinals to be afraid of.
At worst they were only to be a little shaken. Against the
Urbanists, all those Cardinals who were present at the
Fateful Conclave are on the same side: there was pressure,
there was terror.

Significantly enough, from that day to this no man not
a Cardinal has been elected Pope. And since the Dutchman
Adrian VI, who died in 1523, no man not an Italian has
ever been elected. That means there have been only seven
non-Italian Popes in six hundred years.

"Tomorrow," said the Cardinal of Florence on Saturday,
"we will make all the obligatory blunders."

"How so?" cried the Bishop of Castro.

"Yes," continued Florence, "what we are doing all adds
up to nothing."

It was Easter Day, at sunrise, on the steps of the Basilica of Saint Peter, when Cardinal Orsini took up in his hands and placed on Urban's head the high, rounded hat adorned with the three crowns. This headdress harked back to Persia's diadem, an ornament Rome had hated once; indeed, when Caligula made use of it, Rome had thought it madness. But as the Republic waned, and became a memory, the diadem had been copied by Diocletian surnamed Jovius, along with robes of silk (silk that had been forbidden to Roman males) and of gold, and shoes ablaze with precious jewels. Becoming Emperor in 284, Diocletian introduced the old Persian ceremonial along with the symbol, so that a Roman graced by reaching his Sovereign at last, had to fall prostrate on the ground before him, and adore him, hence the *Adoratio* still offered in our day to the Roman Pope.

Cardinals and lesser prelates, riding black horses decked out in white trappings, came after Urban on his white palfrey through the streets to Saint John Lateran for the rites of the *Possessio*. Ahead of him, Robert of Geneva carried a staff and with it pushed the people to one side. Young Cardinal Orsini brought up the rear. The cortege straggled along, some here, some there, the Pope sparsely attended. Non-Urbanist witnesses remembered that most of the Cardinals' faces were clouded over. Some raised up their eyes to heaven, some bowed their heads low, "as a man does when he has a nosebleed."

From his windows, Thomas degli Ammanati watched them all go by: "As d'Aigrefeuille passed my house, he leaned with one hand on the front of his saddle, and with the other he beat absent-mindedly against his chasuble as if not aware of his surroundings."

The ceremonies had taken and would still take several hours. Presumably the same marble chair, parts of which were already a thousand years old, was there then as now to receive the Pontiff as Bishop of Rome. A feast had been laid, and Urban VI, still in tiara and vestments, sat himself down and crammed some food into his mouth (it was before forks existed), but especially sucked away at his beaker. "Eight separate times he emptied his beaker. I counted," the Cardinal of Brittany said afterward.

Pierre Gandelin, commandant of Castel Sant' Angelo, later deposed, "When I saw him there at that table, I said to myself, 'You now have before you, combined in one person, all the Devils of Hell. . . .' As for the Cardinals sitting by him, they looked as dazed as I."

In any case that seems to have been the last of the good food, the fowls and wine. At dinners and suppers thereafter, Urban offered his Curia only bits of fish and indifferent meat.

4 THE ANGRY BLOODSHOT EYES

Duurin g holy week, everybody went through
the prescribed motions, asked for and obtained rich patron-
age from new Pope Urban, gave him gifts, showed themselves about him as his Cardinals. Even d'Aigrefeuille
came with a present. "Holy Father," he said to Urban, "as
a symbol of my strong attachment, I give you this ring.
Take it. It was my mother's." For these acts of obedience
the uncomprehending future would reproach them later on.

Like the Cardinals, the populace now hailed him. They
said he had chosen the name Urban for *urbs*, the city. As
he rode among them they shouted: "Long live our Pope,
that we, not others, have made Pope! Holy Father, remember Rome, for it was Rome that made you Pope!"

One citizen drew out his sword and cried, "Do you see
this blade? This made you Pope!"

Meanwhile, Urban hastened to dictate letters to the
various crowned heads, announcing his "unanimous" election. Entrusting them only to selected messengers, he carefully read over these missives before they went out.

Nine days after the enthronement, the entire Sacred
College then in Rome wrote this—Urban breathing over
their shoulders—to the Cardinals who had remained behind in Avignon:

Very reverend Fathers and Lords, *as rumor can easily
cover up truth with clouds and false colors, especially in*

times of stress, we deem it proper hereby to inform you, by this missive which contains the very truth, of all that has happened during these days in the Roman Church, of which you, even as ourselves, are honorable members and pillars. Thus you may not place any credence at all in those who may have told you or written you of the events in a different light, and being well convinced that we write you in a state of perfect security, you may remain at peace yourselves. Know, therefore, that after the death of Gregory XI, our Lord and Father, which came on the twenty-seventh of March, to be followed by eternal life, as we have no doubt, resting ourselves on the mercy of God: and after having performed the funeral ceremonies for so great a Pope, we entered on the seventh into Conclave in the Apostolic Palace, having first implored the grace of the Holy Spirit, to deliberate on the election of another Pope. The day following, enlightened, as we devoutly believe, by the rays of that Sun that never sets, about the hour when the Holy Spirit Paraclete came down into the hearts of the Apostles, having all directed our votes unanimously and freely upon the person of the very reverend Father and Lord in Christ, Bartolomeo, Archbishop of Bari, distinguished equally by his merit and by his virtues, we elected him Pope with one common voice, and as such we announced him to an incredibly great multitude of Christian folk. Having then been placed on the ninth of the month on the Apostolic throne, in the presence of the faithful, he took the name of Urban VI, and on the day of the resurrection of our Lord, he was, according to custom, in the Basilica of the Prince of the Apostles, and to the acclamations of an innumerable crowd, solemnly crowned. We apprise you of this that the sadness occasioned by the death of Gregory XI may be succeeded by the joy you should now feel at this gift sent down from Heaven.

The Cardinals, of course, wrote their private letters too. Against the above, for example, must be set one by the *socius* or Conclavist of Pedro de Luna, which reports these momentous happenings substantially as they appear in the foregoing pages. Or yet another, by Pierre de Cros—d'Aigrefeuille being present—to the King of France, advising him to put no faith in anything the Cardinals might say or do while they remained in Rome, for they were, he wrote, under restraint at all times. There was as well that oral message, secretly dispatched by the Cardinal of Marmoutier through Wenceslaus Stirnandus, for the Holy Roman Emperor: "Pay no mind to whatever Prignano or the Cardinals may write. . . . We will send you our own messengers, once we are free."

Except in secret here and there, the Cardinals seem not to have discussed the new situation among themselves as a body, feeling that they were captives, and none of them quite sure where the others stood. Each one believed that while he had not, in his heart, elected Urban, perhaps some of the others had. Each thought Urban's conscience would oblige him to abdicate. Too late, they woke up the next morning to discover that the man had no conscience. Urban had exploited their dilemma. Urban was the interloper who, noting the confusion of his betters, saw and grabbed his chance. It was not the first time such a thing had taken place in the world, and would not be the last.

Two things were now going on: the non-Italian factions, maddened at having lost their *situation acquise*, their entrenched position, were secretly planning to make things come right anyhow. And Urban was revealing himself in his true light. This was a moment when the fate of Western Christianity hinged on the character of one man.

It is a mystery how the new Pope managed to curb himself long enough to be elected. Even Pedro de Luna must have been taken in, for he had suggested Urban's name to a fellow Cardinal at the Conclave as a possible compromise. Perhaps the election itself had dealt Urban's reason its *coup de grâce.*

In any case, once chosen, the short, thickset Urban VI never governed himself again. His somber face would grow darker yet and an almost maniacal fire would kindle in his brooding eyes. When he had exhausted himself—but never his fury—politics, reputations, personal loyalties, lay in ruins. Unlike many people with occasionally blazing tempers, he could neither forget nor forgive. Hate stirred continuously under his hair shirt and burst out in rages that instead of relieving the man, devoured him.

Anyone else, knowing himself to have been elected under a cloud and by the unwilling, would have tried to strengthen his position, to win over the Cardinals, high prelates, probably-friendly sovereigns. Not Urban.

Every Consistory began with Urban's faultfinding. Monotonously naggingly, he reproached the princes of the Church for immorality and greed. They panted after gold, he tirelessly reminded them; they lived in barefaced luxury, they surrounded themselves with huge suites, they purposely embroiled affairs of state for their own gain. Individuals were singled out: Orsini, to his face, was "a maniac," Robert of Geneva was "lewd." One day he turned on the Black (i.e., Benedictine) Cardinal of Amiens, Jean de La Grange, who had come back from Pisa when Pope Gregory died, but arrived too late for the election. La Grange had, shouted Urban, prolonged the war between France and England to line his own pockets; for the same purpose he had stirred up quarrels between the Kings of Castile, Aragon and Navarre. "This Black Cardinal," he went on, pointing at the Benedictine, "has set up false gods. In all these affairs he has but sought his own self-interest. He is a traitor to the Church."

La Grange pushed back his chair. He drew himself up, threw a furious glance at the Pontiff, raised his fist. "Telling you not as Pope," he shouted, "you puny and insignificant Archbishop of Bari, you lie!"

With this, the Black Cardinal and his partisans marched from the hall.

Or there was the business of Queen Joanna I of Naples. Delighted that a Neapolitan, one of her subjects, now sat on the papal throne, Joanna celebrated the event with fireworks. Then, to pay him homage, and not homage alone, she sent up a delegation loaded with costly gifts and forty thousand gold crowns. To these gift-bearing ambassadors, Urban ranted against their Queen, climaxing his tirade with: "I will shut her in a convent; I will trade off her scepter for a distaff!" (That time, he kept his word: for he would excommunicate Joanna in September, knowing the excommunicated have no rights and could be preyed upon at will. Then he preached a crusade against her, stripping churches to pay for it.)

Or there was his treatment of Otto of Brunswick, current husband of the same Queen. As consort, this Prince came up to Rome to be enfeoffed by the Pope with the Kingdom of Naples. Otto knelt down before Urban, and offered him a cup of wine. The Pope, his lips twisted in malice, hugely enjoying Otto's servile posture, sat and stared at him, making no move to take the cup. The pause lengthened out. Embarrassed, one of the Cardinals spoke up: "Holy Father," he said, "it is time you drank."

At a private Consistory, Urban rose from his chair in a rage, to strike the Cardinal of Limoges. Robert of Geneva threw himself in front of the Cardinal, and cried, "Holy Father, Holy Father, what are you doing?" Forcibly, he sat Pope Urban back in his chair.

Truth to tell, Urban's reproaches were not always off target. Other Popes had said as much before him. Jean de

La Grange, for example, was known as the French King's
man. Secular monies did come in, paid out by princes to
the hierarchs. These last-named personages, as a rule, were
anything but angels. And—although a previous Pontiff had
awarded her the Golden Rose—the same could be said of
Joanna, that matrimonious if not murderous Queen. It was
simply that people would not take such treatment from
Urban—because of something lying deep in Urban himself.
French historians, who worship the golden mean, the *juste
milieu*, comment fastidiously that he was carried away, he
was *fantasque*. That is, the man was alien and impulsive,
one never knew what he would do, and stories about him
soon blew from mouth to mouth, from the hierarchy down
to the last servant, and out *urbi et orbi* so that in weeks the
Christian leaders had the word.

So soon as the Tuesday following his election, a group of
young probationers, about ten of them, were on the stairway
of Saint Peter's that led to the papal apartments in the
Vatican. They met the Cardinal of Milan coming down,
and he asked them, "To whom do you go?"

"We go up," said the eldest of them, "to pay our respects
to the Pope."

The Cardinal turned pale. Shaken, he asked again, "To
whom do you go?" Then he raised his hands skyward and
cried: "O God, save Thy Church!"

Essentially what happened was that the Cardinals, given
the choice between a corpse and a madman, had chosen
both.

The dubiety as to Urban's credentials was general; even
foreigners in Rome, particularly Germans, discussed the
matter, for Urban's own doubts were contagious. Why, on
the Friday before Easter, had he forbidden the Romans to
kiss his foot? The Aragonese Inquisitor would comment
afterward: "Urban often said that he was indeed the true

Pope. But Roman Pontiffs had never been wont thus to express themselves."

Gandelin, commandant of Castel Sant' Angelo, made a deposition partly in Latin, and its second part, which goes much further, in Provençal. At his last audience with the dying Gregory XI, he had promised never to yield the Castle without consent from Avignon. Urban now offered Gandelin showers of gold in perpetuity to relinquish his trust. The commandant steadfastly refused, explaining his reasons.

Urban cried out: "So you take the advice of those accursed Limousin traitors! Know then that I served the Cardinal of Pamplona for fourteen whole years, and I never once got a good word out of him. When he gave me an order he would not even deign to look my way, he would turn his back on me and grunt like a calf: like a calf! Ah, you will suffer!"

In the end the commandant agreed to one thing: he would hoist a banner, bearing Urban's arms, over the Castle. But Gandelin held on to the keys.

5 THE RIDDLE OF FONDI

Now it was May and warm weather was on the city. On the sixth, Cardinals d'Aigrefeuille and Poitiers slipped out of Rome. They left supposedly because of the oncoming summer, yet rumors persisted of a split between Pope and College. Even before Coster and Gutenberg, before increasingly dazzling news media, people seemed to find out everything, so that you wonder again whether secrets ever really exist. "That which escapes the twain," Islamic tradition has it, "is known everywhere." The twain, say commentaries, are the two lips.

The Cardinal of Viviers was the next to leave. Early in June others followed, still others in mid-June, and by June 21, 1378, all the non-Italians were together at Anagni. This was a likely enough gathering place in the circumstances, because the late Pope Gregory had made it the summer residence of his court. Nevertheless, Thomas degli Ammanati deposed, "I thought then and still think . . . that they could not have managed such an exodus unless God had a hand in it."

Pedro de Luna was among the last to go. Far from precipitate, his mind was slow and sure, and he was persuaded that the Pope should be in Rome. Speaking pure medieval language, he finally remarked: "All the Cardinals have left for Anagni and why should I, de Luna, stay here with the Pope, who does nothing whatever that I ask? Assuredly, I would never serve God Himself, if God did me no good."

On July 27, Marcile, who was chargé d'affaires of the Uni-

versity of Paris at the Papal court, wrote this letter from
Tivoli:

> . . . *Not for a hundred years, in my opinion, has the
> Church been in such imminent danger of schism, may
> God preserve us from it. As I already wrote you, the Pope
> now resides in Tivoli and with him are the Cardinals of
> Florence and Milan, also Saint Peter's and Orsini. The
> others, thirteen in number, are at Anagni. The Italian Car-
> dinals, the Roman people and the commoners of Italy, say
> that the former Archbishop of Bari is truly and rightly the
> Pope; the other thirteen Cardinals, according to what
> people say, affirm the contrary: that is, because of the vio-
> lence done by the Romans to the Cardinals, the election is
> null and void, not having been free, and consequently the
> former Archbishop of Bari is not truly the Pope.*
>
> *For these reasons the abovementioned Cardinals have,
> to guard their persons, summoned both Breton soldiers and
> mercenaries from other parts. . . . What do the Cardinals
> really want with these armed men? In general, nobody
> knows. Some say they will proceed to a new election.*

About now there seems to have been a *pro forma* embassy back to Pope Urban, demanding he step down and
leave the electors free to choose again, and holding out
the promise of choosing *him,* this time freely and by
canon law; hardly a hopeful request to make of a man who
said he would never renounce the tiara, though to keep it
he must confront a thousand swords. On July 16 the Anagni
Cardinals themselves acquired some swords: they called in
Bernardon de la Salle, fire-eating captain of mercenaries
and onetime comrade-in-arms of Du Guesclin. He came at
the head of two hundred Gascon lances, besides the Breton
soldiers aforesaid. Marching from Viterbo they had to cross
the Tiber by the Salaria Bridge, not far out of Rome. The

Romans ran up in great numbers to block the bridge but
Bernardon rammed his men through and killed many. Seeing the slaughter Urban was virtually out of his mind. He
forgot his recent slurs on Queen Joanna and begged Naples
for help, whereupon she sent up a hundred foot soldiers
and two hundred lances. Her ambassador tried meanwhile
to reconcile Urban with his runaway Sacred College, to
small avail.

The Anagni Cardinals have left a letter which tells what
they did once they were safe out of Rome and had their
little army to protect them, and their statement is filled out
by details from the Cardinal of Saint-Eustache:

*The first thing that was settled was to draw up a written
account of the case. . . . After each had looked it over, a
few corrections were made as to certain points, concerning
which some Cardinals had a clearer memory than others.
The whole work was then presented to the assembled Cardinals and attentively read to them in three successive meetings. Finally, having agreed on every point, they decided on
the text and each one certified that the work was in every
detail in conformity with truth.*

They then spent considerably more time going over the
rights and wrongs of the situation, appointing a committee
to make an even closer examination of the facts and further
deliberating together, by twos and threes, and finally they
concluded unanimously that Bari was not the Pope. Even
after this decision, one man asked them to take still more
time to think the question through. This was Pedro de
Luna.

"My lord of Geneva is inclement," de Luna told them,
when Robert of Geneva objected to the delay, "saying that
I am too conscientious. It is certainly the case that I wish
to see clearly what Urban's rights may be. I tell you in all

truth, were I at this moment in Avignon, united with those who are there . . . and were I to learn that, legally, Bari was the rightful Pope, I would still come over to him, if I had to walk to him barefoot."

Thus braked by prudence, they meditated further. They also called in legal experts not from among themselves. In the end everyone agreed that Urban was an interloper, seated unlawfully in Peter's chair.

The Anagni Cardinals then summoned the Roman Cardinals to join them. Convincing Urban that for the sake of unity they must gather with their fellows, the Roman Cardinals in effect abandoned him on July 26. They did not, however, proceed to Anagni, but met Anagni's deputies at Palestrina, where they urged that an Ecumenical Council be summoned. Only three of the four Italians presented themselves, incidentally, for old Tibaldeschi was dying, and he had nowhere on earth to go.

Next the Anagni Cardinals made a public, historic, irretrievable move: on August 9, 1378, exactly four months after the supposed election of Urban, deciding to wait for the Roman Cardinals no more, they read out in the Cathedral at Anagni, following a Mass of the Holy Spirit, a solemn document, which anathematized the Archbishop of Bari as an intruder, declared his papal claims invalid, and the Holy See vacant. Inevitably the same instrument, which was directed to all the courts of Christendom, stigmatized its authors as cowards, liars and cheats.

Consumed by their zeal for the House of God, [the Cardinals wrote] they cannot see without anguish how Peter's bark is well-nigh sinking; how the Ark of the Covenant has been carried off by Philistines; how, in the hands of a blasphemous Belshazzar, the sacred chalices of the Holy City of Jerusalem are now held high. Their conscience forbids them to leave the mystic, Seamless Robe where it might be

rent asunder; their silence would impair the purity of the
Faith, the rigor of the discipline, the edification of Chris-
tian folk.

They had been compelled, the Cardinals said,

to elect an Italian Pope that the Holy Spirit had not chosen.
A half-crazed mob forced out of us the temporary election
of an apostate, a murderer, a heretic stained with every
crime there is. He had acknowledged that his election could
only be provisional, no more; and then, his word meaning
nothing, he forced us, threatening us with death, to raise
him up to the Apostolic chair, and to set on his disdainful
brows the triple crown. . . . Notwithstanding the nullity
of his election, his blind ambition keeps him on the throne.
. . . Now that we are safe from his anger, we solemnly de-
clare that he is an interloper, a usurper, an anti-Christ; and
we pronounce our anathema against him and against who-
soever may bow to his rule.

"I was there," said Thomas degli Ammanati later on. "I
heard it all."

Rome being still too close for comfort, the Cardinals
went on to Fondi in Campania.

"Fondi," was Urban's comment when he heard, "Fondi,
where we have it from Saint Gregory, the Demons once
gathered together in council." Of their summons to him to
disappear, he said, "I have no intention at all of resigning
from the Papacy. I will not resign to make way for the Devil
and his crew. I will stay. In the name of God I will fight
them all."

His three Italian Cardinals still sent their messages, but
they did not return to Urban. They wandered for a time
from place to place, and like so many would-be mediators
incurred the wrath of both sides. The truth is, they them-

selves were not sure how to proceed, or what to believe. It is said they were at last lured to Fondi by a secret promise, made to each of them separately, that he would be elected Pope.

On September 6, 1378, old Tibaldeschi retired from the scene, his few lines spoken to history, his role ended. It is ironic to reflect that, had he accepted his play-acting enthronement—had he taken the move away from Bari—during his remaining five months of life peace might have been restored, and a compromise Pope might have been elected. Or was compromise impossible, and the underlying question not which Pontiff, this man or that, but which people: France, or Italy? Who can tell?

The runaway Cardinals easily picked up as allies people, such as Queen Joanna, who had been gratuitously damned by Urban. Joanna was for them now, and so was the powerful Governor of Campania, a man whom Urban had driven out, dismissing him from office and refusing to repay him a just debt of twenty thousand florins. The King of France, Charles V, who naturally wanted the Pope back in Avignon, wrote to promise men and funds. This Charles, of the high cheekbones and little, slanting eyes, was referred to as "the Learned." He is the one who, with a thousand manuscripts, founded the Bibliothèque Nationale of France.

The prelates next invited this king, a recent widower, to be Pope himself. If they thus risked the friendship of rival European rulers it was because they foresaw the need of strong military support in what was already shaping up as a bitter struggle for power. They were within their rights to choose a king for Pope, since theoretically any male Catholic, married or single, would be eligible. The King, however, wisely declined. It was rumored that he would have said yes, except that his arm was lamed from poison administered to him by Charles the Bad, King of Navarre, making

it impossible for him to celebrate Mass. He could, of course,
as Pope, have dispensed himself from this canonical impediment, but he preferred, doubtless, to be the power behind
the tiara.

After that they looked about them and concentrated on
two of the Conclave. One was dark. He was Pedro de Luna,
the Aragonese. His country was known for its implacable
men and implacable mules. This man, through his mother,
went back to the Arabs—to Saïd ben-Alhakam, King of
Majorca, that Muslim who, captured by Christians, had had
himself baptized. (Since, as a Muslim, Saïd believed in
Jesus and His Virgin Mother anyhow, he had doubtless concluded that life was well worth a Mass.)

De Luna sat before them now, solid and yet so charged
with energy that he seemed caught in midflight. He was
short in stature but he sat tall. His brows were slightly
drawn together, his eyes wide, peremptory, showing much
white, like an Arab stallion's. He had a beak of a nose, firm
lips, a bit of beard under the lower jaw. They knew that
before his Avignon days he had won his doctorate at Montpellier, and had stayed on there and brilliantly taught canon
law.

The other was fair, a "German," or as we would say, a
Swiss. He was Robert of Geneva, the one who had done
brutally at Cesena. Robert had a slight squint; he also
limped somewhat, but had taught himself to disguise it,
and his height and handsome bearing offset these small
handicaps. Like de Luna, he too was of royal lineage; his
brother was Count of Geneva and he was related by direct
blood or collateral line to most of the rulers of Europe. The
Cardinals thought of him as a Pope's Legate, a Prince, and
no stranger to the battlefield. They deliberated and made
ready to vote.

And so the day came, September 20, 1378, at the palace of
the Count of Fondi, in quiet and with the Camerlengo from

Castel Sant' Angelo as guard at the door (he having brought along the tiara out of Urban's treasury), when the Cardinal of Limoges declared: "I perceive that the French want a Frenchman, the Italians an Italian. I name a man who is neither a Frenchman nor yet an Italian; I name one who is of the German nation: my lord Robert of Geneva. I name him Sovereign Pontiff."

At once all the Cardinals, one following the other—all except the nominee and the three Italians—advanced and cast their ballots for Robert.

Later on the three Italians drew up their own *casus* wherein they stated: "At Fondi, on Saint Matthew's Eve, the Cardinals from beyond the mountains, being thirteen in number, . . . and ourselves being present, twelve of them unanimously elected as Roman Pontiff and pastor of the Church the most reverend lord, then Cardinal Robert of Geneva, today Pope Clement VII. No objection was raised by us to his election. We acknowledged it then, we acknowledge it now: his election was canonical."

The same College of Cardinals had now elected two simultaneous Popes. And when the news of Robert's crowning reached him, the King of France declared: "The Pontiff is I, myself."

On the night of April 8, 1378, there had been quite possibly two Popes in the Vatican: the Archbishop of Bari and the Cardinal of Saint Peter's. Or else there were two non-Popes, or two presumptive electees. The voters themselves, the electing Cardinals, did not know for sure. The people were certain enough of old Saint Peter's election to sack his palace, as was the tradition when an ecclesiastic was thus elevated. The Roman leaders were certain enough it was Bari, since they came genuflecting or trying to force him to renounce. Bari did not decide, at first, that he was Pope—although papal jurisdiction begins at the moment of election: on the morning after, the Friday, April 9, he forbade the Bannerets to kiss his foot. The Cardinals, having throned him, fled, thus expressing better than in words their opinion of Bari and his Popedom. They declared Bari anathema and his election void. Old Tibaldeschi died. Bari continued on as Pope Urban VI, while the same Cardinals who elected him (or had not elected him) gathered at Fondi and elected Robert of Geneva as Pope.

Catherine of Siena, who had not questioned the election of old Tibaldeschi, now supported Urban VI. As she later wrote the King of France: "That one whom they elected out of fear, that was my Lord of Saint Peter's: this is obvious to all; but the election of Pope Urban was done according to rule."

In after days partisans of either side compared the way in which Urban and then Clement accepted the purple. Glandève reported: "Bari screamed out at the top of his lungs: 'I accept!' But Clement wept, and said he was unworthy. Another would do better, another should be chosen in his place. He flung himself on the ground till we begged him and made him to consent."

Whatever the calm tone of their *casus*, the three cheated Italians could hardly contain themselves; and it was rumored, true or not, that the youngest of them, Orsini, sickened and died of rage.

So ended this phase of an episode which cracked the Western World—perhaps for forty years as it is in the books, perhaps forever.

6 TWO BEGINS DIVISION

MANY DID NOT see things the Cardinals' way. In the first place, Pope Urban did not. On November 29, 1378, he excommunicated Pope Clement.

Then there was Catherine of Siena, who raised her voice in dissent. The letters she now wrote were tinged with horror, for after all, had this not been her own doing? Had she not traveled to Avignon and with all her unearthly power forced Pope Gregory back to Rome?

Even before the irreparable break between Urban and his Cardinals, Catherine, deeply troubled, had written Pedro de Luna:

I seem to have heard that inharmony is setting in between the Christ of the earth and his disciples. From the terror of heresy I experience indescribable pain. . . .

May I behold you shorn of that self-love which weakens every reasoning creature, rich in that one true love which is founded on Christ. . . . In that love, the soul is ever strengthened, for it has burned away whatever held it back. Not only, then, is the soul powerful in itself, but often to its neighbor it can communicate this power.

To Pope Urban she wrote privately: "In the name of Christ crucified, moderate a little those too rough impulses that nature has given you."

Catherine often admonished Queen Joanna, writing her such lines as: "O sweet and venerable Mother, how ashamed should the creature be to pride himself on his rank and state, when he sees his Creator humbling Himself so low, hastening with such ardent love to His abject death upon the Cross!"

After the Schism, when Queen Joanna declared herself against Urban, for Clement, Catherine wrote Joanna in October, much of her letter consisting of an apostrophe to the Cardinals:

. . . you say that he, Urban, is not the true Pope, because you named him out of fear, dreading the wrath of the people. That is not true; but even if it were, you would merit death for choosing a Pope in the fear of men, and not in the fear of God.

Think not that God will spare you out of any concern for your scarlet caps . . . come back to yourselves, and purge away the poison of self-love.

Then addressing Joanna again:

I do not attack their station, but their wickedness; for they made another Pope, and after they made him, people said it was done by your hand; and you believe he is Pope. . . . Your taste has been perverted, like the taste of the sick.

In November, 1378, Catherine threatened the Queen with violent death. Joanna had shown, she says, "not a heart generous and virile, but a woman's heart, without firmness, shaken like a leaf in the wind." (As with Héloïse before her, as with so many other women great and small, then and now, "virile" to Catherine was a meliorative term.)

You have subjected yourself to a lie, and to the Devil who is its father. . . . Alas, again alas! Unless you abandon so monstrous an error, over you can we mourn as over the dead; for you are cut off from the life of grace: dead as to soul, dead as to body. Perish you must, and you know not when. Neither your riches, nor your power, nor the pomp of the world, nor your nobles, nor the peoples who are your subjects so far as the body goes, can defend you from the sovereign Judge of all. . . . Sometimes, indeed, He uses such as them for executioners that they may castigate His foes. . . . Lest the Hellish wolf devour you, come back, poor lamb, into the fold!

Again and again she returned to the attack. We have three enemies on earth, she told the Queen: "The Demon— weak unless we strengthen him by our consent; the world, its honors and delights—weak if we do not love it too much; and our own feebleness—compensated by the crucified Christ." Fervently, she tried to snare Joanna with the ecstasies of Faith.

When God took on man's nature, [she once wrote] His reasoning creature then became His bride. O sweetest love Jesus! To show Thou wert taking the creature to wife, eight days beyond Thy birth, at the circumcision moment, Thou gavest her with Thy most soft, most holy hand, the nuptial ring. You know it well, O venerable Mother, when those first eight days were done, He yielded her a circle of His flesh, as pledge of all He would yield up on the holy Tree, that day the spotless Lamb, the heavenly Groom, would be offered up, and shed from all His body streams of blood to wash away the stains and sins of humankind, His wife. Note well: His burning love bestowed on us, not a golden ring, but a ring of His unsullied flesh.

And then there was Catherine's letter to the Italian Cardinals:

. . . I Catherine, slave of Christ's servants, I write you in His precious blood, longing to see you return to the

truth and the light, out of the thick darkness into which you have fallen. . . . Like flowers you were, destined to waft abroad their sweet odors, set on the breast of the Church; like pillars were you, to bear up the mystic Building of Christ; like torches high-placed, to light the faithful's way. Have you, now, reached the aims for which you were raised up? Alas, not so. . . . And what tells me that you are nothing but ingrates and mercenary men? Is it not this very persecution you are inflicting on the Church? . . . Know you not, better than any, that Urban VI is the sole legitimate Pope, chosen by canon law . . . ? What led you to do as you did? It is the poison of self-love, that poison which has doomed the world, that poison which, out of the pillars you were, turned you to sticks of straw; and out of the sweet-smelling blossoms you were, to foulest slime; and out of the angels on earth you were, to Demons, seeking to spatter upon us the venom within you, pulling us away from obedience to the true Vicar of Jesus Christ, bowing us down to antichrist, who is a Limb of the Devil even as you are yourselves. . . .

You cannot bring us ignorance for an excuse; you did yourselves announce, in your solemn declaration, the very opposite of what you now proclaim. It is not we who told you that Urban VI was the valid Pope. Fools are you! Fools!

As for their claim that they elected Urban only under pressure and out of fear, she continued: ". . . with no risk of failing in respect, since you have made yourselves unworthy of it, I submit that this is false. . . . It is you yourselves who taught me to believe in you no more."

She reminded the Cardinals of how they had performed the ceremony of "adoring" Urban, in which case, if he was not Pope, *are you not idolaters and shams for thus adoring him as Jesus Christ on earth?*

And now you have made an antipope! . . . Whoso be not for Christ, that is to say for His Vicar Urban, is of need against Him. You have then acted wrongfully in choosing this Devil's Limb; for were he, Clement, a Limb of Jesus, he would have died rather than consent to such a crime, for he knows the truth as well as you. . . . Yes, it is pride and pride alone that drove you into schism; because, ere the Pope took you to task—a trifle severely, perhaps—you had confessed and acknowledged him as the Vicar on earth of Christ."

Who was the Pope? The Archbishop of Bari, according to the Cardinals, had made an agreement with the Conclave to step down once Rome was quiet again. But any agreement made by the Archbishop of Bari was not (precedent said) binding on the same man once he was Pope. Did the few months when the Cardinals appeared to acknowledge him constitute ratification of their vote? Or was Urban's illegal election rightfully canceled, according to plan, as soon as the Cardinals were safe? And what of Clement VII? The Cardinals who chose him, not under pressure this second time, were the legitimate electors appointed or inherited by the dead Gregory XI, a recognized Pope. According to the Bull of Nicholas II in 1059, only these could elect a Pope. If Urban really was *intrusus* as these Cardinals said (and whatever Catherine wrote, there is no shadow of a doubt that Urban was elected by the Conclave only because they were under the threat of imminent death), then Clement VII was certainly Pope. Or was Urban Pope, and Clement a bigamous choice and thus nobody at all? Or was neither Urban nor Clement Pope? Like many a case at first seemingly simple and easy to settle, this affair soon became entangled beyond all unraveling.

Before the years wore on, and evils burgeoned, the leaders of Christendom might better have taken a lesson from the *Gulistán,* or *Garden of Roses* where Persia's Sa'dí had written:

> *The tree that fresh in earth is put*
> *One man alone can soon uproot,*
> *But if a while you let it sprout*
> *Never a windlass can pull it out.*

The number two is infamous, a cleric of the day remarked, "because it is the beginning of division, and division is the fountainhead of discord . . ." Two worlds were officially inaugurated on September 20, 1378, at Fondi, and two new words were coined.

The resultant division of the West has been graphically illustrated:

> *Let us imagine a line [writes Valois] cutting Great Britain so as to separate Scotland from England; another line leading from the Channel south of Calais, going up the Rhine from Cologne to Basel, describing a curve around one part of the states of the House of Austria, then cutting Piedmont to end west of Genoa on the shores of the Mediterranean Sea; a third line, finally, separating the Kingdom of Naples from the rest of Italy. . . . After the Schism of the Greeks, one now beheld the Schism of the Latins, and could not but await the final disintegration of which these divisions were perhaps only the initial symptoms.*

Such confusions are further described by the Abbé André:

> *And thus the Schism was established, strong, vigorous, as impossible to settle as an absolute dogma, a devouring purpose, a political conviction, and the world was soon divided*

into Urbanists and Clementines, urged on, each against the other, by an equal hate, a parallel antipathy, a corresponding propaganda. Although, officially, each kingdom espoused one or the other of the two claimants, nevertheless there were always in a given kingdom zealous partisans of the other side. . . . An Urbanist could not so much as look at a Clementine but he trembled with rage, for he saw in him the sole cause of all the ills of Europe. . . . A Clementine beheld in an Urbanist . . . a wild animal thirsting for blood. . . . Later on, when the reciprocal excommunications and censures of each side began to take effect, then hate expanded to infinity, and the very furies seemed to be brandishing their torches over Europe. Moral anarchy soon brought on the saddest of results. Everything could be bought: conscience, oaths, honor, God Himself.

Black had evidently turned blacker; the investigator seems to remember the same charges at Avignon in pre-Schism times. The split at first did not cause, so much as it disclosed, the general corruption; then, by its very existence, it increased the evils. Bought by money or ambition, prelates would anathematize the next day what they had blessed the day before, for commerce adoring what they had burned, burning what they had adored. They passed back and forth from one papal flag to another. Soon, "virtue and religion were to be found only in the books."

Pastor, noted Catholic historian, affirms:

The amount of evil wrought by the schism of 1378, the longest known in the history of the Papacy, can only be estimated, when we reflect that it occurred at a moment when thorough reform in ecclesiastical affairs was a most urgent need. This was now utterly out of the question, and indeed, all the evils which had crept into ecclesiastical life were infinitely increased. Respect for the Holy See was also

*greatly impaired, and the Popes became more than ever
dependent on the temporal power, for the schism allowed
each Prince to choose which Pope he would acknowledge.
In the eyes of the people, the simple fact of a double Papacy
must have shaken the authority of the Holy See to its very
foundations. It may truly be said that these fifty years of
schism prepared the way for the great Apostasy of the 16th
century.*

"Nothing better proves the thorough decadence of the
princes of the Church," says the Abbé André again, "than
the birth of the Schism." He goes on to comment that their
crime lay in handing over the Papacy "to the mockery of
peoples, to the examination of scholars, to the intervention
of Princes." He adds that from that day forward, "the Papacy was only the shadow of what it once had been."

There were to be saints and saintly personages on both
sides of the gulf and the lay public was exposed to a be-
wildering heavenly fireworks of anathemas and counter-
anathemas, double legates, double bishops, visions and con-
flicting visions and irrefutable miracles proving the authenticity of either camp. Four of these spiritual leaders were
Urbanist: Catherine of Siena and Catherine of Sweden,
Peter of Aragon and Gerard de Groote. Three were Clementine: Vincent Ferrer, Peter of Luxemburg and Colette of
Corbie. You could not, of course, rely even on a future
saint to remain stable, or to be strictly accurate. On May 6,
1379, Catherine of Siena wrote the French King: "We see
that all the true servants of God obey Urban VI and acknowledge him as true Sovereign Pontiff, which in fact he
is." And she went on:

*. . . if one blind man leads another, both will go over the
brink. Unless you make amends, the same will happen to*

you. I am astonished that a Catholic man, wishing . . . to live in the fear of God, would let himself be led about like a child, and would not see the ruin to which he is exposing himself, in allowing the light of the Most Holy Faith to be stained by the counsels of those whom we know to be Devil's Limbs, corrupt trees . . . that have sown the poison of heresy by telling us Pope Urban is not the true Pope . . . What! the pillars of the Church, those who are set up to promulgate the Faith, have sought from fear of physical death to drag us along with themselves into death everlasting! They have designated as our Father one who is not!

Yet Charles V himself and many another presumably true servant of God sided with the Cardinals. The University of Paris first pronounced for Urban, then, by an act dated May 30, 1379, reversed itself in Clement's favor, thereby losing some dissident professors to the universities of Vienna and Prague.

As for Saint Malachy, he who, in the twelfth century, had died in the arms of his friend Saint Bernard of Clairvaux, leaving behind a remarkable list of Latin descriptive phrases, one phrase per every future Pope till the end of time—he seems to have been on everyone's side at once. His phrase for the man who would fit Urban's place on the list is *de inferno praegnanti*—out of a pregnant Hell; and indeed, other aptnesses aside, Prignano had been born near Vesuvius in a place called Inferno. Malachy's description of, presumably, Clement VII is *de cruce apostolica*—of the Apostolic Cross; Clement was Cardinal of the Basilica of the Twelve Apostles, had a gold cross in his coat of arms, and was also, say Urbanists, a cross for the Church to bear.

(Skeptics point out that Malachy's prophecy was not published until 1595. Nevertheless, it is also of interest regarding the Popes who *followed* that date; for example, the phrase *aquila rapax*, or ravening eagle, is graphic for Pius

VII (1800–1823), the Pope who was seized and carried off
to Savona and Fontainebleau by Napoleon. If, as many
Catholics believe, Paul VI is Malachy's *flos florum*, from the
flowers on his coat of arms, then after him says the prophecy, there are only four more Popes to come.)

PART TWO

AVIGNON

7 CO-POPE AT AVIGNON

H E W A S Y O U N G, Pope Clement VII, only thirty-six or seven. He was a man who laughed and cried easily. They also say he had a good figure—a feature not, perhaps, particularly essential for a Pope. He could write and speak well, knew Latin, French, Italian, German. His affable manner belied his reputation as the Butcher of Cesena (which title may, indeed, have swayed the voters his way). It is true that he liked war as well as high living, and if he took the name of Clement it was not for that quality but because in some other respects he was similar to the Avignon Clement who preceded him: he too preferred the ways of kings. Much given to fleshly pleasures, he tended to choose mistresses and favorites (says Maimbourg) from among his own relatives, and load them down with riches. He is described as "a worldly prelate, a prince in all the strength of the term." This regality, of course, was his by birth.

What was wanted at this moment was not the Prince Charming in Clement, but the Butcher in him. A well-aimed blow, a dead Urban, and there might have been no Schism of the West, at least not then. But Clement paused and thought, and we can almost follow his reasoning still: he had, on his side, the Count of Fondi and in secret the Queen of Naples; he had the Marquis of Montferrat and could expect help from Viterbo, Piedmont, and the forces of Giordano Orsini. Castel Sant' Angelo remained in Clementine hands and its siege pinned down a considerable number of Urbanist soldiers—Urban himself could not stay on in the Vatican because it fell within the range of the castle's bombards and archers; also, Clement had galleys waiting at the mouth of the Tiber. All this was in Clement's favor but did not offset the fact that most of Italy was for Urban— because Urban was Italian, not because the Italians liked him. Then, there were the two-way mercenaries: the peninsula teemed with them, ready for the hiring, and this brought Clement to the pinch—the gold he did not have. Urban owned the papal treasure, the great, tempting papal take still spouting into Rome.

Whether or not he had to, Clement waited. He moved out of Fondi to Sperlonga, actually to a stronghold close to Gaeta, from which he could look at the Mediterranean Sea. Some say the remove was due to his being sick of a tertian fever: either sickness, or a healthy fear of Urban. In any case, nightly he posted up to fifteen sentries along his battlements, and he also sealed up a number of windows and gates. On the 18th of April, 1379, three bombards together with their missiles were brought in from Gaeta. Wood was cut nearby for a palisade, and Clement thought he would construct on the curtain or joining wall between two bastions a sloping wooden screen to shelter his archers.

When spring finally came, Clement's nephew, the Count of Montjoie (a name which is, significantly perhaps, in this context, the ancient battle cry of France) led down his forces from the north. Nepotism would save the day. Yet before Montjoie could get to Rome, Castel Sant' Angelo fell to the Roman Pope.

Three days later, on April 30, 1379, Urbanites and Clementines—each side marching under banners bearing the Keys of Saint Peter—met head on near Rome. Montjoie, leading the Clementine cavalry, seemed the winner at first, when he swept Urban's hired captain, Alberigo di Barbiano, back toward the city. By evening, however, Clement's

nephew was to see his dead piled everywhere, his remnant
fleeing, and himself a prisoner, along with sixty other high
officers, two of them of equal rank to his own. The Clementine disaster was total: in an ordeal by force Urban had
won. Nevertheless the Clementine army managed to reform and hire away sufficient of the previous day's enemies
to stand up as a wall between the two Popes.

Clement then took to the sea at Sperlonga, and sailed
southward to what he hoped would be the protection of
Naples. There the Queen was friendly, the people not; for
Pope Urban, after all, was one of their own. Crowds spilled
through the streets, looting and crying out: "Death to Anti-
christ! Death to Clement and his Cardinals! Death to the
Queen if she takes their side! Long live Pope Urban!"

Joanna had chosen for her guest the Castel dell' Ovo, and
had joined its rock to the mainland by a causeway. But it
looked to him more like a trap than a haven, standing flat
on the sea; more an end than a beginning. Three days he
shared this hiding place of the Queen's, this Castle of the
Egg, and then he fled north to Sperlonga again. He vacil-
lated here, debated Urban's strength or lack of it, asked
himself should he stay or go, should he flee or fight. May
came. On the twenty-second his fleet stood out to sea, the
rudders swung around, the prows aimed straight for the
Baie des Anges. Clement's immediate goal was Nice, but
what he yearned for now was the impregnable fortress-palace
at Avignon.

This time the voyage was even worse than usual because
war broke out among Clement's galleys, Aragonese fighting
with the men of Provence. Bowmen of both sides took so
many shots at their opponents that Clement had himself
rowed ashore and went on to Nice by land. Peace settling
down again in the fleet, the Pope sailed from Nice along
the coast to Marseilles, making one stop at Toulon. He was
properly welcomed at Marseilles and Aix, remained three

days in each city and on June 20, 1379, entered Avignon. Three years had passed since Pope Gregory XI had taken the Papacy away from here forever. Now it was back, in this palace by the Rock of the Lords.

In Rome, Urban's mobs punished Castel Sant' Angelo, tearing it down, scattering buildings and treasures as if an earthquake had struck. Only Hadrian's cylinder survived, too strong to fall.

France's King Charles V had a younger brother named Louis, the same Duke of Anjou who had begged Pope Gregory to remain in Avignon. Louis was something of a fighter, with blond hair and beard, a taste for circumstance and "a hand always ready to seize on gold." (True, he would spend it afterward.)

To this Duke Louis was brought the Cardinals' Anagni declaration of August 9, 1378, besides a letter dated August 15, 1378, bearing the seals of twelve Cardinals and calling for the Duke to support them. Louis received the word within weeks, for news, although only for the elite, reached those who wanted it and made it, surprisingly fast. (In a dire emergency, Paris could get a letter to Avignon in less than four days.) Following word of the election, Louis at once espoused the cause of Clement VII and declared him Pope in the streets of his capital, Toulouse.

The Duke already had his eye on the Roussillon and the Balearic Islands, but the bait which newly crowned Pope Clement held out to him was in the opposite direction: it was a kingdom, a realm in Italy to be named Adria, which would be sliced out of the Papal States. That Louis must first himself win the future kingdom away from Urban was a minor detail.

Clement next bethought him, it was 1380 by now, that Queen Joanna of Naples had no child, and he prevailed upon her to adopt Duke Louis d'Anjou, well dowered with

Church monies, as her son and heir. If Joanna's assiduous
courtier and kinsman Charles of Durazzo felt displaced by
the move, no matter. Clement also knew that Pope Urban
had excommunicated Joanna. What of it? The fellow had
also excommunicated himself, Pope Clement. True, Urban
had England on his side, but no support was monolithic, no
battle line indelible. Joanna, who had traveled up to Avignon to talk things over, went back to Egg Castle and there,
on June 29, 1380, signed a testament making Louis d'Anjou
her heir. Meanwhile Louis delayed, having his troubles in
Provence, and proving a reluctant sword.

As for England, a useful sidelight on views across the
Channel was provided by Adam Easton, who later became
one of Urban's Cardinals and was rescued from that Pontiff by King Richard II. Cardinal d'Aigrefeuille had, it
seems, approached Easton to ask if Urban's election would
please the English King and barons. Easton replied that the
entire realm of England was more than pleased with the
Italian's election, since French Popes and French Cardinals
were regarded by England's lords as enemies more redoubt-
able to them and theirs than the King of France himself.
Also that had the Cardinals stubbornly insisted on electing
yet another Frenchman, peace between the two Kings would
have ended forever. Moreover, continued Easton, the order
had gone out in England to strip all French Cardinals of
their benefices, and only a letter from Urban to England on
their behalf could save their revenues. According to Easton,
d'Aigrefeuille himself was delighted at that moment with
Bari's elevation.

But d'Aigrefeuille branded this whole deposition as false,
adding most effectively by way of rebuttal that no order had
been given in England to withdraw the benefices of French
Cardinals; that he himself was peacefully enjoying his English benefices, with some three thousand florins coming in
annually; that the Cardinal of Poitiers was receiving two

thousand, and the Cardinal of Albano five thousand, and Cardinal de Vernhio about two thousand, and the Cardinal of Saint-Eustache a very sizable sum, and that many other French, which is to say Clementine, Cardinals were doing as well. (A gold florin of the day is described as being about equivalent to a sheep.)

It was this same d'Aigrefeuille who had cried out at the first election that it was better to elect the Devil himself than die. Such computations were abhorred by Catherine of Siena. Her eyes were fastened elsewhere. The Cardinals of her day made no sense to her, belonging as she did to the timeless, placeless band of those who immolate themselves. She could have been nailed up beside Jesus. She could have been a Persian Bábí, singing to the crowds who had come to watch him die:

> Happy that lover under the Loved One's spell,
> At the feet of Him to whom his soul is wed,
> So drunk with love he cannot even tell
> If he's throwing down his turban, or his head.

D'Aigrefeuille would have made sure it was his turban.

The point was that Clement had, even more urgently than other Pontiffs before him, to send a general into Italy to fight his wars. For the Pope was a temporal ruler in Italy, owning his Papal States, roughly one fifth of the peninsula, which he would keep until Napoleon and then Garibaldi would take them away. (Rome itself, except in the Avignon time his capital for a thousand years, would be last to go, when in 1871 by a vote of 130,000 inhabitants to 1,500, that ancient city would join the new Kingdom of Italy.) Besides, he had often to quell by force of arms one or another of the rebellious Italian republics. In Clement's case the war was the more pressing as he must do battle not only with his subjects but with a hostile co-Pope.

No sooner had Clement allocated Louis of Anjou to Joanna than Urban raised up a rival sword out of the Queen's own household. Charles of Durazzo, called "Charles of the Peace," a nephew-in-law to Joanna, had not enjoyed being ignored in favor of Louis. The redheaded youth, soft-voiced, with honeyed words, everybody's favorite, and known as the "spoiled child of the Naples court," easily sided with Urban and betrayed the Queen who had passed him by. By mid-July, 1381, Urban had crowned him and Charles was ruler of Naples. Joanna was his prisoner, shut in Castel Nuovo, gazing out through her dimming eyes across the Mediterranean, watching from her tower for the new heir, the French champion who never came.

Yes, a good deal of water had flowed under Avignon's bridge since 1343, when her grandfather, Robert the Wise, had left her owner of that city and of Provence, and Queen of Naples. And at the last it was not for a distaff, as he had threatened, but for a winding sheet that Urban would trade in her royal crown.

Meanwhile France's King, the learned Charles V, had pretty well ousted the English, also improved his realms in other ways and in 1380 passed away. Froissart tells how the new King, Charles VI, the Learned One's son, went down and paid a visit to Pope Clement. Arriving at the palace which had been prepared for him in Villeneuve, young King Charles crossed over the Rhône to Avignon and found Clement in full Consistory, the Pope seated in his papal robes on his papal chair, perhaps the same twelfth-century one still there at Our Lady of the Lords, with its miter-shaped back and on each side in bas-relief a winged creature with cloven hoofs. As the King approached, Clement rose up for Charles's kiss. When dinner came, Clement with much state took his seat at a table alone, while the King was placed, also alone, at another table below that of the Pope.

Froissart says that Pope and Cardinals rejoiced at the King's visit and had reason to, "for without his support they would have been in but small estimation. There were no Kings in Christendom who paid the Pope obedience but such as were allied to France."

8 ON THE DEATH
OF FAIR LADIES

It was Catherine who had drawn Pope Gregory out of Avignon to Rome, so that he died in the Vatican where a free Conclave could not meet. Then came the forced election which made the Urbanists, followed by the free election which made the Clementines. Whatever its result, Catherine had succeeded at the first of her self-appointed tasks: getting the Papacy back to Rome.

At the other two, she failed. She wanted the West to proceed against Islam, as it had a hundred years before. But the last real Crusade was over. He that the Christians miscalled Mahound, Muhammad the Iconoclast—from whose name they coined the word *maumet* for "idol"—had won. So far as war in the Holy Land went, the Christians had no stomach for it any more.

The third of Catherine's tasks was to heal the Great Schism of the West. At this the Saint worked, prayed, and failed again. She had rallied to Urban, stormed at the three Italian Cardinals, kept after Joanna of Naples to bring her back into Urban's obedience, demanded that the King of France abandon "Belial's son, the cursed antipope," as she called Clement VII. Reinforcing Urban, she had summoned Charles of Durazzo to head an army against the Clementines. She wrote the Queen of Hungary: "You know it is in the hour of need that love is manifest. The Church has need of you." and she directed Urban to oust the Cardinals and name twenty-nine new ones chosen "from amongst all nations"; to warn Europe's crowned heads of the dangers of schism; and to take over Castel Sant' Angelo. Those letters of hers to Popes and rulers, Princes, Cardinals and Dukes, the lords of cities and their peoples, remain her monument.

Catherine, who bore in her hands, feet and side the five wounds of Jesus, was subject to bouts of black depression (followed, indeed, by the ecstasies). Her confessor, Raymond of Capua, relays a dialogue which transpired, after one of these black moods, between the Saint and Jesus Christ.

Catherine cried out: "Where wert Thou, Savior, while my spirit within me was so utterly cast down?"

And the answer came: "In thy heart . . . there was I, to sustain thee in the battle, and to save thee in the great water floods."

She could not survive the inception of the Schism very long; only two years, and then in 1380 she was gone, still young, at about the same age as Christ crucified.

Her last bed was straw; on it she died of cancer, and surely Jesus was with her in the battle. Her body was decapitated and buried there in Rome, the hacked-off head being carried for a relic to Siena.

For Joanna, threatened by Saint Catherine with violent death, there would still be two more years. First she was a prisoner in Castel Nuovo, shut here by Charles of Durazzo, of the cold heart, him she had befriended, one not even born in her old, great days. Charles told her she must name him, not the Clementine Louis, heir to her realm. But Joanna hedged and promised, still hoping for Duke Louis to come from over the sea.

Then Charles attacked with men and arms, laid siege to her tower, had her treed there, was hurling against her walls projectiles loaded with excrement and human remains. And a champion did try to save Joanna. Otto of Brunswick, the Queen's fourth husband, did respond to her secret cry for help. Sword in hand, leading his men, he slashed his way to the prison tower and was grasping for Charles's flag when he fell, amongst enemy knights. After that she was completely in Charles's power, and he carried her away and locked her in the Castle of Muro—a desolate structure on the edge of a ravine, in dust and eroded land, under beating sun. It was to the southeast of Naples, not far from Venosa, only sixty miles southeast, but removed for all time from her carved throne.

She who had ruled, and owned; who had loved and also killed; who had murdered Andrew, her husband (as Charles proclaimed, for that was Charles's antique excuse for his treason) or had not murdered Andrew, was alone now. She, the first woman ever to receive the papal Golden Rose, had now, by a later Pope, been put out of the Church, and by an upstart defrauded of her crown. The excommunicated have no rights at all; no vows to them are binding, no debts need be repaid. And she was fifty-six years old.

Exactly how Joanna died, at whose hand, is not clear. According to Dietrich of Niem she had gone to chapel that May morning in 1382 and was at her prayers; kneeling there in the candle flicker, her mind perhaps turning backward over the long past. It is said that she was strangled as she prayed, that quick, rough fingers looped a cord over her head and jerked it tight. Surely in the final spasm she had no more time to think, or to see the faces of those others who had paid with their deaths for that forgotten murder of Prince Andrew. It is doubtful if she had a moment at the last there, on that cold chapel floor, to tell herself whether or not she was innocent. Probably she could only remember how gustfully she had breathed in the sweet air.

As for Duke Louis d'Anjou, early in 1383 he finally sailed, and finally marched. There even came a day when he was only twenty-five leagues away from Pope Urban in Rome. Urban on that day was almost unarmed; he was dickering with Sir John Hawkwood, famed captain of mercenaries, who well knew that Louis was approaching at the head of sixty thousand men. Hawkwood had Urban where he wanted him, their bargain was still unclosed.

However, like Pope Clement before him, Louis stayed out of reach. He had brought a jeweled crown along with him and wanted it set on his own head in Naples. Urban could be postponed.

The promised realm of Adria and the throne of Naples shimmered before Duke Louis, a double prize. French lords, aroused against Urban (who excommunicated the whole lot of them and preached a crusade against them, a crusade, he declared, worth the same merit as if they were fighting Saracens in Palestine) were at his side. But Charles of Durazzo, besides plotting with Urban to try poison on Louis, was fighting a guerrilla war. He kept away, he was never there for a battle.

At a day's march out of Naples, which city he could have taken with ease, Duke Louis stopped. He stayed on in Italy to watch thousands of his men gradually sicken under the hot sun and die, and from the jaws of victory he snatched defeat.

9 THE LION IN SPAIN

IF POPE CLEMENT VII was unfortunate in the Duke
of Anjou, he was blessed in another of his chief lieutenants,
Pedro de Luna. Kin to the royal house of Aragon and also
of Navarre, de Luna seemed a born Papal Legate to the
Christian Kingdoms of Spain. Clement accordingly sent
him off, and he reached Barcelona the first week in April,
1379. It was not long before his skill had netted a future
saint for Clement, the renowned Vincent Ferrer. Aware
that a good part of leadership is gathering the right people
about one, he proved equally successful in obtaining as aman-
uensis the clever Francisco Climent Capera from Valencia.
King Peter the Ceremonious of Aragon he found well disposed toward Pope Clement, particularly because the latter
—with promises of the Kingdom of Adria—had whistled off
Duke Louis of Anjou from his designs on the Roussillon
and the Balearic Islands.

Then there was Castile, where de Luna had every reason
to hope for a welcome. It turned out that Urban's envoys
had gotten there first, making overtures to King Henry for
the Roman Pope. The King, however, had not said yes. Unlike many kings, this one did not forget a past favor. He
still saw himself, Henry of Trastamara, lumbering off a battlefield back in 1367, his horse too heavily barbed to run.
He remembered how his monstrous half brother, Peter the
Cruel, winner that day, had galloped his black mount here
and there over the field of the dead, searching through the
bodies and calling out for Henry's blood. That time, Henry

had made it to the palace of Illueca, de Luna's ancestral home. De Luna had saved him, so that Henry went back later on and killed Peter the Cruel. Now, he merely announced that for the moment, all Church revenues would go into the public treasury pending his decision.

Henry died in May, warning his heir not to choose too quickly between the Popes. Young King Juan obediently sent out envoys to Avignon and thence to Naples and Rome, and on the basis of their reports he leaned toward Pope Clement. On November 23, 1380, de Luna was at Medina del Campo, debating the Schism and pleading Clement's cause before King Juan. Two days later, Urban's man, Francesco d'Urbino, spoke for the Pontiff of Rome. Thirty-four Spanish men of the cloth, most of whom had been in Rome at the time of the Fateful Conclave, added their testimony.

While royalty and the intellectuals debated the Schism, the average man gave up; millions then, as in religious questions still, dismissed the whole subject, saying they were not qualified to judge. For men are happy to proclaim there is an area where their minds may not go, where only a particular class of people is, somehow, authorized to venture. Froissart wrote of the Schism: "Such matters do not belong to me." And so that most intimate, most urgent door is closed and padlocked. In every era, if superstition is to be exploited, the strong discover that this willing ignorance is an essential; it is easily maintained by brainwashing the very young, and leaving the rest to human nature, sure as gravity.

Over a period of four months, every detail being fresh in mind, the question was aired and debated to shreds. Thereafter, the clergy of Castile were consulted. Finally, on May 19, 1381, Castile declared for Pope Clement VII. Saint Vincent began to travel about that country winning Clementine souls.

De Luna then went on to Portugal. "I speak of what I

saw and heard," he said there, explaining the Schism to King Ferdinand and his Court: "Men grave and earnest, declaring they had acted in the grip of terror. By these men I mean the Cardinals. We must perforce take their word for it, because they and only they can tell what came to pass."

But England and Portugal had just allied themselves in a war against Castile, and winning Portugal seemed pretty hopeless. De Luna therefore retired to his Castle of Illueca. Actually, he had succeeded better than he thought. Once the war was over and the English had gone, Ferdinand of Portugal did side with Pope Clement. His envoy to Clement was soon slaughtered by the Urbanists, however. Urban's Bull of November 4, 1385, forgave the murderers, since, the Roman Pope said, they had acted only from excess of zeal.

As for Peter the Ceremonious of Aragon, he kept on playing one Pope against the other until January 5, 1387, when he died. Upon learning of this, de Luna hurried down from his fastness of Illueca, and on January 24, using the vulgar tongue, preached a moving sermon in the Cathedral of Barcelona before John, the new King, his Queen Yolande de Bar (cousin to France's Charles VI) and Queen Mary of Sicily. On February 24 Aragon declared for Pope Clement. Still another feather for Clement in de Luna's cap was the King of Navarre. Except for uncertain Portugal, he had thus won over Christian Spain, and Church treasure began to pour from there into the vaults at Avignon.

URBAN BECAME Pope partly by pre-election design, partly by fluke, but it was his own nature which brought on the Great Schism of the West. At whatever point one examines his career, it is much the same. One could indeed read the end of it from the beginning: he would be sure to sickly things over, as a slug will leave its calligraphy of slime, yesterday or tomorrow.

Queen Joanna of Naples was only one victim of this "Pontiff of the massive hates." For example there was the case of his infamous nephew, Francesco Prignano, better known as Butillo, or Fatty. Urban had traded Joanna's kingdom to Charles of Durazzo, hoping for other cities—Capua, Caserta, Aversa, Nocera, Amalfi—to give to Butillo.

Urban was banqueting with Charles, by then on Naples' throne. Toward the close of the feast, wishing further to enrich the infamous Butillo, Urban asked Charles for Capua. Never, replied Charles; never would he make a Prince of Capua out of anyone so worthless as Urban's nephew. At this the Pope turned fiery red and released such a stream of evil language against Charles that he had him seized and led off screaming and shut him up in the fortress at Naples.

Charles was Urban's man, it will be remembered—Urban's sword. Both at this time were in grave danger from the temporarily successful invader, Duke Louis. Urban had come south supposedly to help Charles out—and this was

the result. It was always difficult to say, from the treatment
he accorded them, just whom the Pope considered his
friends.

The matter was mended. Urban, possibly having entered
another phase of his illness, was freed. Nephew Butillo ultimately got Nocera and renounced Capua. Along the line,
however, Butillo had proceeded to kidnap a young nun, and
she was a kinswoman of Charles's. Charles summoned the
ravisher, who refused to appear and was thereupon sentenced by the King's council to have his head cut off. Urban
set the judgment aside. Only he was sovereign of Naples, he
said; without his leave, no one could condemn to death a
member of his house, particularly for such a trifling act.
Moreover, he said, the peccadillo should certainly be overlooked in view of Butillo's youth. (Butillo was past forty.)

In the autumn of 1384, Duke Louis d'Anjou, following
his soldiers, sickened and died in his turn. Charles then
felt strong enough to do as he pleased with Urban, and
marched against him at Nocera, while over in France the
Clementines rejoiced at this new division.

Meanwhile there was the matter of Urban's College of
Cardinals. When the original Sacred College deserted him
in 1378, he had appointed new ones, naturally of his own
choosing. It was not long before a group of these resolved
at any cost to put him off the throne. They hired a skilled
lawyer, Bartolino da Piacenza, who produced arguments to
the effect that the Sacred College could indeed exercise for-
cible control over a Pope whose conduct was detrimental to
the welfare of the Church. The Cardinals could, he said,
either elect another to serve coetaneously with such a Pope,
or else depose the unfit Pope and name his successor—the
same answer that Urban's first College had come up with
at Fondi. (Today Catholics believe that whereas the Pope
does not derive his authority from the Cardinals but *de iure*

divino, by divine right, only he can decide as to his abdication; and that he can be deposed only for heresy and by a General Council.)

When the Cardinal of Manupello betrayed his plotting colleagues they were handed over to torturers. A confession was forced from the Bishop of Aquila (after he had lost consciousness seven times under "the question") that the group of six had planned to take Urban prisoner, try him as a heretic and burn him to death.

One of the six, the fat Gentile di Sangro, was subjected to a kind of torture called the Italian method, or *strappado.* He was trussed up, hoisted to the ceiling by a pulley and repeatedly dropped. Every time he fell he mouthed the words: "I have nothing to confess."

The Cardinal of Venice was treated the same. Urban arranged that this one's torture should be conducted in a room giving on his own customary place of meditation in the castle gardens below. The Pope was pacing there, reading the Divine Office, as his victim continued to gasp out: "Christ suffered for us; we must suffer for Him. Christ suffered for us . . ." Urban, pausing from time to time, listened to these sounds, face tilted up, eyes closed, then resumed his walking and his reading.

Dietrich of Niem, the Pope's secretary, tells how he pleaded humbly, trembling with fright, and in vain, for the tortured, then went away and hid himself to weep. Urban's answer was to keep them chained in cells too short for them to lie down in.

And as Charles was now besieging him, the Pope was both jailer and prisoner at once, his victims below him in their dungeon and he above, hemmed in by Charles's soldiers. Regularly, Urban would appear at his window with bell, book and candle—to the soldiers' loud hoots—and excommunicate the besiegers four times a day. The Pope extricated himself from Nocera by buying up some Clemen-

tine mercenaries who cleared a way out, and so he departed,
dropping treasures along the mountain roads and down the
ravines as he went—jewels, chalices, precious weaves—but
preserving intact his line of tortured Cardinals, lashed to
their pack animals like a baggage train behind him. The
Bishop of Aquila, oldest and most worn of all, proved trou-
blesome at this point, his mount lagging and slowing down
the flight. Urban, eyes aflicker, watched while his soldiers
kicked and mauled the old man and at last left his silent
body beside the road.

One way or another the Pope made Genoa by sea. People
crowded along the port to welcome him, but could not
stomach the chained-up Cardinals. A public clamor began,
and even royalty intervened: one of the six prisoners, the
Englishman Adam Easton, was released when Richard II
informed Urban that otherwise he would pull England out
of Urban's camp. Two Urbanist Cardinals who had dared
speak up for the victims fled to Pope Clement. It is said that
one of them, Pileus of Prato, by way of insulting Urban
burned his red hat in the public square at Pavia. (It is added
that this prelate later abandoned Clement for the Urbanist
Boniface IX, after which he became known as the Cardinal
with Three Hats.)

As for the remaining prisoners, on a stormy December
night in 1385, the five of them vanished away. We have too
much information as to their doom: it is said that their
throats were slit and they were bundled into graves hurriedly
scratched out in a stable floor; that they were strangled,
salted, dried in an oven, and stored each in a separate coffer
on which was a Cardinal's hat; that one had a ravening wolf
shut in his cell; that two were sewn up in skins with live
serpents and flung into the sea; that one died by the method
Urban liked best—in quicklime to his head, so that you
could watch the play of expressions on his face. One version
has it that they were walled up alive—and late in the nine-

teenth century walled remains would be dug up in the Convent of San Giovanni which might have been theirs. Nobody knows.

In those days people inherited their wars. A father would
leave some realm to a son, who would then have to fight for
his legacy. More complications would arise if the son was a
minor: then a queen or princely uncle would be taking over
as regent. The possibilities for turmoil were endless: life for
the ruling class was a deadly game of three-dimensional
chess.

Thus it came about that Naples was disputed not only by
two Popes, but by two little boys. For Charles of Durazzo
was invited over to Hungary to make war and win that
country's throne. Despite the pleas of his wife, Marguerite,
Charles sailed away, leaving Urban, still active, at his heels.
In Buda, Charles briefly wore his new crown; but he was
pierced through by a Hungarian assassin's sword, lingered,
and died on February 5, 1387. His young son Ladislas thus
inherited Naples—but so also did Louis, the son of Duke
Louis d'Anjou, Joanna's heir.

Urban now had a chance to regain his power, by joining
forces with Marguerite, Charles's widow, and driving off
the Clementines. Marguerite begged and pleaded with Urban. And to help him see the light she even kidnapped the
precious Butillo, and now set him free as a special induce-
ment, all to no avail. Urban wanted no part of the hated
Charles. He declared a crusade against both little boys. Otto
of Brunswick, once Charles's captive, reappeared at this
point and won over Naples to Louis' heir, and incidentally
to Pope Clement. A number of other Italian cities, such as
Bologna, also turned Clementine. By this time Pope Clement's "obedience" almost equaled Pope Urban's.

When Urban was seventy-two he had reigned, in effect as
co-Pope, eleven awful years. He had spent the time at war

on many levels, in the world and within himself. He had

led armies here and there and been beaten back. His hands
were purple with the blood of his own Cardinals. He had
rejected Pope Clement's proposal, made through envoys to
all of Europe's courts, that the disastrous double election of
1378 be submitted to the judgment of an Ecumenical Council. Now he dragged himself from city to city, an embarrassment, Joudou says, even to those who were on his side. One
day near Perugia the mule he was riding slid from under
him.

They carried the injured Pontiff to Rome and his ill-fated
wanderings were over. Weakened from his fall, sick, he still
would not die. Then, on October 15, 1389, he was gone,
and as somebody afterward wrote, no man could shed a tear.

And now, you would think, the Schism was ended. Eleven
years before, the authorized electors had produced, instead
of one, two Heads of the Church. Now, only one Head was
left. To us, at this distance, it all looks simple enough. It
was not.

Urban had created and left behind him fourteen new
Cardinals, and whatever the great issues involved, the personal issues were that these fourteen did not care to be
tortured, or jailed—perhaps tethered at the end of a chain—
or to lose their property, or to stop being Cardinals, or quite
simply to stop being.

After the solemn funeral at Saint Peter's they went into
Conclave before Avignon should hear of the death, news of
which only reached that city on the tenth day following, and
they proceeded with all nimble speed to elect one of themselves as Pope.

Historians have called them selfish for not consulting the
rulers, divines and intellectuals of Europe and at least trying
to end the Great Schism, but had they so consulted and so
tried they would likely have lost, if not their heads, at any

rate their hats. Besides, they can always reply from their graves that they considered themselves the true, legitimate line, the only valid authorities concerned, and that had they turned to anyone else this would have been tantamount to disclaiming Urban, from whom their own validity derived. Certainly any such appeal to the outside would mean they had been clustering around an antipope, and therefore deserved at the very least an indefinite occupancy of somebody's jail.

On November 2, 1389, they elected Piero Tomacelli, Cardinal of Naples, as Pope Boniface IX. And the Schism was safe.

The new Roman Pope was his predecessor's reverse: young, good-looking, of noble family, with winning manners. He came just in time for Rome's Holy Year Jubilee of 1390, which means that his war chest at once brimmed over with pilgrims' monies to carry on the Schism.

11 THE WELL-BELOVED CHARLES

THERE IS A crack, they say, in everything God has made. This could well describe the Europe of that day: not only were there two heads to its Church, but the one head of its leading King was split down the middle.

Nature had at first been generous to young Charles VI of France, throned as a boy of twelve when his father, the Learned One, died. He could sit a horse, shoot an arrow and break a lance with the best. At thirteen he would hunt the wild boar. Not quite fourteen, in November, 1382, he took the field and won a great victory against the Flemish at Roosebeke. All his critics could find to say of the popular King was that he threw away money, and threw away love. "Heavy," wrote someone, "was the tribute he exacted from the daughters of his subjects."

When he was seventeen, he married Bavarian Isabeau (granddaughter to the Duke of Milan, a man so unsavory that he had required Petrarch's pen to improve his image). Her father, Duke Stephen of Bavaria, refused France that self-arrogated right to examine the King's intended stark naked. This was a task normally entrusted to ladies of the court, their purpose being to determine—how, is not reported—whether or not the maiden would prove fertile. Much taken with the rompish fourteen-year-old, Charles married her anyway.

Approaching twenty, King Charles VI shook off his four overbearing uncles and replaced them with functionaries who had served his father well, such able commoners as

Bureau de la Rivière and Olivier de Clisson. The discarded Highnesses scornfully dubbed these people "marmosets," by which they meant little, ugly, lowborn men.

It was precisely on account of one of these marmosets that the worst came about. When a certain noble, backed by the Duke of Brittany, almost succeeded in murdering Clisson, Charles saw it as a blow at the King. "They shall pay for this," he cried, "as if it were done to myself." And he marched against Brittany.

Many did not favor the expedition. There were delays and arguments. Charles was always feverish when contradicted, and those about him found him staring and remote. The doctors said he was unfit to ride. He roused himself, however, and on a hot August morning in 1392, resumed the march.

As Charles rode through the Forest of Le Mans, a bare-footed, wild-haired man ran out from under the trees. Pounding up to Charles he seized the bridle of the royal horse. "King!" he shouted, "ride no farther! Go back—thou art betrayed!" The King's soldiers beat him away, out of sight and history. Wordless, Charles rode on.

At midday, under stifling sun, they were crossing a vast, sandy plain. Charles, buttoned up in black velvet, rode by himself. Directly behind him, one following the other, came two of his pages. The page who bore the King's lance dozed off, jerked himself awake, dozed off again. The lance slipped from his fingers. It fell against the steel helmet of the boy in front of him and rang out like a gong.

The King screamed, wheeled, and drew his sword. "Advance!" he bawled. "Advance on the traitors!" He killed four of his people that day, says the *Grandes Chroniques de France*. Then he galloped off, screaming, and they finally managed to ride him down, pinion his arms, and get his sword away. He spoke no further word, but his eyes rolled in his head, showing the whites.

Every possible cure was attempted. A wax figure was made of the King and sent with a great wax taper to Arras, to an abbey where lies Saint Aquaire, who heals the insane. Nor was another psychiatrist saint, Hernier in Rouais, neglected. Prayer meetings were held in the streets, and special alms given. A charlatan was called in to break the spell. Among the doctors one de Harseley, too clever to stay long at Court, made Charles well that first time. "This disorder of the King's," said he, "proceeds from the alarm in the forest, and from inheriting too much of his mother's weak nerves."

But nothing availed for long. For three decades, Charles and France would plunge into and rise from a madness that was all the worse for being cyclical and intermittent. A civil war between the partisans of Burgundy and those of Orléans —the Burgundians and Armagnacs—would rend the country as Charles's mind was rent. The time would come when Isabeau would give France to England by the Treaty of Troyes.

Often the King had to be shut away, and padded back and forth, naked and fouled. If he ate, he wolfed his food down. He had discovered a little fragment of iron, which he secreted in a fold of his body. "They had not," writes Juvénal des Ursins, "previously found out about this and it rotted his flesh away, but no one dared come close enough to rid him of it." A doctor finally sent in some strong young courtiers, wearing protective clothing and with their faces blackened. When he caught sight of them the King was shocked into passivity. He let them remove his rags and the piece of iron, and change his clothes. "He was piteous to behold, his body eaten up by dirt and lice. Whenever they wanted to clean him, they had to go about it in this way."

The young Queen continued to live with her husband for many years. Often, her large brown eyes must have widened in horror as the frenzy possessed him again. She never knew, ahead of time, what state he would be in: presiding at his council, receiving ambassadors, or running here and there like a mad dog, and begging for death. At those periods he could not stand her at all. "Who is that woman?" he would cry. "She obsesses me! Get her out of my sight!" He could remember his uncles and brother and companions and even servants long dead, but not his wife and children. And if, alongside his own, he noticed her Bavarian coat of arms, he would dance before it and make obscene gestures and try to wipe it out.

Meanwhile the ugly marmosets who could have saved France were ousted by the Dukes. The one-eyed Clisson, immediate cause of the disaster, was besieged by soldiers who had enlisted in the abortive war on Brittany and wanted their pay. Bowed by this and other problems, he presented himself one day to the Duke of Burgundy, his haughty and now triumphant foe, and asked what to do.

Answered the Duke: "Clisson, Clisson, you need not trouble yourself about the state of France, for she will be perfectly well governed without you. Quit my presence and leave my house. Let me never see you again: and know that were it not from regard to my own honor, I would have your other eye put out."

There were others, too, who failed to grieve over what had happened that day in the forest. Over in Rome, Pope Boniface and his Cardinals "rejoiced on hearing it. They . . . said the worst of their enemies was severely chastised, when God had thus deprived him of his senses; and that this punishment had been inflicted by Heaven, for having so strenuously supported the antipope of Avignon; that this chastisement should make him attend more to his own kingdom, and that their cause would now be better."

12 PEACE FOR TEN TONS OF HERRINGS

Back in 1391 the Chancellor of the University of Paris, Jean de Gerson, had called on King Charles and the Dukes for an end to the Great Schism. Instead of their military campaigns he asked the King and nobility to fast and pray. The idea gradually developed to follow one of three Ways to Unity: the Way of an Ecumenical Council; the Way of Convention (that is, of mutual agreement between the two Pontiffs); or the Way of Cession, whereby each of the two would step down from the splintered throne.

All this was of course an affront to Clement VII, France's reigning Pope. To answer the University of Paris, Clement selected his Legate, who had come back victorious from Spain, thus giving Pedro de Luna yet another chance to arise and shine. Instead of supporting Pope Clement in this crisis, the Legate, speaking so to say as Crown Prince of the Church, recommended the throning of yet a third Pontiff: himself. He stood, he told them, for the union of Christendom, and if, when the day came, he were exalted to the Papacy, he, de Luna, would willingly take off his tiara and set it aside. "Elect me to abdicate," he told them in effect.

At our distance, it might seem peculiar to invest a man with office for the sake of ousting him: but when we remember that following the death of one Pope his Cardinals automatically elect another, and that here was a man who stood for union, to be achieved if need be by the Way of Cession after he was Pope—we see why this policy statement proved as welcome to most as it looks implausible today.

Now Legate *a latere*—from the Pope's side, specially en-trusted—in May, 1393 de Luna obtained an audience with the uncles of the King of England, asking if he might come over the Channel and preach Pope Clement. The Duke of Lancaster replied: "We follow my lord Boniface. You wish to preach against him in our realm? Then do so. . . . But be assured, since you speak of this ominous split, that you Cardinals of Avignon are the cause of it, and it is you who keep it going and you who make it worse. If I had my way, once peace is signed, you would have either to establish unity once more, or be wiped out."

Pedro de Luna had always been aware that as between himself and Clement, he was the better man, the one who, if not at Rome, should have been chosen at Fondi. He was also persuaded—it had become the theme of his life—that Urban was an interloper and no Pope at all, which would nullify Boniface and anyone else of Urban's line. On the vacuity of Urban's claim he would never yield, not when he was past ninety; not when dying, and his immortal soul atremble in the balance; not beyond the grave.

Journeying here and there, de Luna had indeed won many notables over to Clement, but inevitably, at the same time, over to himself. This fact had not escaped the Pope. Never-theless de Luna had very likely noticed that Clement, though the younger man, was failing. Self-indulged, cos-seted, the Pontiff was not one to stick to the abstinence and cold water, the fig-and-grape diet advocated at this court in an earlier age by Petrarch. And page boys around him were rifer here than ever, their jackets climbing higher: knee length in the days of Clement VI, they were shrinking to mid-buttock or worse.

Whatever de Luna's motives for offering to settle the Schism over the head of his chief, to sacrifice the throne once he was on it and thus reunify the Church, when he got back to Avignon the atmosphere was chill. For a time he even thought of going home to Aragon again.

Suddenly, however, none of this mattered any more. On the morning of September 16, 1394, Clement heard Mass, and as he returned to his chamber felt a great blackness bear him down. He had only a moment left, to seat himself and call for wine.

Six days after Pope Clement's passing, the King of France, who was living at the Hôtel Saint-Pol in Paris, was first brought the news—which might, had it come in record time, have reached him in three and a half.

Charles was luckily sane at the moment and at once gathered his counselors to decide whether or not a new papal election should be permitted. Simon de Cramaud, Patriarch of Alexandria—and no friend of de Luna, who had prevented his acquiring a Cardinal's hat—said that the Holy See should be kept vacant until the kings of Clement's obedience could get together with the late Pope's Cardinals. Although this move would cast doubt on the validity of the departed Clement, almost everyone agreed. Accordingly, bearing instructions to this effect, the King's courier galloped off to Avignon that same day.

The University of Paris also seconded the King's move, and stood for the abdication of the Roman Pope, Boniface IX, to be followed by an assemblage of leading personalities to end the Schism.

King Charles's letter was whirled to Avignon in four days and was thrust into the hands of one of the Cardinals just as he was being shut up with the rest into Conclave.

Eleven of the twenty-one Cardinals were Frenchmen. Still, the French King's letter was not opened. A voice was raised against reading it, since it had arrived when the Cardinals were already assembled and the doors about to be locked. Then de Luna spoke up and said that, for the very sake of Church union, the vacant See must be filled at once. Should Boniface be induced to abdicate, then, in order for Christianity to agree on a Pope, that Pope would have to be elected by a College of Cardinals half of whom would be Urbanists, and half Clementine. And only a valid Pope—i.e., a Clementine—could validate the Urbanist Cardinals, they being schismatics. When someone proposed the election of Boniface IX, Pope of Rome, he was told that only a valid Pope could relieve Boniface from the censures the late Clement had declared against him.

Pedro de Luna had made it clear everywhere that, to terminate the Schism, he believed in the Way of Cession—the abdication of both the Clementine and the Urbanist Popes. He assured his colleagues, there in Conclave, that he wanted Church union as much as the rest of them, and that he could as easily doff the tiara, once it was placed on his brows, as he could throw off his cope. Moreover he was clearly the ablest man present. As protocol decreed, Pedro de Luna induced them to urge him and urge him again, but at last he agreed to be elected—by twenty votes. On the eleventh of October, 1394, they crowned him Pope Benedict XIII.

Later on, fearing for their benefices, the Cardinals wrote King Charles that they had chosen de Luna on a provisional basis only, and that the election was up to the King's pleasure. Froissart, although praising de Luna as "a devout man, and of a contemplative life," comments that his choosing was "subject to the approbation of the King of France and his council, otherwise the election would not have been maintained. . . . Those who were, or ought to have been, free, thus subjected themselves to the will of others whom they should have commanded."

Young Charles and the University of Paris rejoiced at the news of Benedict's election. At last, they thought, the

Schism was going to end, for so the new Pope had promised when he came to Paris as Pedro de Luna. In February, 1395, the King summoned a large gathering of leading clerics, and sixty-nine of them arrived at the capital to confer on the projected union of the Church. Charles had previously settled with Benedict that the assemblage would only consult, and would take no step unsanctioned by the Pope.

They talked two weeks, under the chairmanship of the anti-Benedict Simon de Cramaud. Simon—and actually the rest of them too—stood for the Way of Cession. Nor did they object now to an Italian Pope, residing not in Avignon but in the Eternal City. Now they had a foreigner, a Spaniard, anyhow. So let there be another foreigner—anything to end the Schism—and let him sit in Rome.

Without much appreciation of Benedict's character, a solemn party of dignitaries then floated down the Rhône to tell the Pope what Paris had decided. The party included, with their respective suites, the King's uncles (Dukes of Berry and Burgundy), and his brother Louis, Duke of Orleans. It was May. The Princes were borne rapidly along in their lavishly decorated boats. They, together with delegates from the University of Paris, disembarked at Avignon's ramparts, were received with wine and spices by Benedict and invited to dinner for the following day, then recrossed the Rhône to sleep on French soil.

But later, after hearing them out, Benedict told them: "The Way of Convention is my Way." He meant specifically that the two Popes and two Curias would meet somewhere and consult with each other as to what solution was in the best interests of the Church. The meat would (as a Persian proverb has it) be entrusted to the cat. Benedict was sure that, being right, he could win over the erring Roman Pope Boniface, if only they came together face to face.

The envoys began talking about the Way of Cession, and how that was the King's Way. They collected Benedict's

Cardinals at Villeneuve on the French side and won most of them over. Had not the Pope himself, as Cardinal Legate, declared for the Way of Cession? It now developed that he had meant the Way of Cession, only if all other Ways were eliminated first. For example, he also favored the Way of Accomplished Fact—the *voie de fait*—say a military victory over the other Pope.

Benedict now called in the King's uncles to his palace and had a long tête-à-tête with the Duke of Burgundy. The Pope commented frankly that had he been French instead of Spanish, he would have been treated better. As for his Cardinals, and asking their advice, he told the Duke they often changed their minds. "And why," he added, "should one set underfoot what is at the head, and why should one become the serving man of him who has you for his master?"

Then he spoke in private with each of the other two Dukes, succeeding best with King Charles's young brother, Louis of Orléans, who liked the still current idea of possessing a kingdom of Adria carved out from Italy's Papal States, as had earlier been offered to Louis d'Anjou. The effects of this interview proved enduring. In future years, if the King was sound, and had his brother Orléans beside him, de Luna prospered. If the King was ill and the uncles ruled, de Luna had to struggle all the harder to retain his papal throne. Benedict's star would rise and set with Charles's mind.

Meanwhile things were not going too well at the conference when Avignon's bridge, specifically one of its wooden arches, caught fire and went up in smoke. The guests, thus marooned on the other side of the Rhône, took it personally. They blamed the Pope, who averred he was innocent and set up pontoons. There was a grand scene at the end of these events with the Dukes and all the Cardinals (except only Martin de Salva, Benedict's trusty Cardinal of Pamplona) on their knees begging the Pope to accept the

Way of Cession, the Way which, indeed, he had sworn on the Bible to follow.

It is from this time on, this summer of 1395, that history begins to call Benedict XIII adamant, inflexible and the like. Over and over, in every situation, some version of the term recurs. And yet, however cross-grained, stiff-necked, granitic and obdurate this Pope might be, Benedict, it should be remembered, did what he did because he thought he was right.

Benedict said No. And he apparently could not foresee that thereby he was losing France, and hemming himself in with hostile French Cardinals who had chosen to side with the then neutral (which to Benedict meant hostile) King of France—the country which held many of their benefices, and whose protection they urgently required.

"Rather than take the Way of Cession," Benedict thundered at the great assemblage, "I would be burned alive!"

His guests refused another invitation to dine. "Enough of banquets," they said. "We are hastening back to the King." But first they held a public meeting in the Church of the Franciscans, where they explained the value of the Way of Cession, and roused the citizens of Avignon against their stubborn Spanish Pope.

The Way of Cession would work, of course, only if both Popes agreed to abdicate. Two impossibles do not add up to a feasibility, and the basic reality of the day was that neither Pope would yield. They backed and filled, and sent out abortive embassies. There was a great coming and going, there were spies, battles, manipulations, deceptions, there were supporters who failed. Europe was an anthill stirred with a stick.

All this time, between France and England, the Hundred Years' War which had started in the late 1330s, was off and on again. It would continue until 1453, but it was intermittent only. Indeed Richard II of England, King in 1377, was so much inclined toward France, where he was born and in whose tongue he was fluent, that the English disparagingly called him Richard of Bordeaux.

Unlike his bellicose nobles, he stood for peace across the Channel. In the autumn of 1396, after long negotiations, he married the French King's little daughter, Isabella. The child, born November 9, 1389, was not quite seven. Since the Church had fixed twelve years as a girl's minimum marriage age—for a boy it was fifteen—and the Holy See reserved to itself all dispensations from a matrimonial impediment, only a Pontiff could validate the royal bond. It was Benedict XIII, the Clementine Pope, who was asked to grant the necessary dispensation.

Froissart (who had previously presented Richard with a French book about love, bound in crimson velvet, with silver-gilt roses) describes the wedding, over in France: the plain studded with tents and pavilions, the hundreds of glittering French and English knights weeping for joy, the bareheaded Kings passing together, hand in hand, between their kneeling ranks. He tells of great dining boards set on trestles in the royal tent, of costly gold and silver plate, the Grand Dukes acting as waiters, serving the comfit box and wine. When the banquet was finally over, Queen Isabeau, attended by a great number of pearl-and-diamond-garlanded ladies of the court, led in the tiny bride, who was carried away in a rich silken litter.

For many years there was much galloping and sailing to and fro as responsible lay leaders tried to heal the impossible-to-accommodate Schism. Both Popes maintained aggressive lobbies in Paris, where the general view was that both should resign and the unity of Christendom be referred to an Ecumenical Council.

Froissart also tells of a secret Lenten meeting at Reims

in March, 1398, between King Charles and Wenceslaus,
known as the Worthless, the Holy Roman Emperor. On
this occasion the Germans took delivery of ten tons of her-
rings and eight hundred carp, while the Duke of Orléans
"supplied the company with such quantities of plates of
gold and silver, as though they had been made of wood."
Elsewhere we hear that Wenceslaus at first got himself too
drunk to negotiate, and that only days later, after a forty-
course dinner, he consulted with Charles at a time when the
latter sovereign felt his frenzy returning. Then the Duke of
Orléans took over, and the idea resulting from this and subsequent meetings was that Bishop Pierre d'Ailly would direct each Pope to submit to reelection; if not reelected, each
would then have to abdicate. The club held over the Pontiffs was loss of revenue: should either refuse, he would be,
in vulgar terms, cut off at the pockets.

From Rome, Boniface replied that he was agreeable to
whatever the Emperor, King Sigismund of Hungary and
the King of England should advise, and that "the person
who resides at Avignon, and who styles himself Pope Benedict, whom the King of France and his nation have acknowledged, must first resign all claims to the Papacy"—after
which he, Pope Boniface, would cheerfully attend an Ecumenical Council wherever the Kings should wish.

The truth is, Rome was incensed at the message d'Ailly
had brought from Germany and France. "They were fearful," records Froissart, "they should lose the Holy See,
which was of great consequence, and also profit to them,
from the general pardons, which were personally sought
for, and which obliged such multitudes to visit Rome." So
the Romans called on Pope Boniface to resist, and he told
them: "Be comforted . . . I will not submit to their wiles."

Returning from Rome, d'Ailly met Wenceslaus at Constance, and the Emperor told him: "Carry this message to
the King of France . . . as he shall act, so will I; but from

what I see, he must begin, and when he has deposed his Pope, we will depose ours."

King Charles was desperate for the Church to be whole again, because they had assured him that only then could he be whole himself. He summoned a learned gathering which debated, voted, and assigned a delegation to go down to Avignon with one sole task: to prevail upon Benedict, pending an Ecumenical Council which might well reelect him, to abdicate the papal throne.

Meanwhile, to please his new father-in-law, Richard of England held a meeting and harangued the audience on the miserable Schism, and on France's intention to remain neutral as between the two Popes. He added that Scotland, Castile, Aragon and Navarre were also neutral, while Germany, Bohemia and Italy planned to be the same.

This disastrous meeting was the talk of London. The English prelates cried: "Our King is quite a Frenchman. His only wish is to ruin us. What! does he mean to make us change our creed?"

The citizens parroted: "This Richard of Bordeaux will ruin everything; his head is so thoroughly French that he cannot disguise it. However, a day must come when he shall pay for all."

Obviously, something had to yield. In the end, it was France which created "a schism within the schism." When, in April, 1398, Pope Benedict canceled a tax concession that the French kings had enjoyed for three decades, thus upsetting the national budget, that was perhaps the last straw. Anyhow, on July 28, 1398, almost four years after Benedict was crowned, France publicly withdrew from his obedience.

This withdrawal by France not only removed souls from Avignon's jurisdiction—which was deplorable—it cut off the Pope's revenues—which was fatal. Yet even more serious than the loss of communicants, revenues, and the kingdom that had been Benedict's chief support, were the theological

implications of this act. The phrase "withdrawal of obedience" sounds so mild nowadays that it is easily passed over,
but what it meant was revolution: that Catholic adherence
to the Pope could depend henceforth on Catholic approval
of his actions.

To what extent the withdrawal, voted by prelates and
University spokesmen officially convoked by the King, was
wholehearted we cannot tell. Benedict's champion, the
splendid Duke Louis of Orléans, had temporarily abandoned the fray and left. King Charles commented listlessly
of the business, "Do as you like."

Valois, who in a later age checked the canvas bags of
square, irregular-sized, original paper ballots in France's national archives, says that two fifths of the assemblage were
opposed to the revolutionary step. Government pressure, he
implies, was behind the vote. He comments that France's
act led ultimately to creating a schism "in each province,
in each diocese, in each monastery, almost in each family."

The mission to Avignon, asking Benedict to abdicate, was
foredoomed. So little did France believe in it that Marshal
Geoffroy Le Maingre, called Boucicault, was ordered to go
along with the delegation and, should it fail, raise up an
army and attack the Pope.

Pierre d'Ailly, as Froissart tells it, arrived in Avignon, took
lodgings in the great wood market, changed his clothes, ate,
and went to see Benedict. "On entering his presence," Froissart says, "he made the proper obeisances; but not so rever-
ently, as if he and all the world acknowledged Benedict for
the true Pope." Well versed in Latin and French, the
Bishop "made an elegant harangue."

Absorbing the information that Emperor and King
wanted not only Boniface in Rome but also himself to disappear, Benedict by turns reddened and paled. Then he
cried in a loud voice, "I have labored hard for the good of

the Church, and have been duly elected Pope. I will never consent to resign. Let the King of France know, though it bring me the martyr's crown, he cannot prevent me from my rank, my throne and my opposition till the day I die."

"My Lord," replied the Bishop, "I always thought your Reverence more prudent than I find you to be."

In the end, Benedict agreed only that he would consult with his Cardinals. The next day, watching outside the meeting, Pierre d'Ailly knew from the way some of the Cardinals departed that there had been conflict. What had in fact happened was that the Cardinals assured the Pope and one another that with both Emperor and King united against them, they would lose all their benefices.

Entering the hall, d'Ailly thereupon asked the fulminating Pontiff for a quick answer.

"I will never resign," flamed Benedict, "nor submit myself to any King, Duke, or Count, nor agree to any treaty that shall include my resignation from my Popedom." And he never did.

As for King Richard, he paid at the last for his Frenchness, and all. He lost his throne, and his life. His marriage to Isabella, says the chronicler known as the Monk of Saint-Denis, was never consummated (but the Monk was not there). At any rate, a day came in 1399 when, off to a distant battlefield, he said goodbye for the last time to his small bride—raised her up in his arms and kissed her many times, more than forty times, a French writer affirms. And then he cried: "Adieu, Madame, adieu, until we meet again."

13 WHEN THE CITY BROKE ITS WORD

Many a man, receiving a death blow at seventy, will lie down and die. Not Benedict XIII. "Saint Peter was no less a Pope," he said, "because they did not obey him in France!" This although the Avignon Pope was left now, in 1398, with only one strong ally, his relative by marriage, Martin, King of Aragon. And while Martin did provide men-at-arms, his support was less than wholehearted: when Benedict offered to move the Papacy to Barcelona or Perpignan, Martin's comment was, "Does the priest think that for his sake I will plunge into war with the King of France?"

By this time Charles's Marshal Boucicault had marched down from Lyons to Fort Saint-André at Villeneuve, only the river's width from the Palace of the Popes.

"Your mission is finished," he said to the returning Pierre d'Ailly. "I will now fulfill mine. Go back and tell the King that I shall render him a good account."

There was now more pressure than ever on the Avignonese to abandon Pope Benedict. The King, they were assured, would close off their bridge and starve them to death if they stood by the Clementine. Some took to jeering at him, and calling him Pedro of the Moon and of the Sun, but as things worsened the municipal leaders swore allegiance to him, saying they would sacrifice themselves, their wives and their children rather than give up their Pope.

Alone in his palace, with only five Cardinals and a meager Spanish garrison under his nephew, Rodrigo de Luna, Benedict defied the might of France. He heartened the Avignon- 127 ese and held on to them with promises of help from Genoa and Aragon.

"You worry yourselves too much," he told them. "The city is strong and well stocked with supplies. You take care of the walls, I answer for the Palace."

Optimism, however, is not always convincing; more effective were the threats of the royal commissioners to seal off the citizens and starve them; besides, there was death waiting outside the walls, from Boucicault.

This was when the city broke its word and withdrew its solemn pledge. Avignon deserted Benedict, and went over to the eighteen Cardinals who by now were defying him from the French side of the Rhône. On September 15, 1398, the Avignonese, having seized the Pope's stores of weapons and grain, opened their gates to Cardinal Jean de Neufchâtel, called him their Governor, and on behalf of the Sacred College welcomed him in. Dressed in his red robes, the Cardinal paraded on horseback through the streets, a baton of authority in his hand, at his side a sword. He did not need his escort of armed men, although they made a good show, for he was hailed on all sides with shouts of "Long live Avignon! Long live the Sacred College!"

The day after that, the eighteen Cardinals sent off a message to King Charles assuring him that they had withdrawn their obedience from Benedict XIII. They then composed an apology in which they adduced their reasons for deserting the Pope, and in a later statement by Leonardo di Giffone, Benedict was placed in the same company as Julian the Apostate and that old favorite, Simon Magus—the bad Samaritan for whom simony is named.

By renouncing Benedict, Avignon cast an irrevocable vote against herself. In return for a momentary respite from attack, she sold her chance of world renown. It is always possible, of course, that history would have kept on unchanged had she decided otherwise. But when, in that strange ma-

neuver, directed for the first time in centuries by a King
openly over a Pope, Avignon rejected Benedict and chose
instead to be ruled by eighteen runaway Cardinals, and
highlighted to the Christian world the picture of one stubborn man standing almost alone in his papal stronghold,
abandoned by France, by the majority of those who had
elected him Pope, and now even by his city—she betrayed
not only her own trust but her own interest, which should
have hurried her to his defense.

Boucicault led his troops into Avignon on September 22,
1398, and took over the city, replacing Cardinal Jean de
Neufchâtel and proving to the citizens that they had not
bought peace by turning coats. His men seized the house of
Cardinal Pérez, one of Benedict's loyal five. This "livery"
stood close to the Palace walls and would have provided
cover for future attacks on the papal fortress, but the Marshal's men were driven out, leaving behind the first casualty
of the undeclared war. The Bridge was still defended by
a small band of Pope Benedict's men, who now set fire to
the wooden spans over the Rhône in an attempt to break
the connection with Villeneuve, headquarters of the enemy
Cardinals and the rest of the attacking force. At the same
time, they of the Bridge signaled to the Palace their desperate plight. From the Palace wall, a mortar sent a stone
cannonball arching through the cool autumn air. It was set
off most likely by some too eager soldier and not on command, but Marshal Boucicault, who had been the aggressor
throughout, chose to consider that his troops had been
attacked, and the war was on.

Mines and mortars guaranteed the submission of Benedict's little garrison at the Bridge outpost. Five days later,
on September 27, the flags of Avignon, of Marshal Boucicault, and of the Sacred College whipped in the wind over
Bénézet's Bridge, and the Pope was encircled in his fortress.

Benedict's luck seemed to have run out. Avignon had confiscated stocks of provisions and weapons which the Pope had stored away from the Palace. His only hope, the King of Aragon, dared not face up to France. And as for France, heretofore sponsor and protector of the Avignon Popes, it was her armed might behind the troops and guns of Boucicault, and back of his flag, her royal lilies.

Benedict had, in effect, only one confederate: the Palace itself. It was, and is, gigantic, this Palace-fortress where they hemmed him in. Solidly set on a rocky hill above the town and the river plain, its walls loomed twelve times the height of a soldier peering up at them from their massive base. Cannon, that terrible new weapon, could not crack them— they were six to twelve feet thick. (Even four centuries later, Napoleon's cannon could not pierce the fortress walls at Saint-Jean d'Acre.) The whole mass of masonry sat on its hill like a mammoth letter B, square-formed, with two open enclosures. Rising skyward, above the Palace's 150,000 square feet of area, were eight defending towers, the tallest more than one hundred and sixty feet above the pygmy foe.

In after years, when Mérimée as inspector general of historic monuments came to this Palace of the Popes, he would write that it looked more like the citadel of an Asian tyrant than the abode of the Vicar of a God of peace. Everything there, he said, "has been sacrificed to safety." The inside was as strongly fortified as the outside. Even if an attacker won over the gate and the great court, he would have to begin his siege all over again. Even if he staved in the gate of a second tower and pounded up long flights of narrow, twisting stairs to the Pope's apartments, he would only reach a trap where defending swordsmen could slash him down, destroy him and his fellows one by one. Against this martial aspect, we must remember that in what Froissart called "the loveliest, vastest House in the world" there were frescoes and tapestries and costly ornaments, gardens, soaring vistas and singing birds.

You can see the Marshal laying his armor aside and climbing to the rooftop of a house across from the main Palace gates. Houses huddled beneath the walls in what is now an open square might offer temporary cover for a frontal assault, but bombards could hurl down crushing masses of stone upon dwellings and men alike. And fire could shoot through the sky to turn shelter into trap. Those who escaped would be pursued by clashing, thudding arrows streaming from crenels and cross-shaped slits where archers from Aragon and Catalonia would be measuring the Marshal's men for death. If any of his soldiers ever succeeded in reaching the main portal, searing falls of pitch and oil would drown them as they tried to claw their way through stone.

Boucicault would have searched that expanse of masonry for a single flaw. He would have looked to his left, to study the Cathedral of Our Lady of the Lords, hard by the Palace's north wall. The Cathedral walls, even then some three hundred years old, were solid. He could harass the Pope with fire from the bell tower. Harassment would be all, however. If he mounted an attack from there, his forces would be raked with fire from the Trouillas Tower, the Tower of the Winepress, at the rear, and the Campane Tower which stood almost next to the Cathedral's own. Meanwhile, a deadly direct fire would cut his men down as Benedict's soldiers ranged themselves along the battle stations of the high wall by which the two towers were linked.

On the other side of the Palace, to the Marshal's right, the ground sloped down from the great chapel of Clement VI and the square, buttressed tower erected half a century earlier by Innocent VI which bolstered its defenses. The Marshal would have hungered after the high, narrow windows of the huge chapel, while his soldier's mind showed him the perils of an assault against that place.

Still other obstacles to a successful attack were invisible from this housetop, but the deserting Cardinals would have sketched him a rough plan of the Palace. The crossbar of the B divided the Palace into two halves; and it was likely that if the Marshal achieved the impossible and managed to scale a wall, or smash in an entrance with concentrated fire, or even tunnel his way under the fortress, he would only drive the Pope and his troops into the other half. For the haphazard planning of successive Popes had resulted in the erection of what amounted to a pair of fortresses side by side. An enemy's problem was further complicated by the fact that the defense walls he must storm were the outside walls of a series of connected but virtually independent buildings. Each of these was in effect a separate bastion, each could serve to bottle up the invader.

Still another obstacle, also invisible this one, was the ability of Rodrigo de Luna, Benedict's nephew, who commanded the Aragonese and Catalonian soldiers defending the Pope. He turned out to be a commander full of resources, meeting new emergencies with imagination and skill.

The Marshal must have shaken his head wearily over the prospect of a long war. He was well supplied with weapons for a siege—the more so as his own were now augmented by those from the warehouses of Pope Benedict—but what to do about those implacable walls? Unless he could discover some hidden weakness there, he might have to sweat it out, and wait for slow starvation, that last friend of all besiegers.

Boucicault put his armor back on, rallied his forces and prepared to attack. His men quickly took over the Episcopal Palace across from the Palace of the Popes. They installed themselves in the towers of the fortified dwellings which

various Cardinals had built (though hardly with a view to
making war on the Pontiff) and hauled weapons up into
the bell tower of Our Lady of the Lords. They seized the
houses of all private citizens opposite the great walls; they
drew up their heavy engines of assault. Arrows, catapulted
masses of stone, cannonballs, homed in on the defenders
from all directions. Some of Boucicault's men were so close
to the Palace, according to Valois, that the men on the walls
could hear their taunts.

"Your Pedro de Luna will die in there," they shouted;
"or if he gets out, it will be Paris for him, with a chain
round his neck!"

Benedict was in fact one of the earliest casualties, and
just escaped death. The bombardment of the Palace was
being reinforced by cannon obtained through the Cardinal
of Ostia, who fancied himself as a military man. Unfortunately for the Cardinal, men trained in handling the new
monsters were in short supply. However, he maneuvered his
artillery with considerable skill for a churchman, and on the
twenty-ninth of September one of his cannonballs, or rather
fragments of it, struck Pope Benedict in the shoulder.
(Boucicault was not one to be displeased, when he heard
of it.) Despite his wound, the Pope refused to allow his men
to return the fire because it was the feast of Saint Michael.

The Cardinal's lack of respect for the Archangel and the
person of the Pope received swift heavenly retribution: he
was killed two days afterward, presumably by one of his
own guns. Just how this happened is not clear. We do not
know whether he was cut down by a remarkable display of
inaccuracy on the part of a novice artilleryman, or whether,
as Joudou leads us to suppose, an overheated or improperly
charged cannon blew up.

In spite of heavy bombardment, the Palace defense was
running smoothly. The loss of supplies and weapons was
not serious as yet, and there was plenty to eat. Benedict had

ample forces for defense and he overlooked no detail; every point of danger was well guarded; every tower was manned throughout every hour of the day and night. Guards were stationed in passageways; reserves would hurry to any threatened point. Fresh troops relieved the others after eight hours of duty. The problems involved in dispatching soldiers through confined passages and up narrow stone staircases were carefully studied. A close inspection was established. At frequent intervals, rounds were made throughout the Palace, and in this work the five Cardinals alternated with bishops and abbots in maintaining a never-ending vigilance.

The Pope's inflexible discipline, his rock-hard will, won the loyalty of his soldiers. They were, as well, impressed by his frequent promises that they would not only win earthly glory by standing by him, but would also be rewarded for their help in heaven.

The refinements of modern warfare were foreshadowed in Avignon: civilian homes were bombarded. For this the Pope must bear a full measure of responsibility; if he did not order the bombarding, he apparently did nothing to prevent it. His justification was that the people had backslid. They were traitors. The Papal Palace dominated all of Avignon, and some of the most heavily populated sections were in easy range of the Pope's artillery. The houses with their stone walls and haphazard clutter of roofs were crowded together side against side; they were, in most cases, congeries of small rooms divided by narrow streets, above which neighbors across from each other might almost touch hands. Over and into these cells of sleeping humanity, great chunks of stone would arch silently through the night sky, crashing on bed and cradle. Then with a sweep of orange flame in would fly the fire balls, followed by dust and smoke, the sharp crack of splitting timbers, screams of the dying, the slow paradoxical slumping of masonry, and silence. In

that day as in this, once the dead were collected and shoveled out of sight, the war went on as before.

Sometimes there would be truces, during which each side
spied on the other. Three of the Marshal's negotiators were
able in this way to enter the fortress and learn how batteries
and men were disposed; they discovered a section vulnerable
to fire from the Cemetery of Saint-Symphorien, and later
this knowledge was put to good use. The Pope's men managed to climb up into the bell tower of the Cathedral, but
nearly died there of suffocation when the French built a
bonfire to smoke them down. Another fire was surreptitiously set within the Palace itself: wood piled against the
inner walls of the Winepress Tower suddenly went up in
flames. Almost at once, for it made an excellent chimney,
fire raced up this corner defense of the Palace. Working at
top speed, in intense heat, coughing in the smoke, greasy
with sweat, amateur masons managed to seal up every aperture, thus blocking the draft, and the tower was saved.

One early dawn, Boucicault himself almost ended the
Schism: he had learned of a secret way under the Palace
walls.

Flanking the Tower of the Latrines, built by Benedict
XII, there was a vast apartment with an enormous funnel
of a roof made to carry off great thunderheads of smoke.
This was the Palace kitchen. Here in normal times oxen
turned on their spits, flocks of cygnets, ducks and geese spun
round, fat sputtered into flames, herb sauces bubbled in
copper caldrons and released pungent steam into the rough,
blackened cone through which, if the cooks craned their
necks, there was a circle of blue sky.

To the cellar of this tower kitchen slops oozed down,
mixed with rain water, and slipped farther on to the Tower
of the Latrines. The augmented sluggish flow then passed

through a large sewer that led under the Palace walls and
emptied into the Sorguette River. Completing the impreg-
nability of the Fortress, the outlet here had been blocked
up.

But the *Maître des Portes* at Villeneuve disencumbered
the outlet and one October dawn about sixty armed men,
even the shortest of them hunched over to keep from bumping the roof, started pushing their way into the sewer tunnel
single file. In addition to fifty-three picked men-at-arms,
there was a relative of Boucicault's named Hardoin, two
more knights, four captains, a citizen of Avignon, and the
Maître des Portes who, better than the rest, certainly knew
what he was getting into. They were equipped for anything
including the hauling away of money, for they carried sacks
as well as crowbars, axes, ropes, mallets, chisels, pliers, even
flags bearing the lilies of France to run up from the Palace
walls.

The first man leaned forward, his lantern flickering here
and there against polished slime. The ancient tunnel and
doubtless some of its contents went back sixty years, to
Pope Benedict XII. He pushed forward and waded on,
smeared to the thighs. If he looked backward toward the
dim opening of the tunnel, he saw hunched forms crowding
in after him, blocking his way out.

The burrow turned off somewhere in the blackness;
steeper, more slippery. It had become a vast pit, a hollow
black cube, the bottom thick with reeking filth. Once across,
there was another opening and on the farther side the air
was clean at last. He had reached the dark cellar of the
Kitchen Tower.

The Palace lay heavy in its dawn sleep. The sixty men
climbed upward toward the sleeping Pope. Suddenly one
of the doorkeepers, a man in charge of the apartments
where costly Church ornaments were stored and who happened to be making his rounds, paused as he stood on an

upper gallery and glanced downward. Was it darker forms
that alerted him, moving in the darkness, or the furtive
clank of arms, or did he smell a change in the air? Immediately the alarm blew from the bugles and there came a rapid
hammering on the bell, the sudden thud of feet, and shouts
of "Where? Where?" Men rose out of sleep, grabbing their
weapons, bumping each other as they ran toward the sounds.

A messenger, guards following him, broke into Benedict's
room, and gasped, "They are inside the Palace! They hunt
for the Pope!"

Benedict calmly ordered: "Get back. Get back. Courage!
They are yours."

Quickly, reinforcements blocked the passage to the Pope's
apartment. The main body of the invaders found itself
hemmed within the great kitchen, others were trapped on
the narrow stairway as they climbed the tower, a few made
it back into the sewer. Up the slanting roof of the kitchen
swarmed a squad of defenders armed with iron bars: they
pried stones from the central opening and slammed them
down on the men beneath. A rain of soot drifted down to
mingle with the flying ash kicked up from smoldering fires.
Heavy work tables were overturned, pots clanged to the
floor, it was over.

The Marshal's beaten men were penned up in the Tower
of the Winepress, while their leaders were salted away in
the Treasury: was this a bit of papal irony, because Benedict
knew that the invaders had come in with sacks to carry
away his gold? Or was it simply the safest place in the Palace for objects one did not intend to lose? In any case, the
officers and the mountains of treasure were locked in together.

Except for the alertness of that one man, the Western
world might now have come to rest. Had even a handful
surprised the drowsy guards and crept to where Benedict
was sleeping, they could at will have led him out in chains

and sent him to Paris (as had been promised) or, in all that darkness and confusion, have quickly settled the Great Schism by the Way of Accomplished Fact: *videlicet*, the knife.

Boucicault was not stopped by his failure at the sewer. He knew the walls to be untakable, and knew that the Kitchen Tower was now effectively blocked off. He decided, therefore, to tunnel under the whole massive pile. A war of moles began. The Marshal launched a three-pronged underground attack; sealed out in one direction, he would try another, and again a third. One subterranean passage led in from the front, its objective the Tour de la Gâche. To the right, sappers dug their way in the direction of the Gate of the Peyrolerie. Opposite this, close to the north side of the Palace, and on the attackers' left, was the Cathedral, Our Lady of the Lords (parts of which, some say, had been repaired in the days of Charlemagne). The Cathedral offered the most promising entry into the Palace, as work could be begun there without detection, and the distance to the Campane Tower was short.

Made aware of the danger either by spies or by sounds of burrowing, the defenders took up picks and shovels themselves. They dug countertunnels of their own, and engaged the enemy below ground. These dark battles were not confined to hand-to-hand fighting: they cut the assailants down with volleys of arrows, or even smashed them with blasts of catapulted stones. Lime, boiling oil and pitch were hurled. They set fires to burn out the wooden supports that held up a gallery, so it would collapse on the invaders. To prevent the spread of flames, in moments of great emergency the bronze doors of the Cathedral were used as fire walls. Sometimes a gallery dug by the besiegers was set on fire by the diggers themselves, they hoping that its collapse close to the Palace might damage one of the massive walls and make it vulnerable at last to bombards and mangonels. This operation was once almost successful against the outer walls in the neighborhood of the Campane Tower, opposite Our Lady of the Lords. It was here that Boucicault mounted his strongest assault.

Trying to uncover their subterranean foes and engage them outside the Palace, the defenders had dug three countertunnels to their own peril. Despite the shoring up of these tunnels with timbers—with which Boucicault was far better provided than Rodrigo de Luna—the foundations of the Palace wall in this sector were weakened.

One or more of the defenders' galleries then intercepted the Marshal's, and he, seeing his surprise attack foiled, and dreading defeat in the underground war, set afire the supporting timbers in the defenders' tunnels as well as his own. At this the entire population of the Palace had to be rushed to the weakening foundations to prevent the collapse of the walls. Scullery boys worked with Bishops to set braces, while above them the great walls shuddered and swayed under the pounding from the Marshal's artillery as his engines hurled against them huge masses of stone weighing anything from three hundred pounds to above a quarter of a ton. What with everyone, except only the Pope and his Cardinals, sweating and straining at the dangerous labor, the foundations were saved. The peril was over, and again Pope Benedict had won.

14 WHITE SHAPES IN THE SKY

ROUND THE MIDDLE of November Marshal
Boucicault was relieved of his command. Thus ended a
boast he made when the war began, that the citizens of
Avignon would, within days, be dancing in the Palace of
the Popes. Actually, the Marshal had come closer to success at Avignon than his backers knew. They were aware of
his self-esteem; they did not realize how close he had come
to seizing the Pope in that daring attack through the sewer,
or how nearly he had managed to broach the thick walls
with his underground tunnels. In any case, almost meant
nothing to them.

The new commander—chosen by the Cardinals and other
leaders of the city—was Georges de Marle, Seneschal of
Provence. He kept on with the burrowing tactics of his
predecessor and the besieged countered with more of the
same. One day, perhaps weary of being moles, the Palace
soldiers took the offensive, and shielded by screens of wood
called mantelets, they climbed down the wall, and attacked
the tunnels from above. Before clambering back, they had
set fire to a number of covered stalls and houses surround-
ing the Palace.

A truce effected November 24, 1398, by the new commander stopped this war, as damaging to the Church as to
the Palace and the homes of the Avignonese. The fighting
was halted, but the blockade of the Palace went on.

Shortly before this, a tongue of flame had been seen from
the terraces of Villeneuve: it stretched across the Rhône,

and licked at the Rock of the Lords. Also, a nun saw a Cross
leaning over on the Tower of Lead, and soon after a cannonball did in fact twist the Cross decorated with orna-
mental lilies which surmounted that tower. Later on, white
shapes and bright lights moved on the Palace summits in
the middle of the night. Best portent of all, so far as Benedict XIII was concerned, the enemy Cardinal de Neufchâtel
was struck down by a fever and died in four days.

Already, the Cardinals were afraid they had gone too far.
The indignant King of Aragon was threatening them and
the Avignonese, and Pope Benedict's envoys had raised up
an expedition in Catalonia. The clergy of Tarragon province
donated a half year of tithes toward outfitting a flotilla of
eighteen galleys, eight ships propelled by oars, and a number
of smaller boats as well. In command was yet another stal-
wart relative of Benedict's.

By January 10, 1399, this expedition had come up the
Rhône as far as Arles, twenty-six miles from the war. The
Cardinals proceeded to fortify Avignon's Bridge, and to stop
the boats they fastened an iron chain across the Rhône.

When the besieged, watching from their high walls above
the water, saw all these preparations going forward, their
hearts, worn by the long confinement, pounded for joy.
Their countrymen were coming at last; they would soon be
free. Impatiently, they waited for the boats which they
thought must be hard by. As each day passed, and they
strained their eyes to make out the floating banners of Catalonia, they told one another how the rescuers must surely
camp a while first, after the long sea voyage, the better to
help them store up strength. Then a message got through
that the flotilla was at Lansac, in the neighborhood of
Tarascon. This was only fourteen miles away, though of
course, downriver.

But here the boats stuck. The water was too low at this

time of year to carry them farther. Every morning Benedict's soldiers studied the dawn skies, looking for signs of rain that would lift the river. Prayer after prayer went up from the Palace, that the warm *Föhn*—Favonius, the western wind—would unlock the snow water held fast in the distant Alps. When they could see from their ramparts that the water did not rise, they scanned the gray-and-yellow plains for the glint of sun on armor that would tell them help was coming overland.

For some twenty days after the fleet had reached Lansac those in the Palace wore their eyes red with looking. Help was but fourteen miles away. Yet the rescuers, apparently, were staying by their useless boats. Perhaps they dared not leave them to an enemy at the rear; for those boats meant going home.

Hope is rugged. Though each long day went emptily by, still the besieged knew that the next day help would come. And then at last, in mid-February, 1399, black news: one by one, the boats were casting off, hauling in their ropes to float downstream toward Spain. The charters for the boats were expiring, and the whole lot had to be home again.

In spite of constant danger, the growing casualty list, the inroads of disease, the shortages of food and fuel, courage had until now been high. But hunger, ally of Boucicault, was also his successor's tactic. True, the Palace still had wheat to be ground into flour but it made a tedious, unwholesome diet when there was little else. Only a meager supply of dried vegetables remained to be doled out, and what meat reached the table was either heavily salted, or spoiled. To many an eager hunter, the Palace rapidly lost its population of cats, rats, mice and sparrows—these last, doing duty as ortolans, no doubt, being reserved for the table of the Pope, who indeed was "as fond of these as of fat fowl." The besieged now drank water and vinegar mixed:

in the beginning, they had been too free with their casks of wine.

Benedict's forces, ill-fed though they were, escaped, says one chronicler, an epidemic which raged in Avignon. There the townspeople, many of them enjoying full tables as always, died "like pigs." (We note in passing how gluttony has lost ground as a sin; in the Middle Ages it ranked as one of the seven deadly ones, the other six being anger and covetousness, envy and lust, pride and sloth. Demoted, it is now only an error.)

During all the siege, some say, only one man died within the Palace walls, a priest who was almost cured of a wound, but failed to follow his prescribed diet. Just how he could have followed it in the circumstances makes a nice problem. Less rose-tinted accounts tell of scurvy, and of men dying of wounds and sickness for lack of medicine and proper food. They must have sickened, too, from the clammy chill. It is possible to be warm in Provence in winter, when the sun is shining and you can sit close to a south wall out of the hammering wind. But these men were confined in cold stone rooms; in the damp, cumulative cold of many Januaries, they moved through halls where the sun never comes; their pallets were on stone floors, under high, vaulted masonry, colder than the winter sky. No wonder they ached with rheumatism as they stood watch along the parapets under the fierce whip of the mistral. And such was the shortage of fuel that roof beams had to be ripped down in order that the monotonous meals might be prepared and the sick given a measure of protection against lung congestion and death.

With all this was the weight of a long siege on the spirits of men confined for months and then for years. Help had come so close and gone. Did it mean they must stay here and starve? Confident at first that their cause was just, they began to doubt, when victory never came. They were holding an island in the sea; a single wave could carry them off.

A man is beaten only when he knows it, and Benedict was at all times sure he would conquer. Day after day, into many a night, key supporters were working in the countries of Europe to encourage those who had remained loyal to the Avignon Pope, and to show his enemies that their actions harmed the Church. At France's court, the brother of the King, the glittering Duke of Orléans, was a strong partisan. His influence could be traced in the growing belief that France's withdrawal of obedience from her Pope had been unwise.

Duke Louis of Orléans had black damask gowns ornamented with golden collars and bells; also cloaks of black and crimson satin with golden stripes, and bracelets of rubies, and belts studded with golden nailheads shaped like hearts. He was a Prince Charming who charmed, in addition to everyone else, his brother's Queen.

In 1399 alone, six times Charles had been laid low. His heir the Dauphin was born in 1403 and lived haunted by the shadow of illegitimacy (although Joan of Arc, to whom he would owe his crown, assured him he was Charles's son). Femmette, the Queen's maid, left no record. As one French writer reminds us, "we cannot know the secrets of the royal alcove." But it was probably from 1404 and thereafter, when she had had, it seems, eleven pregnancies, that Isabeau— exhausted with fright, sudden outbursts and blows, endless days of her husband's prostration, jumbled words whose only clear meaning was hate—became completely separated from Charles and became engrossed in the pleasures of her licentious court.

And as he had, somehow, to be fed, clothed and washed, the King had also to be provided with a wife. It could no longer be the Queen. No one wanted to see, some early morning, the hacked-at corpse of a foreign princess on France's hands. Accordingly they cast about and found him a young girl, Odette de Champdivers. Suitable arrangements were made for Odette: she received as payment the two beautiful manors of Créteil and Bagnolet. In exchange she stayed with Charles at all times, and was publicly referred to as "the little Queen." She was good to look at, remained by the King over a long period, and earned her two manors: the couple had a daughter, Marguerite.

Meanwhile in private, sealed-off gardens, back of locked gates, or sometimes under the same roof, Isabeau and the magnificent Orléans were joined by rank, politics, and love—this being, perhaps, not only adultery but, for the times, incest as well.

15 ANOTHER WORLD WATCHING

MEANWHILE THE Muslims had it in mind to exploit the Great Schism of the West.

They seemed to be everywhere lately. Back in 1338, when a great Khan sent envoys to Benedict XII, Avignon had gaped. Now, that unfamiliar world was getting nearer all the time. In 1361 Sultan Murad I, known to the West as Amurat, took Adrianople and made it his capital. Next, the Ottoman conquered Bulgaria, and in 1389, Serbia, before he was stabbed to death in his tent.

Not long before Charles lost his mind, he held a peace conference with England, footing the bill for two hundred English lords, from Calais to Amiens and back. To them, France's King disclosed among other matters the hope of a French-English expedition against Amurat who, he said, "presses very hard." "Amurat," added Charles, "is a man of great valor and enterprise but of a sect contrary to our Faith, which he daily oppresses."

Nothing came of it, but when the next Sultan, Bajazet, invaded Hungary, the Roman Pope declared a crusade against the "infidel," and Sigismund of Hungary led Europe's armies, predominantly French, against the Muslims. Bajazet trounced them all at Nicopolis in 1396. (The English, reportedly, were not displeased. The Duke of Gloucester remarked to a confidant: "Those rare boasting Frenchmen have been nearly annihilated in Turkey.")

Bajazet saved out various French nobles for their rich armor and also exacted a huge ransom: white gerfalcons, tapestries from Arras, linens from Reims, scarlet and crimson cloth. These treasures were loaded on six sumpter horses and sent off.

Ransomed and home, the Duke de Nevers reported that many Muslims felt Christianity had been "corrupted by those who ought to have kept its purity," and believed that Bajazet was destined to destroy it and rule the whole world.

"Such was the language the interpreter translated to me; and, from what I saw and heard, I believe they are perfectly well acquainted in Turkey, Tartary, and Persia, and throughout the whole of the infidel countries, with our schisms in the Church, and how the Christians are at variance one with another respecting the two Popes in France and Italy."

It was Bajazet's plan, de Nevers said, to march on Rome and feed his horse on the altar of Saint Peter's.

Pope Benedict stayed on as a prisoner in his palace at Avignon, but the fighting was not renewed and even the effort to starve him out was gradually given up. Negotiations took the place of underground war; rats were no longer a delicacy. Nevertheless, there were harassments: Benedict found that obstacles would be thrown in the way of restocking his larder; safe-conduct passes were more often promised than delivered. The blockade was eased rather than lifted. The war could be resumed at any time; dark threats were made, presumably to force a favorable decision in the endless parleys over the Way of Cession.

By the spring of 1401, after two and a half years of siege and blockade, Provence spontaneously came back into the Pope's obedience. One François de Cario even started a plot to hand him back Avignon, but this unfortunately proved premature. On November 26, 1401, de Cario's head was found swaying on a pole in the Square of Saint-Didier; his right and left arms appeared respectively on the gates of Saint-Lazare and Saint-Michel; his right leg was fastened to the gate called Limbert, his left one to the gate of Our Lady of Miracles, while his bowels were exposed in a flat basket in Saint Peter's Square.

With the growing influence of Duke Louis of Orléans, Pope Benedict's fortunes rose. True, the King's uncles, who so often ruled France during Charles's frenzy, were strongly anti-Benedict. But Louis, at first agreeing with them, now actively opposed them, particularly the Duke of Burgundy, Philip the Bold. Louis did not help Benedict entirely for love: the Duke had grown ambitious, on behalf of his line as well as himself. His wishes, however, did not always prevail: when he asked Benedict for a dispensation to marry his daughter Marie to the Dauphin, Burgundy blocked him, arguing that Marie was too young for matrimony. She was then four weeks old.

The Duke of Orléans stubbornly continued faithful to Benedict. To the Cardinals on September 19, 1401, he complained of their treatment of the Avignon Pope. On the same day he wrote him: "By every means, I swear to you, I will not leave this work undone." His ardor on behalf of the captive Pope gave color, but not truth, to the widely spread rumor that, in exchange for being crowned Holy Roman Emperor, he would turn Roman co-Pontiff Boniface IX over to Benedict.

There was a time in 1401 when the prospects looked bright for a conference among those countries which had originally supported Pedro de Luna. It was hoped that an agreement could be reached to end the schism within the Schism—with the ultimate aim of ending the Great Schism itself. But Pope Benedict, always wary of such projects, wrote to Orléans on December 4, 1401, asking him to oppose this conference, and stating that it would not properly conform to canon law.

In Paris fighting almost broke out between the Dukes of Orléans and Burgundy, but toward Christmas they reached a peaceful settlement. As a by-product of this peace, the Pope's affairs improved.

The universities of France began to make their voices heard. In 1401 the University of Orléans protested (if somewhat tardily) that it had not, as the royal ordinance claimed, concurred in the withdrawal of obedience of 1398. Now the university went further. In February, 1402, it reaffirmed that it had not agreed to the withdrawal, and advised the restitution of obedience.

The University of Toulouse joined Orléans in supporting Benedict, as did the University of Angers shortly after. The chancellor of the University of Paris, who had kept quiet ever since the withdrawal of obedience, now spoke up: Pope Benedict was neither a heretic nor a schismatic, he said, and it would be most unsuitable to open an action against him on such grounds.

The clergy had previously welcomed one aspect of the withdrawal from Benedict: they had expected a lightening of their tax load—only to find the hand of the King's tax collector still heavier than the Pope's. They now hoped to revert from the fire to the frying pan.

In the secular realm, although at some cost, Benedict gained a new ally. Duke Louis II of Anjou, crowned King of Naples in 1389, had taken no side in the Schism, leading Benedict's supporters to credit Louis' subsequent loss of Naples and Taranto to Heavenly displeasure. On August 27, 1402, King Louis spent a night in the Avignon Palace and the financial settlement that resulted in his adherence to Benedict was large but not generous, for it was squeezed from a cornered Pontiff, obliged to secure aid wherever he could, at whatever cost.

About this time, the Carthusians returned to the obedience of Benedict after electing a partisan of the Avignon Pope as General of their Order. A coalition of those who had unwillingly accepted the withdrawal was now forming.

A growing number of leaders saw the deleterious results of their too hasty act in 1398.

The King of Castile had agreed ahead of time with France's withdrawal of obedience. But he had begun to waver in his lack of faith as early as 1399. By the spring of 1402, he was clearly inclined toward Benedict and sent ambassadors to Paris. The Pope was so sure of his coming back into the fold that around the first of 1403 he instructed the Bishop of Ávila to give absolution to this King and all his Castilian subjects as soon as they submitted themselves. The Monk of Saint-Denis wrote that during the years from 1398 to 1403 one could see the general law being proved in France that no church may shake off the authority of the Pope without falling under the yoke of the lay government. "The first fruit of the withdrawal of obedience," says the chronicler, "was to expose the Church of France to persecution by the secular arm."

"Shall I enumerate the further disadvantages of the withdrawal of obedience?" asked Valois. "The abasement of the Cardinals, degraded to the role of agents and courtiers of Princes; the oppression of the lesser clergy by prelates against whom they no longer had recourse to the Holy See; the harshness exercised toward those clerics who obeyed the voice of their conscience; the humbling of that Pope considered to be legitimate, which at the same time raised higher the position of the 'intruder.'" He sums up: "All these disadvantages had been foreseen and, from the beginning, set forth by foes of the withdrawal of obedience. The time had come when more than one, even among those who had promoted that radical measure, acknowledged that even the most pessimistic of predictions had been realized. If they did not say so aloud, many confessed to themselves in a whisper that France had taken the wrong road."

16 THE BEARD OF POPE BENEDICT

THE SENTINELS posted outside Avignon's Palace were bored. Nothing had happened for a long time; nothing would ever happen. Benedict had been a prisoner here for four and a half years. It was March 11, 1403, and black night.

Pope Benedict was now seventy-five years old. His eyes were as lively as ever, as clear, as piercing. The strong, aquiline nose conveyed the same fierce lordliness. His body was hard and lean, because of frequent fasting to attract Heavenly support. His store of vital life was undepleted. Except for one thing, there had been no change, certainly none in that agile, penetrating mind; the one thing was his beard. He had vowed to grow a beard and never have it cut off again until he should stand up a free man.

There had once existed, before hostilities began, an opening in the Palace wall, a link between the Palace and the deanery of the Cathedral. Stones used to close up this breach were square-hewn, probably fitted without mortar. Some of these blocks were now surreptitiously removed. A man could get through.

Tonight Benedict's slight figure was muffled in the habit of a Carthusian monk. With him, the men at his side had come through fire; he could trust them. For the same reason, he had just, without a qualm, handed over the Palace to Rodrigo de Luna. But what of those who waited outside the breach in the wall? He might be escaping into a trap.

Close beside him was Robert de Braquement, a Norman

gentleman. Duke Louis had entrusted Benedict to his safe-keeping. But de Braquement was a commander under Bou-cicault and his successor; as such he had come and gone into the Palace, his shift in allegiance undetected; and a man who has secretly changed sides can always change again.

De Braquement, according to plan, was to leave him now and go out by the main gates. Approximately at that moment, Benedict, issuing from a long, dark passageway, would step through the secret opening in the wall. Beyond the barricades—the second obstacle to flight—he and de Braquement would meet.

Was he sure of this man? Once Benedict had left these thick, protecting ramparts and passed, almost alone, into Avignon's dark, winding alleys, could he rely on him? After all, the Pope was a coveted prize. As Benedict waited, his heart beat fast against the silver box he carried at his breast: in it was a consecrated Host. Under his monk's robe he had his letters from the King of France, especially that one in which Charles denied any connection with, any responsibility for, the Cardinals' war on their Pope.

De Braquement left. The moments passed. Men knelt before Benedict, and asked his blessing.

"Fear nothing," was his last goodbye to them. Then he turned and started down the narrow way. He reached the hidden opening, carefully felt his way through. Nine years before, as Pope, he had entered this Palace with panoply and splendor, the trumpets blowing triumph. Those years were gone in a single breath and here he was, creeping out like a thief in the night.

It was three o'clock. The sky was clear, with low-hung stars. He and those with him—his doctor, a chamberlain, a noble from Aragon—stood outside the massive walls. There was no sound from the watch; as ever, the sentinels drowsed. Easily, the furtive little band passed through the barricades, and out to the empty lane where de Braquement waited.

They came along after him, a shadowy line of men, one of them a nondescript Carthusian who carried under his monk's coarse robe the letters of a King. At the Inn of Saint Anthony, however, hard by the gate which led to the Rhône, their way was blocked. They had to wait here, pacing out the night; for the city gates were closed at night, the enemy locked out, and all the inhabitants, for better, for worse, locked in.

At last, the birds began. It was dawn, the gates swung open. Country people entered the town, and those townsmen who were up early and had business across the river at Villeneuve or along the Rhône walked out through the western gates. Among all these was Pope Benedict XIII.

Once through the gate, Benedict was nearly at the river's edge. He glanced quickly about, at first not seeing the boat. But it waited there, a long craft with fourteen powerful men at the oars. He stepped hurriedly in, they cast off into the rapid current, the oars dug into the green water, the boat whirled away downstream.

He was nearly betrayed by a friend. A man who watched from the shore, unable to contain his joy, and being, also, one of those who always have to come first with the news, cried to a passing acquaintance, before Benedict's boat had cleared the bend: "Even if it spoils his breakfast, go tell the Cardinal of Albano that the Pope has gone!"

The news spread through Avignon like dust twisted along by the mistral, but it was too late to stop Benedict. The Rhône and his oarsmen were too swift and strong.

The Avignonese, southerners that they were, did nothing, except that, rather petulantly, on the day of the Pope's escape they allowed no food into the Palace. They could hardly dream that their glory had departed; that with a flick of the Rhône, a shove of the mistral, Avignon had ceased, forever and ever, to be the city of the Popes.

They turned where the Durance enters the Rhône and rowed upstream. They reached a point that is six miles overland from the Palace, though farther by boat. Here on the riverbank, waiting with horses and an armed guard, was the faithful Cardinal of Pamplona. Swiftly, Benedict disembarked, and after the hasty greetings mounted, and they galloped upward toward the twin fortified towers of the as it were symbolically named Château Renard. It was still only about nine o'clock in the morning.

Straight out of the flat land rose the steep hill crowned by two round towers. From the side of the hill the party zigzagged up, along the slope, under pines and cedars squeaking in the wind. Way below was a crazy jumble of roofs, and spread out all around, the valley of the Durance, home of the earliest vegetables and fruits.

The castle where Benedict now came—yet another of his endless High Places—is today diminished mostly to the one "Tower of the Griffon," its second tower being a ruin, crumbling and hollowed out. As he reached the summit, the Pope could look back on long chapters of history spread out: the Charterhouse of Bonpas, Petrarch's retreat near a castle at Vaucluse, the fortress built by Good King John, the square tower of Philip the Fair. There, too, mightiest of all, was Benedict's own Palace of the Popes.

Did Benedict know, as he stood on that height and gazed about him, that he should not have been here, watching from far away, from the outside, his mighty citadel? For if the Popes erred when they came to Avignon, they erred again when they left it. Centers and institutional places can have a significance as well as people; for generations, Avignon had been a point men turned to, a Mecca, a Rome. Within that stronghold Pedro de Luna saw himself as trapped, but from a different vantage point, from beyond those walls, he looked enthroned. After that he was still the same man, still Pope Benedict XIII, but people did not

know where to think of him as being. In their minds, thereafter, he was displaced, and fugitive.

For a Pope to wear a beard was not usual in Latin Christianity, and Benedict's enemies had been swift to comment.
He had a ready precedent, however: Avignon's unmistak-
ably bearded Innocent VI. By the time Benedict stood up
a free man, here at Château Renard, his pontifical bush had
grown down to mid-chest. They say he looked like Abra-
ham, or at least like medieval representations of that
Prophet of God.

As a barber prepared to shear away the magnificent
growth, Benedict asked the man where he was from.

"I'm from Picardy," answered the barber.

The Pope chuckled. "I make the Normans liars," he said.
"They boasted *they* would have my beard."

He bestowed his shorn-off beard on Louis of Anjou, a
signal honor.

The feel of Provence soil was good under Benedict's feet,
after so many years of walking the stone floors of his Avignon Palace. Even better was the surging loyalty which he
could sense, and on which he could rise to a power and glory
greater than any he had enjoyed before.

A procession of jubilant, or more often penitent, pilgrims
climbed up to Château Renard. The Comtat Venaissin submitted. The College of Cardinals sued for peace. According
to the Monk of Saint-Denis, the breast-beating Cardinals
fell to the ground at Benedict's feet, weeping and humbly
promising to serve him faithfully all the rest of their days.
Prostrate in the mud, Cardinal di Giffone confessed to
grave sins and even lies.

Benedict invited them all to a splendid feast. From
heaped platters, the Cardinals ate, blessedly relieved to be
thus let off by the Pontiff they had tried to destroy. At the

height of the banquet, however, they heard a sudden martial tread and clank of armor and looked up to see shining halberds in a tall hedge around the tables. With mouths gone dry and food blocking their throats, they saw themselves held, tied, then the flames licking at their legs. They waited, white to the lips. But at a sign from Benedict and as suddenly as they had marched in, the soldiers marched out. The Pope had made his point. Afterward he could not help, on occasion, smiling about this with his faithful Francisco de Aranda, that one who was not so much loyal as loyalty itself, who had never wanted anything from him, except to serve.

In Paris, too, the lines of allegiance shifted in his favor. The same two Cardinals who had previously fought for withdrawal of obedience were sent there to present the case for restitution. The Pope's most unforgiving enemies could not brush away these facts: the withdrawal had been worse than useless; Benedict had proved unbeatable; his cause had not withered away, but prospered. Many, assaying this man who had been tested by desertion, war, and the soul-searing blockade, now found in him those qualities of leadership necessary to carry the Church through troubled days ahead. The weight of theological opinion tipped the scales toward restitution.

As for Avignon, the city wanted him badly, now that he was gone. She did not even wait for approval from France before swinging over to the Pope. Within three weeks of his hegira, in April, 1403, a popular assembly voted an immediate return to obedience. The man who had been forced to flee in secret was now presented with the keys to the city— to add to those two of Heaven. Her houses were brightly illuminated for the reconciliation, her streets were lit by the fires of burning barricades, cries of "Long live Pope Benedict!" rang from squares and towers. To silver trumpetings, the banners of the Pope were run up over the Palace and on public monuments throughout the city. Two hundred children paraded, holding high the flag of Benedict XIII.

But he never went back. The Avignonese, who boasted of having thirty-two regional winds, veered to every one of them. Benedict had had enough of the Palace by the Rhône. Nevertheless, he did not pursue those who had fought him; beyond seeing to it that Avignon repaired the damage to the Palace, he exacted no indemnities. Demonstrating his attitude toward the new order, he restocked that stronghold with ammunition and food, and relieved the weary garrison with fresh troops.

On the fifth of May, 1403, to show Avignon where she stood, he made a triumphal entry into Carpentras.

PART THREE

PISA

IOHANNES XXIII. PAPA.

NEAPOLITANUS.

ALIAS BALTHASAR DE COSS.

dictus, Sede motus in Concilio Constantiensi
Anno 1415.

17 OPPORTUNITY KNOCKS TWICE

O N M A Y 30, 1403, King Charles VI of France, at the moment *compos mentis*, rode to Notre Dame Cathedral where he watched as Pierre d'Ailly climbed up the stairs to the pulpit and read out the King's declaration:

Nearly five years have now passed by since that day when the clergy and lords of France, in Council assembled, proclaimed that to end the Schism, both Pontiffs must be required to come down from Saint Peter's chair. . . . Our Kingdom withdrew from the obedience of Benedict XIII . . . the success we hoped for from this measure was never realized. We had thought the intruder Boniface would be abandoned by his partisans, but in his obstinacy he has stiffened more and more. That antipope, while Benedict truly offered to submit to reelection, refused to step down from the Holy See. And now, since the Cardinals, the final judges . . . after having separated themselves from the Holy Father, have returned to his authority again, we can no longer remain beyond the pale of his obedience.

By all these considerations, on the advice of our uncles, the Dukes of Berry and Burgundy, on the advice of our brother, the Duke of Orléans, on the advice of our principal lords, on the advice of the prelates of the Universities of Paris, Orléans, Toulouse, Angers and Montpellier, we declare that from this day forward, the withdrawal has ceased. We restore to Benedict XIII a complete obedience for ourself and for our kingdom, expressly commanding our Jus-

161

tices to cause this decree to be published and to punish such as contravene these our present wishes, to the full extent of the law.

Charles stood before the altar. About him, tense and solemn, were grouped the leaders of the Church. The King, hands on a crucifix, voiced his oath.

"I too," he said—and the crowd drew to itself each slow word, as their monarch uttered his testimony in the presence of his God and as one seeking to be whole again—"I restore obedience to my lord the Pope. I will keep for him all my life, by this Holy Cross of the Lord, an inviolate obedience, as unto the Vicar of Jesus the Christ. I swear that I will cause him to be obeyed throughout all my realms."

The ailing King then knelt and intoned the *Te Deum*, and many were seen to weep, while churchbells pealed the news. Their ringing spread through Paris and on into neighboring towns, and waves of reverberating joy circled outward through France.

This jubilation was not shared by Charles's uncles, for his brother the Duke of Orléans had arranged all this behind their backs. They were not even present; but having learned the reason for the ringing bells, the uncles broke in on Charles that evening, their anger spilling out in bitterness.

The King stood his ground. He told them that his brother's loyalty to Benedict was shared by a majority of the prelates of France. Furthermore, he told them, he had not taken this momentous step without first extracting certain promises from the Pope. Apparently Louis, Duke of Orléans, had negotiated with Benedict, through the Bishop of Uzès. He had secured the following concessions, the terms of which the King now triumphantly read:

Benedict would issue a papal Bull similar to the one of March 30, 1401. This would bind him to abdicate in case

the "interloper" at Rome, Boniface IX, died, was deposed,
or ceded his claim to the Papacy. All those statements that
Benedict had made against taking the Way of Cession at
the time of France's withdrawal of obedience would be revoked. So, too, all the proceedings instituted because of it.
Such articles as were of interest to the King and to France
in the treaty Benedict had recently signed with the College
of Cardinals, would be confirmed by a Bull. And concerning the previous withdrawal of obedience, Benedict would
let bygones be bygones.

The last concession was the most important: in a year's
time the Avignon Pope would call a council of those under
his obedience and this council would deal with the problems
of union, reform, Church independence, and the shifting of
taxes and other burdens from the backs of the French clergy.
Benedict agreed to abide by the rulings of this council.

His victory was now complete. It had cost him a good
deal in the way of cash and promises, but after five years of
what had amounted to a French national Church headed
by King Charles, Benedict stood supreme in France.

Should the Avignon Pope, at this moment, have renounced his tiara? If power could ever be freely relin-
quished, he now had the opportunity of becoming one of
the great heroes of the Church. Had he shown the will to
sacrifice himself and end the Schism, the wave of enthusiasm so engendered might well have swept his rival, Boniface IX, off the papal throne. Would Benedict then have
been reelected as Sovereign of a united Church? It seemed
clear to him that if he renounced the tiara now, he would
never again be Pope. He might be eulogized throughout
Christendom; he might in time be named a saint; but he
would never again rule. Practical politics would prevail; his
cause would never gain ground in Italy; Church union
would require a noncontroversial figure, someone accept-

able to all sides, a neutral, perhaps a nonentity. Benedict was none of these.

Besides, he was a fighter. He could not give up what he had just won, at such cost, against such odds. The qualities that made him great in adversity made him difficult now. He would carry out no concessions which might cost him his throne, not even to end the Schism. He honestly and unshakably believed that he and he alone had the right to sit in Peter's chair. To step down would violate his principles as much as his nature. We therefore witness the paradox of a man defending his deepest convictions by a series of promises which he intended to retract whenever an increase in his power permitted.

It was all going back to the time before the war. Benedict was, as ever, opposed to the Way of Cession. He did appear ready to hold a council on the Schism, but all was kept vague. He gave the anxious Cardinals no specific ideas on how he intended to unite the Church. He refused any formal commitment as to the Way of Cession and whether he would travel it to the exclusion of any other Way. When the College of Cardinals protested and said they still considered the oaths taken in the Conclave to be binding, and reminded the Pope of various offers made by him at different times but not fulfilled, Benedict assumed a lofty tone. He did not feel himself bound as Pope by the oath he had sworn as Cardinal. He felt free to consult or refuse to consult the College of Cardinals. He would treat as he best judged, those who had secured benefices from the Cardinals. He would not even guarantee to the Cardinals themselves the future possession of their benefices. He was not bound, and would not bind himself to show them respect, affection, even good will. He could not in any way approve revolt or withdrawal of obedience. And he most positively affirmed his intention to give up no portion of his authority, no jot nor tittle. In short, the more things changed, the more they kept on being the same, and Benedict's stubbornness was at the same time his salvation and his doom.

Where once he had promised, as we have seen before, to abdicate in the case of Boniface's death or cession or expulsion, we find him in seven months' time having second thoughts. He expressed the sentiment that it had always been his intention spontaneously to abdicate at the moment when this action would result in reunion. He remained of this intention still. He was even ready to give up his life, should this be required. Nevertheless, and here he dropped vagueness to be specifically firm, these matters were for his decision alone. As Pope, he could not permit any man to restrict his freedom, nor was he subject to the jurisdiction and control of men.

Benedict spoke much of sacrificing his life if that would unite the Church, but it was obvious that, short of this drastic solution, he intended, as he always had, to maintain himself on the papal throne. As he saw it, he was the legally elected Pope, and Boniface the intruder. Therefore he, Benedict, was Christ's Vicar on earth, and as such he would betray his trust if he placed the disposal of the Papacy in lesser hands.

Over in Rome, Boniface IX was equally adamant, equally sure that he alone was Pope. In Rome, they rejected the theory that his predecessor, Urban VI, had been elected under duress. And if Urban was rightfully elected, Boniface was the legal Pope. This was the Roman position and Boniface IX can scarcely be blamed for adhering steadfastly to what he considered the legitimacy of his claim.

The Catholic world faced a stalemate. Was it really to solve this that Benedict sent four ambassadors to Boniface in the autumn of 1404—or was this another delaying action, and a means of embarrassing his rival Pope? As it turned out, the envoys were unable to eliminate Boniface's objections to cession; but as an indirect result of their arguments, Boniface himself was eliminated.

Too wary to trust themselves in Rome without guarantees of personal safety, Benedict's ambassadors waited at home until they received safe-conduct passes. Once in Italy, their welcome had been gratifying. But when the preliminary politenesses were out of the way, things got rough. They discussed with Boniface the steps to be taken to ensure mutual cession, the necessary journeys, the meeting-place. He promised an answer. They waited eight long days. He then said illness prevented him from traveling, as he suffered most painfully from gallstones and gout. Incidentally, it was not Benedict's envoys who suggested a popular remedy for Boniface's trouble: the Pope was advised that the stone could be cured by sexual intercourse. Boniface's indignant reply was that he would rather pass away than live in shame.

On September 29, 1404, they had a last meeting. With firmness, the Italian Pope rejected all proposals to end the Schism. Sometimes he simply said no, without giving any particular reason, as he did when Benedict's ambassadors argued that the rival Sacred Colleges should meet together with full powers to act. He likewise rejected a plan to set up a group of arbiters who would meet in safety and without pressure, their decision to be final and binding. Also turned down was the request that Boniface order his Cardinals not to elect a new Pope in the event of his death until they had made arrangements to end the Schism.

We are told that Boniface then accused his rival, Benedict, of having offered him ten million gold florins to give up the Papacy. He demanded that Benedict's ambassadors admit it. They swore on oath that it was Boniface himself who had tried to buy Benedict, and they countered with a charge of simony.

The simony charge came after the ailing Roman Pope's intransigence had so upset the ambassadors that they replied in kind to Boniface's name-calling. To explain the flare-up of tempers, here is Valois: "Boniface IX was always the same. Neither the lesson of experience nor the peril of the Church nor the approach of death had changed him in the least . . . always this refusal to negotiate on a basis of equality with a rival whom he judged scarcely worthy of pardon." Somewhere, his famed affability had been lost.

With their Pope damned as a heretic and antipope, Benedict's envoys might seem to have defended him feebly enough with their countercharge of simony, surely less serious than heresy. Rather, they struck Boniface in a vital spot. Whereas the charge of heresy could hardly be proved against either Pontiff, Boniface seems to have been vulnerable on the grounds of simony, for it is said that he not only annulled "acts, grants, indulgences and dispensations" of his predecessors in order "to regrant them for five years with new fees," but he also canceled his own awards for the same purpose.

Boniface burst into a rage at the accusation of simony and ordered the ambassadors to leave. They reminded him of the safe conducts that had been issued them and said they would make good use of these documents. In this they were mistaken.

Following the stormy audience, Boniface took to his bed, suffering a rising temperature and increasing pain. The next day, the doctors gave him up. He sank into a coma on the morning of October 1, 1404, two days after the charge of simony had so enraged him. He died that afternoon.

The ambassadors, their safe conducts ignored, were thrown in jail. There they remained until a ransom of five thousand florins was handed over. The asking price had been ten thousand, but perhaps the Florentines, who footed the bill, were better bargainers than the Romans. Later on, the Florentines got their money back from Benedict, whether or not with interest we do not know. They appear to have been willing to risk their gold on behalf of a Pope denounced as a heretic and antipope. His legitimacy might have been in question but his credit was good.

Here, then, was another chance to end the Schism; and as when Clement VII was gone, and when Urban VI was gone, the opportunity was thrown away. National self-interest won out over the welfare of the Church. The French had not been willing in 1394 to accept the jurisdiction of Rome. This time as well, it was not so much loyalty to Benedict which kept the French with him, as fear of losing power to the Italians. And the Italians were just as opposed to the continued presence of the Holy See beside French soil, nor could they be so selfless as to risk giving over the ecclesiastical power into predominantly French hands. Instead of sacrificing power and politics for the good of the Catholic world, the Italians insisted on having an Italian Pope.

The abortive negotiations which followed between Benedict's ambassadors and the Italian Cardinals show this clearly. The Italians asked the envoys if they were empowered to abdicate in Benedict's name. Obviously they were not, nor would they have been so disposed. The Italians then indicated a willingness to delay their election while the ambassadors got in touch with Benedict and arranged his abdication. But it was useless to ask Benedict to place himself at the mercy of his foes.

On October 17, 1404, sixteen days after the death of Boniface placed in their hands the fate of the Schism, the Italian Sacred College elected Innocent VII, one of themselves, to be Pope of Rome.

About now little Isabella, erstwhile Queen of England, touched Benedict's life again. After King Richard vanished, France demanded their Princess back, and eventually she was sent weeping from Dover with her ladies, her rich dowry gone. Then they planned to marry her to Charles d'Orléans, son of Duke Louis, resplendent brother to the King. Bride and groom being cousins, the marriage could be legalized only by a special dispensation from the Pope, for it would have been incest otherwise.

This was the same Charles d'Orléans who grew up to become one of France's leading nobles, was imprisoned twenty-five years in England, and afterward fathered a King —but will be remembered because he wrote fresh and delicate verse: little wisps of poetry that float away at a breath.

Benedict dated his dispensation at Tarascon, January 5, 1404—the year Charles, the bridegroom, was thirteen. And they say Isabella cried at the wedding, either because it was a comedown to be married to a Count after having been a Queen, or because, married once as a child and again to a child, she was *toujours jeune fille*.

18 POPE OF THE SEA

Innocent VII, the new Italian Pope, was born of poor but pious parents and made a poor but pious Pope. He was either gentle and humane, or the plaything of his passions, according to the authority selected.

The emphasis, then, during Innocent's two-year incumbency was not upon him but upon his so different rival, Benedict XIII. And wherever Innocent proved astute, he appeared to have learned his sleights and feints from the Pope of Avignon.

Like Benedict, Innocent had sworn prior to election that he would do everything in his power to reunite the Church, that he would of his own free will even abdicate if this should prove in the Church's true interest. Being himself the judge of the Church's true interest, he never found the situation likely to benefit by his abdication.

When Benedict's ambassadors (no longer in jail but still without guarantees of safe conduct home) informed Innocent of their Pope's willingness to confer with him at some point in Italy that would be both neutral and secure, he put them off. Innocent said he felt obliged, before he could take action, to summon a council of the ecclesiastics of his obedience. But this proposed council, like the one promised by Benedict after his escape from Avignon, was to be held only after a delay of one year.

At first peripatetic rather than aquatic—he later would be styled Pope of the Sea—Benedict had moved to Berre, to

Salon and to Orgon before settling on, but not settling
down in, Marseilles. He had turned back briefly to Tarascon
and Beaucaire, but the great harbor on the Gulf of the
Lions called him back. There, in the Abbey of Saint-Victor
not far from the waterfront, he prepared to become the first
maritime Pope.

For this, he needed money. Accordingly he borrowed
200,000 florins from Aragon, urged his tax collectors to get
busy again in France, and secured promises of help from
the Duke of Orléans and the King. The Knights of Saint
John of Jerusalem engaged to provide him with galleys and
galiots: the fourteenth-century equivalents, although on a
far smaller scale, of our cruisers and light cruisers.

Once equipped, the Clementine Pope saw before him an
open road to Rome.

This was no foolish dream of an admittedly optimistic
man. The opportunity of establishing himself in the Vatican was indeed at hand. Provence stood back of him, the
neighboring Ligurian coast had recently come under French
influence, Genoa was solidly his, mercenaries carried his flag
forward in the States of the Church, a number of his negotiations with Italian princes were advancing favorably, there
was dissension in Rome. Full of confidence, Benedict left
Marseilles for Nice, where the castle overlooking the harbor
had been readied for him by the Count of Savoy.

Here the Pope remained through the winter storms, planning and negotiating for a triumphant passage south. He did
not sail until May 7, 1405, his fleet consisting of six ships.
After three stops along the coast, he reached Genoa at noon,
May 16.

He was given a thundering welcome by the Genoese, even
though Urban VI had made Genoa his papal headquarters
for a time, after his disastrous experience in Naples, and
Genoa had been Urbanist for twenty-five years. Benedict
had every reason to believe that the enthusiasm with which

he was greeted meant that thousands more would welcome him with equal fervor on his way to Rome. Though he often talked of meeting with Innocent so that they could end the Schism, his eyes were on the Vatican.

The massed citizens knelt by the harbor to receive Benedict's blessing, their voices crying his praise across the water. Processions brought down to the shore the most sacred relics of churches and monasteries to testify to the clergy's and people's acceptance of his rule.

In the months that followed, Benedict outplayed Innocent, seizing on the latter's evasions to further his own campaign to become Pope of Rome as well as Avignon. Against the clumsy obstinacy of his opponent, Benedict displayed his skill at appearing to move forward toward compromise while remaining firmly anchored in what to him was right. Aided or blocked by France as the wind blew there, he carefully spread the idea that to unite the Church, he might have to oust his rival and install himself at Rome.

The game was perilous. As Benedict advanced into Urbanist territory, his enemies back in France took heart. The University of Paris did not wish to see the Catholic world united under the Spaniard, for he would be too strong. What they wanted was a manageable Pope. Besides, grumbling rose, even among his friends, over the way funds were pouring out of France. Benedict was buying Italian support with expensive entertainment and expensive gifts, and most of the money for this had to come from the ever-reluctant French, who were quite likely to get nothing in return.

Aware of the danger as he must have been, Benedict did little to allay it. Then, early in August, 1405, an event occurred which seemed to justify all the risks: Pope Innocent was driven away from Rome. Civil war had broken out in that city of eternally divided and shifting concerns. While mobs raged through the Vatican, the Italian Pope had run for his life to Viterbo.

Now was the moment for the march on Rome. And yet, at this time of Benedict's peak opportunity, fortune turned another way. In that same August, Louis II of Anjou (son of that first Louis who died in Italy) was leading troops to support Benedict against Innocent, when he was summarily ordered back by Bavarian Isabeau, the Queen. Once before, Benedict's dream of taking the road to Rome with French forces, led then by the Duke of Bourbon, had collapsed when the King in a period of sanity required that his uncle remain near the throne. Here was the identical situation again. Of armed men immediately available to him now, the Pope had less than three hundred.

Worse followed. Dysenteric plague drove Benedict out of Genoa, making him retreat to Savona, only to be forced away from there by the same enemy. Finally, in midsummer, 1406, he was back at Nice, with the road to Rome barred, the Cardinal of Pamplona, staunchest of friends, dead, and the University of Paris pushing France toward a new withdrawal of obedience. All this in a single year.

Like an acrobat in mid-air, whose partner at the one possible split second has failed to catch his wrists, Benedict was falling toward disaster. It is easy to write off the Italian move as too bold a leap. If Louis of Anjou had not been called back, and if, before him, the Duke of Bourbon had marched south with a French army, history might well have applauded Benedict for his daring.

Then, in 1406, after a reign of only two years, Pope Innocent VII died in Rome, and again everyone had new hopes —or rather, renewed the old ones: France, that the way was clear to place a single Pope over a united Church; and Benedict, that he would be that Pope. Benedict needed a dramatic move, to seize on the minds of men. Otherwise he was bound to be defeated—by his own nature no less than by his foes.

Of these he never lacked. Influential doctors at the University of Paris were always against him, notably Simon de Cramaud. Others, anxious for a Pope who could be led, opposed him on principle. Still others, and perhaps they were in the majority, had been disillusioned by his obvious unwillingness to take one honest step along the Way of Cession. They knew nothing of power and its tentacles.

Benedict's lordliness displayed itself in levying taxes. He was himself a frugal man, but the cost of the Schism was high. He needed money for his fleet, for buying Italian support, for missions to other Urbanist lands, for the never-ending struggle in France. All this was heavy on his people.

Especially burdensome were the sums that had to be paid into the papal treasury by the excommunicated clergy desirous of absolution. Their numbers had snowballed during the withdrawal of obedience and they were now being forced to pay for the defection. It was a day when most problems ended in the exchange either of blood or of gold. Giving up such large sums did not warm their French hearts toward Benedict. All through France his collectors, while they raked in funds, were alienating friends. An estimated 1,200,000 francs was gathered in France in the years immediately after the restitution of obedience. In spite of the disastrous results of the first withdrawal, people began to murmur about withdrawing their obedience all over again. Soon the murmur swelled to loud debates, during which Benedict was labeled not only schismatic and heretic, but a leader of heretics and a debauchee to boot—charges intemperate and false, but heralding the rising storm.

Thus, when Pope Innocent's short reign came to an end in 1406, there was little chance that the two halves of the Church would unite on Benedict. Optimism, however, was

growing as to union under a different Pope. This time the
Roman Cardinals postponed the election of a new Pontiff
while they wrote the King of France, and France hurried
off a reply. France believed that Benedict might at long last
abdicate. In any case, she was willing to merge the two
Colleges of Cardinals, and to prove that she was not playing
for national gain, she offered to make Rome the Holy See.
Avignon, abandoned by Benedict, was now sacrificed by
France. The French court also entered into negotiations
with England, and the two countries were still working out
Church unification plans around the first of the year—when
they learned that the Italians had already crowned a new
Roman Pope, more than a month before.

The new contender, elected November 30, 1406, was the
Venetian, Angelo Corario, who became Pope Gregory XII.
Gregory was nearly eighty when he got to be Pope, and he
surprised everyone by living another eleven years, nine of
them as Pontiff. Prior to his election, he had achieved a
reputation for gentleness, discretion, humility and saintli-
ness; afterward, he was regarded as a hypocritical old man,
undecided about everything except remaining in office.

Certainly Gregory yielded to none in noble sentiments.
In tears at his coronation, he said his only fear was that he
might die before he could unite the Church. "Anathema
upon the Schismatics," he cried to his Cardinals. "Anathema upon them whatever be their power and their rank.
Anathema upon me also if I do not use all my efforts to end
the deplorable division which harms and dishonors Christianity. Yea, my brethren, I swear from the height of the
throne of truth, that despite my age and my infirmities, I
will go to the council which shall be convoked to reunite
the two obediences, and to whatever place it may assemble.
If I have no galley, I shall confront the open sea in a small
boat. If I have no horse, I shall set out on foot, a stick in
my hand." These words were often quoted back to him

when he and Benedict kept missing one another along the Italian Riviera.

Gregory XII was one of those individuals who are almost incapable of any action, even to the delegation of authority. Business usually managed by the Cardinals passed into his hands but rarely through them. In one week, two thousand supplications came in. He crammed them into a bag which served him as a file. Out of the lot, he dealt with ten. The matter of meeting with Benedict to end the Schism made similar progress.

Although the substance of the new Pope's first communication to Pope Benedict was respectful enough and packed with right thinking in regard to union, it opened in a way little calculated to win a friend. The letter began: "To Pedro de Luna, whom some nations during this miserable Schism call Benedict XIII."

Benedict countered with: "To Angelo Corario, whom some in this pernicious Schism name Gregory XII." Round even. That Benedict was also not to be outdone in proper sentiments is evinced by this further quotation from the Clementine Pope: "Haste you, delay not, consider our age, the shortness of life; embrace at once the way of salvation and peace, that we may appear before the Great Shepherd with our flock united."

To begin with, an insuperable obstacle: Where to meet? Rome was proposed, and then the list began to read like a timetable: Viterbo, Siena, Todi, Lucca, were advanced by the Italians. Benedict was at Marseilles. He favored that city for a meeting place, but offered successively Fréjus, Nice, Genoa and Savona. They at last compromised on Savona. but getting the two Popes there was another matter.

No sooner had the meeting place finally been agreed upon than Gregory found it unsuitable. Lengthy negotiations followed. Gregory prepared a long objection, listing twenty-two arguments against Savona. He thought Carrara, Lucca, Pisa

or Leghorn might be better. For a man who had offered,
should Church unity require it, to venture out to sea in a
small boat, he brought up a strange reason for not meeting
with Benedict: he did not have as many galleys as the other
Pope. These rival vicars of the Prince of Peace were both
vastly concerned about their armaments. Another serious
objection was that Gregory could not by a long chalk equal
Benedict's magnificence.

From the three-week-long debates at Marseilles which set
up the physical conditions for the proposed conference to
the ultimate attempt to bring Gregory another handful of
miles to Pietrasanta, we find the Clementine patient and
accommodating, the Urbanist reluctant and afraid.

On April 21, 1407, the terms for a meeting at Savona
were drawn up in final form and duly notarized. Gregory's
representatives had made certain that everything should be
equal at the confrontation of the two Pontiffs scheduled for
September 29 of that year, or without fail, for All Souls' Day
a month later.

Each Pope was to arrive with the same number of galleys,
this number to be set by Gregory, with eight as the top
limit. Each could have only two hundred men-at-arms, one
hundred crossbowmen, equal forces of lawyers, prelates, professors of theology and valets, down to two notaries per
Pontiff. For every category, whether cardinal's servant or
Pope's, there was a one-for-you, one-for-me specification.

Separate but equal applied to Savona, too; half the town
and half the harbor for Gregory, half for Benedict.

Nothing had been overlooked. There were to be hostages
to guarantee performance and safety, search and removal of
arms from the houses and the inhabitants of Savona, safe
passage to and from the conference city, ceding of territory
to the two Popes from the time of their arrival until mutual
cession was achieved. Even the rents were to be controlled.

All this meticulous equality should have satisfied Gregory. On the contrary, the timorous old man found much to criticize. The security measures were not strict enough, for one thing. And, although full of talk at his accession about setting out staff in hand, he now stuck at the idea of an overland journey. Instead of a willingness to trust himself to the open sea in a small boat, he balked at borrowed galleys. He expressed doubt about cession itself.

Benedict on the other hand was all conciliation. He seemed to hasten to meet his fellow Pope. His Mediterranean cruise took him to the presumed conference at Savona ahead of schedule, and as if to demonstrate his eagerness, he sailed on, and reached Porto Venere with its narrow watchtower houses on the tip of the peninsula back of which lies La Spezia, protected by a bay. Gregory himself was at Lucca, about fourteen miles from the seacoast, and some forty-odd miles from Benedict at La Spezia. This was as close as they were ever to get.

A year after the continually missed rendezvous of the two Popes, Ladislas (son of Charles of Durazzo and King of Sicily) seized Rome, giving Gregory a dubious reason for not trying any more, and the long negotiations were scrapped.

Meanwhile Bavarian Isabeau was living in Paris at the Hôtel Barbette, and it came about that she gave birth to her twelfth child. The resplendent Duke Louis arrived at the mansion and sat down by her bed. He was strong in France at this time, but the people did not share their Queen's love for him. He seemed to control the King; the people said that Charles "was sick or well at the whim of Monsieur d'Orléans." As Louis lingered at the bedside, the King's equerry came with an urgent summons from Charles. It was about eight o'clock, on November 23, 1407, when Duke Louis said goodbye to Isabeau.

He left with an escort of some ten men, a few of them

torchbearers, some mounted, others on foot, most dragging behind. He himself was on a mule; he was bareheaded, playing with a glove, singing to himself. Suddenly mortal cries interrupted the song, and there he was, kneeling on the ground, masked men beating him to death, he putting up his arms to ward off the blows. The murderers—hirelings, it became known, of John the Fearless, Duke Louis' cousin and foe—quenched their torches in the puddles and vanished as swiftly as they had struck, as swiftly as they had put out the Duke's splendor and left him stretched out in the street. With him, too, passed Benedict's last great chance.

Quite against reason, one could almost believe that some women, like some jewels, are carriers of bad luck. After little Isabella was married to Richard, that King lost his throne and life. When she was taken into Louis' household, that Duke was murdered. Then, seeking justice, her husband Charles could be seen riding into Paris, dressed all in black, on a black horse—alongside his mortally grieving mother in her black-draped litter that bore in large letters the words: "No longer is anything mine." As for the Pope who twice made marriage possible for Isabella, he became a wanderer, without a home.

By 1409 Isabella, twenty years old, would be designing a splendid canopy for the bed on which she would give birth: it bore the four Evangelists in fine gold on a green taffeta ground. But that September, having had a daughter and being not yet washed from childbed taint, she died staring at them. "Only last month," said one, commenting on that short, doomed life, "the Lady Isabella was buying horses to ride to the hunt, and her husband, gloves, hoods for the falcons, and pouches for game."

Not at that hour but in happier time, Charles had written his famous lines on spring:

The year has laid his coat away
Of icy cold and wind and rain,
And wears a broidered dress again,
And sun so shimmering fine and gay.

No bird or beast but has its say;
Each in its tongue cries this refrain:
The year has laid his coat away,
Of icy cold and wind and rain.

River, brooklet, fountain spray
Have put on livery all ashine
With silver drop and golden chain;
Each dresses up in new array.
The year has laid his coat away
Of icy cold and wind and rain.

The flourishing days immediately after Benedict's escape from Avignon in the spring of 1403 had long since withered. Nearly five more years had passed, and the Church was as divided as ever. Despite his performance, France had no illusions as to the Clementine's intentions. When one after the other, two Roman Popes had died, Benedict had only held the tighter to his own tiara. Then he had negotiated with Gregory in apparent good faith, but France, knowing him well, was not so sure. France must force his hand.

Accordingly, on January 12, 1408, the King's advisers drew up an ultimatum: unless real progress toward unification had been made by May, the French would declare themselves neutral. Experience had taught its bitter lesson. France now threatened a move less theologically drastic, less dangerous to the Church than the old withdrawal of obedience, but one which would deprive Pope Benedict of French support. If France went neutral, he would lose the main pillar which held up his throne.

Foreseeing this, Benedict, who was still at Porto Venere, had already prepared a stringent Bull against those who might oppose him in France; having received the ultimatum, he executed a milder Bull, and then, hating perhaps to waste his literary efforts, sent off both. The men who delivered these Bulls to Charles were promptly jailed, either as a warning to the Pope or simply to punish bearers of bad news. Following the assembly that considered the Bulls, the two envoys were paraded through Paris in a garbage cart. Their heads were adorned with paper miters which conveyed the information that they were traitors to Church and King. The mock-ecclesiastical gowns of black linen in which they were trussed bore on one side a picture of the prisoners offering the Bulls to Charles VI, on the other Pope Benedict's arms upside down. For two days, prior to being jailed, they stood exposed on a scaffold to the insults of the crowd.

This exhibition served publicly to announce the work accomplished by the assembly of May 21, 1408. Nobles, churchmen, representatives from the university, and members of Parliament heard Jean Courtecuisse preach on the text from Numbers 15:31, "His iniquity shall be upon his head." The speaker read out thirteen charges against Benedict XIII. The Avignon Pope was a perjurer and a heretic; his Bulls treasonable as well as illegal, and also an insult to the King. Gerson, chancellor of the University of Paris, having been ordered by King Charles to deal with the Bulls as they deserved, tore the Bulls in half, handing one part to the French nobles and the other to representatives of the Church and University, and both bodies tore their halves to bits. More, the declaration of neutrality was voted. It was a strange kind of neutrality, for Benedict was to be arrested.

France also published a proclamation in Italy calling both Popes traitors, perjurers and heretics. Churches of all lands were told they should reject both.

Truthfully, the conduct of neither had been edifying. As

Milman says: "These grey-headed prelates, each claiming to be the representative of Christ on earth, did not attempt to disguise from the world that neither had the least reliance on the truth, honour, justice, or religion of his adversary. Neither would scruple to take any advantage of the other; neither would hesitate at any fraud, or violence, or crime."

About this time, May, 1408, Gregory, still at Lucca, strengthened his hand by naming four new Cardinals. This was directly contrary to the agreement between the Popes not to change the voting proportion by adding to either Sacred College. Gregory's Cardinals protested vigorously. One fell at the Pope's feet and begged him to refrain from thus packing the College; another cried out, "Let us die first!" Nothing budged Gregory. Nine Cardinals promptly abandoned the Roman Pope and left for Pisa.

This was the moment when placards showed up on the walls of Lucca, flaying Gregory XII. They summoned the Pope to appear on a certain day to be degraded; they accused him of being a shedder of blood, a drunkard, a man of dishonor, a slave to carnal appetites, a hypocrite, madman, heretic, even one who sought to overthrow the Church. As a final touch, the summons purported to have been authorized not only by the Cardinals and the entire Papal court, but also by the lowest of the dishwashers and the man who cleaned out the stables.

Implicit in these placards, invisibly written on these walls, was yet another great split in the Church.

19 AND NOW, THREE POPES

WHEN THOSE nine Cardinals—the majority of his College—deserted Pope Gregory, Pope Benedict saw at once that the defection was to his own strong advantage.

He was at Porto Venere then, and still prepared to confer with Gregory; it was May, 1408, a few days before the assembly in Paris declared against them both. The runaway Cardinals wrote Benedict from Pisa and asked him to join them in Leghorn, which meant a forty-five-mile sail from Porto Venere. (Leghorn had lately been considered as yet another possible meeting place between the two inappetent Pontiffs.)

Anxious to win over Gregory's erstwhile Cardinals, Benedict sent four of his own to confer with them in Pisa, while he made ready to go to Leghorn. He could already appraise the effect on the Christian world when the majority of the Urbanist Sacred College should join with his own Clementine Cardinals to announce that he, Benedict, was the one and only Pope.

Unfortunately, Benedict's envoys could not get to Pisa, being unable to obtain safe conducts; for the same reason, he had to stay on in Porto Venere. When a meeting of the two Colleges took place at Leghorn, the results were not at all what Benedict had visualized: freed of the presence of both heads of the Church, the talk was all of an Ecumenical Council and the election of a new Pope.

The real blow fell on June 5, when word reached the Cardinals of France's declaration of neutrality and the imminent arrest of Benedict XIII. Those Cardinals who were closest to him hurried back to Porto Venere to warn him and urge that he put out to sea.

Pope Benedict's six galleys sailed from the harbor on the morning of June 16, their destination Port-Vendres, near Perpignan, a long voyage away on the Mediterranean's farther coast. There, in view of the Pyrenees, he could expect the protection of the King of Aragon. With him were four Cardinals, the loyal core of his College, most of whose members were about to desert him for the second time.

The flotilla made a minimum number of stops along the shore, putting in only where the fugitives could be relatively safe. Swept on by a storm, they reached Port-Vendres July 1, 1408. From here, Benedict traveled overland to Perpignan, and established himself in the palace which had once belonged to his kinfolk, the Kings of Majorca.

Out from its vaulted arcades at seven o'clock on the morning of November 15, under a canopy carried by four lords, walked the slight yet majestic eighty-year-old Pontiff, preceded by the banner of the papal troops, the Cross, and many notables, including Vincent Ferrer. As the Pope went by, the crowds knelt down and bowed their heads. A great array of nobles and soldiers followed Benedict, and after them came the papal treasurer, scattering *missilia* coins to the multitude with a lavish hand.

In this manner, to forestall any ecumenical council the Pisa Cardinals might call, Benedict opened his own Council of Perpignan, first by celebrating Mass, amid brocades and tapestries and hundreds of candles, at the Church of Sainte-Marie-la Réal. The next day the assembly got down to work.

Whatever else it was, Pope Benedict's Council of Perpignan had been summoned in accordance with canon law. Some three hundred prelates were there: nine Cardinals,

four Patriarchs from the East (or at least four churchmen
so designated), some from Scotland, the Archbishops of
Toledo and Saragossa, some from Savoy and Lorraine who
had traveled here in disguise, a few even from southern
France, but with the preponderating membership out of
Aragon, Castile and Navarre.

During session after session (seven in all), a Cardinal
read on about the pontificate of Pedro de Luna, Pope Benedict XIII, while at the tenth session the Pope declared Gregory and also his Pisan Cardinals anathema, lamented the
state of the Church, and said he was ready to die for her.

As weeks and months went by, the delegates began to
melt away. By now, although neither Holy See was vacant,
a majority of the Cardinals of both obediences assumed
control of the Church and sent out a call to attend their
own ecumenical council at Pisa in March, 1409. On the
twenty-fifth of that month, the Council of Pisa formally
began. All this was contrary to canon law, since only the
Pope could summon a general council, and neither Benedict
nor Gregory ever appeared at Pisa.

Finally, what with being irascible and adamant about his
rights, Benedict had only about eighteen delegates left at
Perpignan. These advised the Pope to send legates to Pisa
authorized to renounce the Papacy in his name.

"That is not the unanimous opinion of my Council," said
the Pope.

"Holy Father," the remnant answered, "there is but one
man here who is of a different opinion."

"Well," said Benedict, "that one man is right."

Actually, Benedict was not alone. Among many adherents
was Saint Vincent Ferrer, who had championed the Clementine cause for years, and written a treatise saying that the
election of Urban was null and void, and the election of
Clement VII valid beyond the shadow of a doubt, because

there had been violence done at the Fateful Conclave in Rome. Saint Vincent, a Dominican born at Valencia in 1357, was more than a man, people claimed. "You are the Angel of the Apocalypse," wrote Gerson, chancellor of the University of Paris.

Constantly traveling, Vincent was a familiar figure in many countries. From the back as he rode along, people recognized his small donkey's two hind legs and tasseled tail, above it the cowled, woolen form; and wherever he passed, Italy, Languedoc, Brittany, Spain, he drew mobs. After him in later years followed his Flagellants, men and women in white and black robes like himself, sleeping on the hard ground, living from unasked alms. They came singing the hymn he had written for them, and when they reached the church porch of a town they would kneel—up to three hundred of them, their faces veiled, their backs and shoulders bared—and as silent thousands, hardly breathing, waited, the Flagellants would begin the rhythmic scourging of their bodies with a "noise as of heavy rain."

Saint Vincent was credited with many converts out of Judaism and Islam, including a man of such rank as the Chief Rabbi of Valladolid. In this missionary zeal he resembled the Clementine Pope, although Benedict, no doubt from his birth and environment, had absorbed something of Muslim tolerance. (One of the charges which would later be brought against Benedict was that he was friendly to Jews and heretics. Muslims were considered heretics; in Dante's hell, torn and maimed for being schismatics and heretics, walk the great Prophet Muhammad, and 'Alí, first of the holy Imams.)

Traditional Muslim tolerance was sadly needed. "Let there be no compulsion in religion," the Qur'án said, "Summon thou to the way of thy Lord with wisdom . . . debate with them in greatest kindness" (2:257; 16:126). On June 4, 1391, crazed multitudes, whipped to frenzy by the mouth-

foaming tirades of the spiritual leader, the archdeacon of
Écija, had burst into the *judería* at Seville and murdered
four thousand people. That summer, in city after city, the
judería was burned out. In Écija and Carmona, Christians
exterminated the entire Jewish population. Some Jewish
communities, like Barcelona's—which had been there continuously from the eighth century—could not be reestab-
lished. Only under Muslim protection were the Spanish
Jews safe. The toll of murdered for that summer is placed
at fifty thousand. The Jews had been driven out of England
in 1290, out of France in 1306 (and would be again in
1394), out of German cities at the time of the Black Death,
but in Muslim-oriented Spain they had long enjoyed pros-
perity and peace. Now, however, they came forward to be
baptized as Christians in order to keep on living. Several
thousand would be converted at Benedict's theological congress, held at Tortosa in 1413.

All who flocked to hear Saint Vincent, whatever their
own language, could, people said, miraculously understand
his Spanish tongue, and those on the outer fringe of the
crowds of maybe ten thousand could hear him best. All
were, on occasion, disconcerted to see him sprout wings in
mid-sermon and temporarily float away.

One of his miracles out of so many was the inducing of
a husband to stay at home. "Have a cup of water handy,"
Vincent directed the wife, "and when your husband comes
home, take a mouthful and hold it in your mouth without
swallowing." Even more noteworthy was the time when
Vincent had promised his superior to stop performing miracles and a builder fell off a scaffold. "Wait!" he cried to the
hurtling workman. "Wait till I ask permission!" The builder
duly waited in mid-hurtle. Vincent ran for permission and
rescued him from afar.

Such was this great ally of Pope Benedict's. Personality,
healer, psychic, Saint Vincent had the character and mag-

netism to attract and profoundly influence the people of his times.

The Council of Pisa ground slowly by. Dignity was lengthily maintained. Nearly a month passed before the Council shook with the demand that both Popes be deposed. It is true that this had been present in men's minds, but now here it was, to be acted upon by those who had all their lives bowed down before the pontifical power. They were being asked to approve a statement that read: "Seeing that the contending prelates had been duly cited, and, not appearing, been declared contumacious, they were deprived of their pontifical dignity." The followers of Benedict and Gregory, if they said No to the sentence of deposition, would be stripped of their honors, offices, and worse still, of their benefices. And they might well be turned over to the Church's dreaded secular arm.

In this crisis of the Church, it cannot be said that the Council of Pisa failed widely to represent the Catholic world. Lists of those who attended show that of Cardinals there were in the beginning fourteen (seven of Gregory's, seven of Benedict's). This number swelled to twenty-six. The Patriarchs of Alexandria, Antioch, Jerusalem and Grado also traveled to Pisa. So did twelve Archbishops, while fourteen more sent representatives with full powers. Eighty Bishops joined with one hundred and two prelates acting for absent Bishops. Eighty-seven Abbots came; two hundred sent proxies. The Generals of the Franciscans, Dominicans, Carmelites, and Augustinians were there. Bandied about were such imposing titles as the Grand Master of Rhodes, the Proctor General of the Teutonic Knights, the Prior of the Knights of the Holy Sepulcher. Delegates from the universities of Paris, Orléans, Toulouse, Angers, Montpellier, Bologna, Florence, Cracow, Vienna, Prague, Cologne mixed with those from Oxford and Cambridge. It should be especially noted that there were present three hundred doctors

of theology and of canon law. Also seeking lodgings and a
place at the Council were envoys from one hundred chapters of metropolitan and collegiate churches.

Since politics and religion were partners, there was also
an impressive array of ambassadors, although the Kings of
Spain refused to be parties to the Council, considering
themselves under the obedience of Benedict XIII. Nor had
this Pope been deserted by Hungary, Scotland, Sweden,
Norway or Denmark, however shaky their support. As for
Gregory XII, he had only a single monarch on his side,
Ladislas of Sicily and Naples.

The Council of Pisa charged both Popes with heresy. It
had no alternative. There could, obviously, be no agreement
on which Pope was legitimate, however badly that question
needed an answer. But if both Popes could be proved heretics, then the Council could act to depose them. Certainly
a heretical Pope could no longer continue to rule. The theo-
retical impossibility of a Pope's being a heretic appears not
to have disturbed them at all (nor is papal heresy considered an insurmountable assumption today, not even since
Pius IX's new dogma of papal infallibility, promulgated in
1870). The main point, it seems, was to rid themselves of
their embarrassment of Popes.

On the question of heresy, they were somewhat short of
grounds. They noted that attachment to power did not constitute heresy as generally understood, nor did subterfuge,
nor failure to carry out promises. They therefore tried to
prove, for example, that Benedict had shown an odd tend-
ency to be soft on heretics, while at the same time being
extremely hard on the orthodox clergy, hanging some, including Menendo, the Bishop of Bayonne, and sending
others to the torture chamber, or to forced labor in the
galleys. As for Gregory, it was recalled that at one time the
Inquisition had been hot on his trail.

Sorcery was also brought into the case, apparently to be

marshaled as a last resort. This accusation was never openly made, but would have been in order, since devils were still an acceptable part of everyday life; psychopathology had not yet replaced them. Besides, the charge of heresy needed bolstering somehow, and then as now there were witnesses capable of swearing to anything. That the sorcery witnesses never had a public hearing was due to the fact that the long-drawn-out proceedings had grown so tedious it was finally decided that no more testimony need be given: the misdeeds of Benedict and Gregory were simply declared to be of wide notoriety.

Gregory's sins in the line of sorcery are disappointing. In order to determine his future, especially as to whether he would retain his tiara, he had consulted a doctor named Elias, who, according to the Catholic witnesses, was not only a Jew but given to necromancy.

As always, Benedict cut more of a figure: it was testified that he had at his disposal two demons, whom he kept handy in a small purse. After his coronation, he was said to have looked everywhere for books on magic, finally securing two in Spain and a third from the Muslims. To divine the future and to discover what people were saying about him, Benedict would place one of these volumes under his pillow before going to sleep. Valois wonders if this was the book that was found in the Pope's bed when he set off from Nice, and continues: "He had also shown an ardent desire to possess a work composed by a Jew in which the magical character of the miracles of Jesus was demonstrated." It seems, however, that Benedict, at first unskilled, could not get the full good out of these books. Whenever he heard of any magicians, even if they were in jail, he accordingly sent for them at once, to improve his techniques. Some of his entourage were accomplished magicians; high on the list of these was a hermit with a stable of three demons who were going to put Benedict in charge of Rome as well as Avignon.

It was also reported that when Benedict was at Nice,
and busily engaged in magical pursuits, a thunderbolt had
struck a nearby tower. Neither did people like the way he
had dried up a storm in the Gulf of Genoa as he was en
route to Porto Venere. It was asked with unanswerable
logic: if Benedict did not have the assistance of diabolical
powers, how was it the storm retreated at exactly the same
rate as his galleys advanced? (When saints performed the
same wonders they were called miracles.)

The Council of Pisa yet again summoned Benedict XIII
and Gregory XII to appear before it. Again the Pontiffs did
not come.

On June 5, 1409, the Council of Pisa formally and un-
equivocally deposed the two Popes. The gates of the Cathedral opened, the Patriarch of Alexandria came out, and
publicly read these solemn words:

*The Holy Universal Council, representing the Catholic
Church of God, to whom belongs the judgment of this case,
assembled by the grace of the Holy Ghost in the Cathedral
of Pisa, having duly heard the promoters of the cause for the
extirpation of the detestable and inveterate Schism, and the
union and reestablishment of our Holy Mother Church,
against Pedro de Luna and Angelo Corario, called by some
Benedict XIII and Gregory XII, declares the crimes and
excesses, adduced before the Council, to be true, and of
public fame. The two competitors, Pedro de Luna and Angelo Corario, have been and are notorious schismatics, ob-
stinate partisans, abettors, defenders, approvers of this long
Schism; notorious heretics as having departed from the
Faith; involved in the crimes of perjury and breach of their
oaths; openly scandalizing the Church by their manifest
obstinacy, utterly incorrigible . . . and though by the can-
ons they are already rejected of God, deprived and cut off
from the Church, nevertheless the Church, by this defini-*

tive sentence, deposes, rejects and cuts them off, prohibiting both and each from assuming any longer the Sovereign Pontificate, and declaring for further security the Papacy to be vacant.

Solemnly, measuredly, determinedly, a General Council thus denied the supreme power of the Pope. He was far from infallible. He was subject to the approval or disapproval of the Catholic world. He was an office functionary who could be impeached. He could be deposed.

Having, as it thought, done away with two Pontiffs, the Council of Pisa, on June 26, 1409, elected one of its own, the seventy-year-old Franciscan, Petros Philargos, who took the name of Pope Alexander V.

In short, Pisa's Council was as much out of line as her tower.

In Perpignan, Benedict had finally budged a little: he had agreed to send ambassadors to Pisa to plead his cause. Once arrived, they found themselves passing through angry crowds to be confronted by twelve Cardinals who were only too pleased with the completed work of the Pisan Council and in no mood to hear anything about Benedict. If the envoys could guarantee that their Pope would submit to the will of Pisa, said these Cardinals, well and good. Anything less would land them in the mortal peril of supporting a heretic.

The envoys thought for a moment of fleeing to the dubious welcome of Pope Gregory; but they would have had to pass through the territory of the horrifying Baldassare Cossa who had promised faithfully that if he got his hands on them he would burn them at the stake. The result was that, nothing accomplished, they hurried back to Perpignan.

As for the Perpignan Council, it ultimately named a committee to draw up its findings. Their text shows that this Council accepted Benedict as true and lawful Pontiff, but begged him to follow the Way of Cession and to abdicate should Gregory XII do the same. With their Pope an octogenarian, they were, otherwise, not at all reassured as to what might be in store.

Meanwhile Gregory, not to be outdone, had called his own personal council, but unlike Benedict's and that of Pisa, he was unable to rally a representative gathering. When at last he managed to assemble a meeting of sorts in out-of-the-way Cividale del Friuli, the Council of Pisa had already reached its momentous decisions, and the old man had only a scattering of ecclesiastics to hear him assert his disregarded rights and to listen—if they did listen—while he pronounced weak anathemas against those who had cast him out. Ultimately one night he had to run off in disguise, for adherents of Pisa were coming after him.

Things had come to such a pass [writes the Catholic historian Pastor] that besides the new theory of the superiority of the Council over the Pope . . . it was said that it mattered little how many Popes there were, that there might be two or three or ten or twelve; or that each country might have its own independent Pope. Again, it was suggested that it might be the will of God that the Papacy should be for a time, or even permanently, divided as the Kingdom of David had been, and after the example of human governments which are subject to change.

The Schism had now lasted thirty years. For three decades Christianity had watched competing Popes, who could not give up papal power once they had tasted it, no matter what oaths they had sworn before their coronation, or what promises they had made afterward. Public cynicism was now chronic. A saying went the rounds: "One Pope is too much for the Catholic world, no Pope would be even better."

20 BENEDICT PLEADS HIS CAUSE

Iℕ JULY, 1409, when the plague drove Benedict out of Perpignan, he crossed the Pyrenees with his Curia, en route for Barcelona, where King Martin the Humane had placed the royal palace at the Pontiff's disposal.

As Benedict came on, King Martin suffered a tragedy: his Crown Prince, Martin of Sicily, died of the fevers, leaving only a bastard behind. Such a one, under Aragonese law, could not inherit Martin's costly silver throne. At once the Cortes ("Courts") met. These Spanish parliaments, which were divided into four estates—clergy, greater and lesser nobles, and commoners—preceded both England's Parliament and the French États-Généraux. In the: fourteenth century a number of them had wide powers, that of Aragon, particularly, serving as a check on the ruler.

This body formally requested grieving King Martin to marry again, and provide an heir. Pope Benedict confirmed their decision and Martin made no protest.

Martin was a king who liked to sit in the garden and read Seneca. He was ailing, and too fat to stir around. He let the Pope and Saint Vincent Ferrer and the others choose his bride, and as between the two hopefuls at court, a young noblewoman named Margarita was selected, perhaps because she had served the late Queen, María de Luna, and came of a house that staunchly supported Pope Benedict. These weighty matters delayed Benedict's ceremonial entry into Barcelona, which finally took place September 29, 1409.

194   In May of the following year Queen Margarita's ladies

busied themselves with serving King Martin a specially fattened roast duck. Even with Saint Vincent officiating at his wedding, Martin had had no issue and it was thought the duck would prove of some avail. Martin swallowed down a few mouthfuls and suddenly cried out with stomach pains. Two days later he was dead, leaving Pope Benedict to weep at his funeral. De Luna was eighty-two, and the penalty for arriving at such an age is losing friends.

Several tried for the throne, then, and Benedict finally intervened to prevent mounting chaos. He bypassed his own relatives for Ferdinand of Antequera (so named because he had won that town from the Muslims), advocated and supported a commission appointed by several *Cortes,* and through Saint Vincent Ferrer's influence, ultimately prevailed upon its members to crown Ferdinand. This accomplished (on January 15, 1414), Benedict had every reason to think of King Ferdinand as loyally his.

Three Popes now demanded obedience of the Catholic world. One of the three, and one only, was legitimate. It could not be Alexander V, the new Pope elected by the Council of Pisa, for by canon law the council itself was illegal. The council had not been convoked by a Pope, nor did either Pope honor it by attending. That the Council acted for the majority of Catholics can hardly be questioned, but Popes are not elected by democratic processes; they are supposed to represent the will of God, not the will of the people. Moreover, a new Pope cannot be elected while the preceding Pope is still living, unless he has abdicated—in itself a questionable procedure, something for him to decide alone, and certainly free of pressure from without. The legitimate Pope—whichever one it was—was still very much alive. He had not convoked the Council of Pisa. He did not attend. He refused to be deposed. So now there were three Popes.

Benedict XIII absolutely and irrevocably believed himself to be the true Pontiff. He knew canon law; thirty years of controversy had made him an expert. After Alexander's election, he wrote *De nova subscimate*, using all his informed skill, his "ironic force" and "vigor of argument," to demonstrate that the third Pope had been illegally elected, and showed the fox side of his nature, as he had the lion before.

The Cardinals were inconsistent, he wrote; indifferent, then overbold; quick to swear fidelity, impulsive in declaring war. First, they laid siege to him, then threw themselves at his feet. Again they joined his enemies, disloyal Cardinals whom they had flayed before, and proceeded at Pisa to a ridiculous election. As for this charge of heresy they had brought against him—they had absolved him of it when they came back to his obedience in 1403. Five years later they still considered him anything but a heretic; they invited him to their conventicle. Had he changed since then? How so? By what reason could any man believe the Holy See was vacant? Had he abdicated? Was he dead? The people of Barcelona saw him every day, speaking, eating, drinking. His faith was sounder than ever. He challenged his foes to prove that a Pope is a heretic simply because he refuses to renounce his legitimate rights.

Benedict concludes with his proofs of legitimacy, the most intriguing being that if both Urban VI and Clement VII were of doubtful legitimacy (as claimed by one side or the other), the Cardinals created by those two Popes should be set aside. This would leave as legitimate Cardinals only those who had been appointed by Avignon's Gregory XI or Urban V who, no one has ever doubted, were canonically valid Popes. He, Benedict XIII, was chosen after the deaths of both Urban VI and Clement VII, by those very Cardinals who alone had been named by unquestionably legitimate Popes. Therefore, writes Benedict, his title to the

Papacy is clear, since it goes back to Gregory XI, a true Pope in the legitimate succession.

What Benedict neglected to add is that both Urban VI and Clement VII enjoyed the suffrage of those same legitimate Cardinals, whose number included Benedict himself.

"A s bishop rich, as Cardinal poor, as Pope a
beggar"—thus the new, third simultaneous Pope summed
up the results of his own prodigality. Petros Philargos, Pope
Alexander V, was born poor, of unknown parents, was raised
by the begging order of Saint Francis, and is chiefly remembered for giving out with both hands. A non-Catholic historian calls him "blameless, studious, holy." Another writes
of his modesty, frankness and loyalty. Pillement adds to his
other qualities the French tribute that he loved good wine.

Alexander had both learning and eloquence. He was free
from nepotism, for he had no nephews. He made up for
this lack, however, by treating his Order as if it were his
family, as indeed it was. From their schools he had gone on
to Oxford and the University of Paris. Unfortunately, his
studies in theology were no help to him in European politics; here he was all thumbs. People have accused him of
being the tool of Bologna's monstrous Baldassare Cossa,
who may well have desired an interim Pope until he was
ready to take over himself.

Within a few months of his election in 1409, the new
Pope issued a sweeping Bull. He struck down seven articles
of doctrine put forward or approved by other Popes, his
chief target being Avignon's second Pontiff, John XXII.
Alexander appeared to concern himself very little with the
problem of papal infallibility. Previous Popes had been doc-
trinally wrong, he seemed to say, therefore they should be
set right. Instead of quietly forgetting the charge of heresy

against John XXII, he stirred things up again by writing that one of John's doctrines had been promulgated while he was under the shadow of that accusation.

But the big storm raised by Alexander was not over dogma. When he granted the mendicant orders the right to perform acts previously reserved for the clergy, he dealt the latter a crushing blow. Pope after Pope had fought the begging orders with restrictions, prison, torture and the ultimate bonfire. Now these Orders were handed powers which has always belonged to resident priests. This seriously undermined those who had the charge of souls in a given parish. What adulterous wife, what seducer, what corrupter of boys, would not prefer to confess before a wandering stranger? The day-by-day affairs of a parish would still be led along by the local priesthood, but their inside knowledge of their parishioners was now being taken from them; the subtle power that came from knowing what went on in the secret places of the houses and hearts of those about them was being stolen away; their one great lever under the public, auricular confession, given them by the Fourth Lateran Council two centuries before, in 1215, was struck from their hands.

No wonder the University of Paris could not believe this Bull of Alexander's to be genuine. They sent him delegates to make sure it was not forged. Even the round, leaden *bulla*, or seal of authority, with Peter and Paul on one side and its owner's name on the other, fastened on silk that hung from the document, could scarcely convince them of its authenticity. Alexander had written that the Bull was composed upon the advice and with the consent of the Sacred College. The Paris envoys accordingly took each Cardinal aside and asked one question: Had he been consulted about the Bull? The new attitude toward the Papacy is clearly shown. Here was a university questioning the veracity of the Pope, a university's envoys playing detective, polling individual Cardinals as to whether the Pope was or was not a liar. The Cardinals denied having had anything to do with the Bull at all.

History says there may have been a connection between the third Pope's poverty and the size of his household, as witness the following list from the Protestant historian Creighton, attributed to someone formerly in the service of Benedict XIII:

First amongst the officers of the household come the Chamberlains, who are of three classes: some honorary; some prelates, generally four, who are intimate with the Pope, read the Hours with him, serve at Mass; some domestics, generally two, who sleep in his chamber and wait upon him. Of the prelates, one has charge of the Pope's private letters and receives his instructions about the answers to be given; another has the care of the Pope's jewels; a third, of the wardrobe; a fourth, of the medicines and drugs. The prelates discharge the duties of their office without salary, except in cases when they are poor. The domestic chamberlains have board for themselves and two servants, and have an underling to sweep the rooms and do the dirty work. Besides these, two Doorkeepers have charge of the audience chamber, where they generally sleep.

Next in importance is the Controller of the Household, who receives the Pope's orders about his meals and entertainments, issues invitations, and orders the service of the banquet. Every night, he receives the keys of the Palace when the gates are shut, and lays them on the table at the Pope's supper hour. Every night also, he receives and examines the accounts of all subordinate officials, which, after receiving his signature, are presented weekly at the Treasury. He is generally responsible for the order and decorum of the household, and has under him a clerk and one or two servants. The Pope's personal attendants are Squires of Honor,

generally eight or ten in number, who receive pay or allow-
ances, and frequently hold some other office. For each
article consumed in the household there is a separate depart-
ment. Two ecclesiastics, each with two servants under him,
hold office over the Bakery, and provide bread and fruit,
have the care of the table linen, knives, forks [since forks
were rare even in Shakespeare's day, we wonder at this item.
There were, indeed, pitchforks at this time, and certain
pronged instruments available to cooks, no less than Devils]
and salt cellars, and have the duty of laying the table. In
like manner, two ecclesiastics, each with two inferiors, discharge the office of Butler, providing the wines, keep the
cellar books, and take charge of the drinking vessels. One
ecclesiastic is enough to have charge over the water, and the
number of his subordinates varies according to the difficul-
ties of obtaining it; his office extends to the care of wells and
their cleansing. Another ecclesiastic, with two inferiors, has
charge of the candles and candlesticks and all that concerns
the lighting of the Palace. Another officer has care of the
beds and tapestries; he has to arrange seats at consistories,
and see to the proper covering of the Pope's chair at church
and elsewhere. The Keeper of the Plate has the arduous
duty of seeing that the plates and dishes are kept clean and
are not stolen; every day after dinner, the gates of the Palace
are kept closed until he has counted the dishes and certified
that all are there. The Master of the Kitchen supervises all
the cooking arrangements; the Steward does the marketing
and hands the produce to the Keeper of the Larder, who
also receives all presents of game and suchlike that are made
to the Pope. The Master of the Hall arranges the tables,
places the guests in order, and sees that they are properly
served.

Besides these officers, the Papal household contains a
Master of the Works to see after the repairs of the Palace;
a confessor whose duty it is to regulate the services in the

*chapel and to vest the Pope; a Master of the Palace, gener-
ally a Dominican Friar [hardly likely in the case of Alexander V] who lectures on theology and proposes questions at
the Pope's bidding; an Almoner and a Choirmaster for the
chapel services. Cooks, doorkeepers, physicians, registrars,
messengers and grooms make up the remainder of the
Pope's retinue.*

At least fifty separate people are mentioned here, and no
one may ever have known how many others were involved.
The quality of the services rendered was most uneven; in
many cases orders were doubtless passed right down the line
until finally the lowest slavey did the work. Servants prac-
ticed nepotism as well as their masters, and those who did
the buying would certainly have received perquisites from
the townspeople and peasants to add to their "squeeze."

Alexander had hardly settled into his vast household
when the plague swept Pisa, possibly as a result of the floods
of people inundating the town now that it was one of the
three Holy Sees. He moved first to Prato, then to Pistoia,
and then, fatefully, his patron, Cardinal Baldassare Cossa,
beckoned him on to Bologna.

It was December, 1409, when Pope Alexander set out
over the Apennines to see Baldassare. All might have gone
well with him in Bologna, but once arrived the restless Pontiff wanted still more travel; this time, he said, he was off for
Rome. In that he erred, because suddenly, on May 3, 1410,
ten months and three removes after being elected, Pope
Alexander was dead. He had lived, indeed, to be more than
seventy, and may have departed peacefully, in the way of
nature, but this is not what was everywhere believed. He
"died most pitifully," Monstrelet says, by poison, adding
that "His bowels were interred, his obsequies performed, in
the Church of the Franciscans."

Alexander's body was embalmed "with fine spices" and

dressed in the papal robes, after which he rested in state, "his face uncovered, gloves on his hands, but his feet naked, so that whoever pleased might kiss them."

22 JOHN XXIII

I f POPE ALEXANDER was not poisoned, it was at least convenient that he died in Bologna, where Cardinal Baldassare Cossa had troops with which to intimidate the ensuing conclave. Should menace fail, Baldassare had money for bribes.

The ruler of Bologna had been a pirate before he turned Cardinal, and two of his brothers had been hanged for the same occupation. It was not their unfortunate example, however, which sent him ashore, nor was it the perils of his erstwhile trade. He never really discarded his grappling irons; he seems merely to have decided that the right pirate could do better on land.

He took up selling as a way of life: he began with a line of preferments, then progressed into blackmail, after which he secured a wholesale distributorship of Indulgences. His methods were carefully developed. Aware that the amount to be realized from preferments was limited by the available supply, he made use of an ingenious device: the holder of a benefice well knew that his tenure might suddenly be suspended, whereupon he would have to buy it all over again —and so Baldassare filled up his coffers by selling "protection" to owners of rich livings who dreaded losing them.

He would send in his agent on a supposedly friendly visit to an ecclesiastic's domain. The agent would be thought to have just come from the Pope. He would admire the property, comment on improvements, and then hint of powerful enemies about the Pontiff who must have intrigued against the incumbent. The prelate's fears would expand as his guest described the Pope's displeasure; poverty loomed before him, perhaps even banishment to the care of souls on some lonely island, who could tell? Baldassare's agent waited patiently for the moment that always came, when the ecclesiastic would cry: "You know the ways of the Papal Court. You are well connected there. What would you advise?" After that the agent would explain that Baldassare Cossa could save the day. From there on, it was simply a question of large amounts of cash.

Although his only conscious intention was to get richer and richer, Cardinal Baldassare helped in his own way to bring on the Protestant Reformation. Earlier the cry had gone up that everything was for sale in Avignon, everything was for sale in Rome, but these new methods gave the reformers more grounds than ever. Baldassare did not believe in waiting for the customer to come to the shop; he took the goods to the customer, and if there was no market, he made one. Milman gives this account of him:

To him was attributed the enormous abuse of Indulgences. Already Priests and Friars loaded with these lucrative commodities, travelled through Germany, by Thuringia, Swabia, Saxony, into the northern kingdoms, Denmark, and Sweden . . . entered the principal church, took their seat before the altar, the floor strewed with rich carpets, and, under the awnings of silk to keep off the flies, exhibited to the people, notwithstanding the remonstrances of Priests or Bishops, their precious wares. "I have heard them," writes the biographer of Baldassare Cossa, "declare that Saint Peter himself had not greater power to remit sins than themselves."

These Indulgences were, in effect, "licenses to sin," and it was not so much spiritual concern for his soul which moved the buyer, as panic brought on by descriptions of

Hell. To know what crawled in the dark of medieval minds, to know from what they were agonizedly trying to buy themselves and their dead relatives free, it is enough to look at the paintings of Hieronymus Bosch. Indulgences were overflow, extra merits piled up by holy beings—a spiritual capital distributable to sinners, and to which the Pope held the key. It was stated a hundred years after this that a papal indulgence could save a man "even if he had violated the Queen of Heaven."

At Bologna, Baldassare consoled himself for not being in Rome by keeping a household reportedly including "two hundred maids, wives, and widows, with many nuns." We read also that after their stay with Cossa, many of them were put to death by their jealous husbands and kin.

The Cardinal taxed prostitutes and gambling houses as well as millers of flour, bakers of bread, and vendors of wine. He preyed upon nobles, but with democratic impartiality also ground the faces of the poor. He was a one-man plague; his cruelty was bubonic. ". . . day after day such multitudes of persons of both sexes, strangers as well as Bolognese, were put to death on [various] charges . . . that the population of Bologna seemed dwindling down to that of a small city." Often the Cardinal was out of patience with his executioners, for they dawdled over the killings.

Like many another dictator, the ex-pirate did achieve an iron peace during his nine-year rule as tyrant of Bologna. Those who survived were inclined to cooperate. The still-living may even have benefited from his business acumen; Leonardo Aretino, his secretary like Dietrich of Niem, rated him at the top among men of affairs, but thought his spiritual standing should be zero, "or minus zero," as he so much preferred preying to praying.

This was the individual who in May, 1410, entered into Conclave with the other Cardinals after Pope Alexander's

death, and terrified them with an account of what he might
do. He then asked for the stole of Saint Peter, saying, "I
will place it upon the one man who most deserves it."

The long silken band was brought in. Baldassare took it
up, looked at it, draped it around his own neck, and declared: "I am Pope." They crowned him John XXIII.

(This is no misprint. It is Catholic practice to blot away
an undesirable Pope by having another take over, at some
time in the future, both his number and his name. Clement
VII of Avignon was blotted out by that Clement VII who
reigned in the days of Henry VIII—the Pope to whom Catherine of Aragon tried to appeal against her husband's "career
of persevering matrimony," but all in vain. Pedro de Luna,
Benedict XIII, would himself be blotted out by the one
who became Pope in 1724. Clement VIII who followed de
Luna was done away with in 1592, by that Clement who
issued a new standard Bible, the Clementine Vulgate, from
the fourth-century Latin of Jerome. The John XXIII of
modern times took this title to efface Baldassare Cossa,
the evil John XXIII who followed the first Pisan Pope,
Alexander V.

The fact that Boniface IX, Innocent VII and Gregory
XII never were blotted out shows that the Catholic position
favors the Urbanist line; yet for obvious reasons, the Clementines cannot truthfully be called antipopes.)

The vote of the Cardinals was unanimous. Milman, dif-
fering from others, says the new Pontiff was never accused
of bribery for the Cardinals dared not raise the question—it
would have been "a condemnation of their own weakness
and want of Christian courage." Later the Council of Constance certainly condemned John for his purchases, and
John's own secretary, Dietrich of Niem, would write in his
Invecta that this Pope hacked his way to the papal throne
with an ax of gold.

By the time John XXIII arrived at the palace in which his predecessor, Alexander V, had lived, Bolognese mobs had, in the good old way, sacked it and carried off all the dead Pope's furnishings. Not a door or a windowframe remained.

On the following day [writes Monstrelet] the Pope celebrated Mass in the Church of Saint Peter, having the Cardinal de Vimers near him to show him the service. [This was necessary because the new Pope had only the day before become a priest; a layman could be named cardinal then, and he was already prince of the Church.] The Marquis of Ferrara had brought him fifty-four knights, all clothed in scarlet and blue, having five trumpets and four companies of minstrels, each playing on a different instrument. . . .

When seated on his throne, which was covered all over with cloth of gold, he was surrounded by Cardinals . . . having tufts of tow in their hands. The Cardinals lighted their tufts; and as the flame was suddenly extinguished they addressed the Pope, saying, "Thus, Holy Father, passes the glory of this world." This was done three times.

The Cardinal de Vimers then said prayers over John and crowned him. The lowest of the tiara's three crowns, circling the forehead, was gold; the middle one was gold and silver; the third, of very fine gold, surmounted the whole.

John was then led out and helped onto a horse with scarlet furniture, his prelates' mounts being caparisoned in white. And we have a glimpse, here, of the Middle Ages sowing the wind, breeding the whirlwind for our own times to reap: In state he was

conducted from street to street, making everywhere the sign of the cross, until he came to where the Jews resided, who presented him with a manuscript of the Old Testament. He took it with his own hand, and, having examined it a little,

threw it behind him, saying, "Your religion is good, but this
of ours is better."

As he departed, the Jews followed him, intending to
touch him; in the attempt of which, the caparison of his
horse was all torn. Wherever he passed, the Pope distribu-
ted money, that is to say, quadrini and mailles of Florence
[coppers] with other coins. There were before and behind
him two hundred men-at-arms, each having in his hand a
leathern mallet, with which they struck the Jews in such
wise as it was a pleasure to see.

When John paraded back to his palace the next day, his prelates were in crimson with white miters. Besides, there were

thirty-six bagpipes and trumpets, and then bands of min-
strels playing on musical instruments, each band consisting
of three performers. There were also singers, as well as those
belonging to the Cardinals and from different parts of Italy,
who rode before the Pope loudly chanting various airs, sa-
cred and profane.

When he arrived at the palace, he gave his peace to all
the Cardinals, who, according to their rank in the College,
kissed his foot, hand or mouth. . . . He then gave his bene-
diction to the four elements, and to all persons in a state
of grace, as well to those absent as present, and bestowed
his dispensations for four months to come, provided that,
during this time, three paternosters should be said by each
in praying for his predecessor, Pope Alexander.

Pope John then went to dinner, as it was now about
twelve o'clock, and this ceremony had commenced between
five and six in the morning.

There was feasting for eight days in his honor. He soon held a Consistory, followed by a feast, dancing and music.

"The ensuing day, the Pope revoked all that his predecessor had done, excepting what he [John] had confirmed, or what had been taken corporal or spiritual possession of."

We learn elsewhere that the general public was considerably less than delighted with the new Pontiff. When, early in 1411, John XXIII left Bologna for Rome, it is true that he went with the cheers of the multitude ringing in his ears. But what they were shouting was: "Long live the people!"

By going to Rome, John demonstrated his courage. The city's inhabitants might rise against him; even if they did not, there was still the threat from the south. King Ladislas, sometime protector of Pope Gregory XII, had taken Rome twice and could take it again.

Arrived at Rome, John proceeded to summon a council, which opened in January, 1412. The council began eerily enough. The Mass for the descent of the Holy Ghost had just been concluded when a great owl flapped in and circled about screeching, its staring eyes fastened on the Pope.

"A strange shape for the Holy Ghost!" someone muttered.

Many were visibly shaken. John immediately ended the meeting, but the next day the assemblage had no sooner reconvened when back came the owl again, its dark wings fanning, its unblinking yellow eyes staring at John. It was driven away at last, with sticks and stones, but the memory lingered.

For the moment, owl or no owl, John prospered. The Urbanist Pope of Rome, Gregory XII, was steadily losing ground. What strength he had came from the support of King Ladislas of Naples. As for the Clementine Pope Benedict, a new war was now launched against him by France, with help from John, and Benedict's grip on his territories was weakening.

The Palace of the Popes at Avignon, Benedict's great
stronghold, was again under siege. His nephew, Rodrigo de
Luna, still held it. Should it fall, Benedict's last hope of
holding the Comtat Venaissin would go.

Of course, the Clementine was still the most powerful
man. He had the palaces of those Cardinals who had worked
against him at Pisa torn down and their arms scratched out.
Rodrigo was still rector of the Comtat. Avignon's magis-
trates had sworn to keep the city loyal to Benedict though
it cost them fortune, family, even life; but all this had a
familiar ring to Benedict, and these days he took such oaths
at a discount.

John XXIII paid for the largest share of the new war
against the Palace of the Popes, and the monasteries of Avignon stripped themselves to reinforce him. The backsliding
town incurred debts that hung over it for years. A crusade
was preached against Benedict's men in the Palace, with
indulgences to whoever took part. Carpentras, scene of
Benedict's past triumph, sent volunteers and siege weapons
to attack him; Lyons floated down barges loaded with huge
blocks of quarried stone to be made into projectiles. One
day the household of Cardinal de Thury watched thirty-
six massive horses being whipped along, their muscles straining, as they drew an enormous mortar up to face the Palace
gates. It was a present from Aix-en-Provence.

Doubts as to the wisdom of this war must have assailed
Charles VI, for the mad King ordered his troops evacuated
in August, 1410. But Pope John's Cardinal Legate and the
people of Avignon managed to have the order counter-
manded that September 15, and the siege went on.

Both sides now utilized an early version of germ warfare.
They filled casks or wooden crates with filth of all kinds,
including excrement; these were then catapulted at the
enemy, smashing and scattering their contents over a wide

area. This was not one of France's many firsts in scientific fields: in 1347, Kipchak Khan Janibeg while besieging the Genoese trading port of Kaffa had catapulted dead plague victims into that city, and excrement was also hurled at Naples by Charles of the Peace.

Otherwise the siege proceeded just as it had when his hostile Cardinals had imprisoned Pope Benedict here in the Palace for so many years. There were tunneled attempts to get within the walls, iron chains across the Rhône to prevent a rescue by boat, another unsuccessful expedition of relief from Catalonia. Rodrigo proved again that he was an aggressive commander. His troops made three sorties and set fire to the wooden section of the Bridge, to cut off the besiegers from supplies and reinforcements. As the flames leaped sky high, the men from the Palace shouted: "Hey, you French, run and get some water to put out the fire! Go tell your crazy King and the traitors from Avignon to come and put it out!"

Benedict's troops, however, were fighting a war they could never win. In September, 1411, they accomplished the difficult, if historically reprehensible, feat of demolishing one of the stone arches of the Bridge; but on November 22, after a year and a half of useless bravery, they had to capitulate. Marching out of the Palace of the Popes, they gazed up at its towers for the last time, and turned toward Spain. Although the conquering French and the people of Avignon took possession of many valuable objects that happened at the time to be available within, the Avignon Palace of the Popes was now owned by the Pisan Pope John XXIII.

PART FOUR

CONSTANCE

23 THE FOX PIT

THE CHURCH itself could act. It could depose the two rival Popes and elect someone else. So had thought the Council of Pisa—a Council representing the main body of believers—in 1409.

The men of Pisa had approached their problem in a kind of democratic spirit. For one thing, they were not hampered by the dogma of papal infallibility: it would not be established until 1870. (Even now it is difficult to discover which *ex cathedra* papal statements on faith and morals are meant to be infallible.)

Whatever the charges brought at Pisa against Gregory XII and Benedict XIII, the fact remains that neither Pontiff was a heretic nor by the standards of papal history unfit to rule. Those charges were only a screen set up to hide the delegates' one unswerving purpose: to end a Schism which had already lasted thirty-one years. That the election of Alexander V did not solve the problem, but only resulted in Western Christendom being divided among three Popes instead of two, was the direct product of Pisa's refusal to solve the key issue: which individual, Benedict or Gregory, was the Pope?

The Way of Mutual Cession, if it could ever have been carried out, would have been the ideal solution. The complicated problem of legitimacy, entangled as it was with national and personal ambitions, would have been bypassed. It is easy to see why the men of Pisa hit upon deposition as the hoped-for remedy, after all those unsuccessful attempts to induce the contending Popes to abdicate at the same time. From trying to force abdication upon those stubborn old men it was only a short psychological step to deposing them by decree.

After the Council of Pisa, events and men moved swiftly toward still another council, ready for a yet more striking revolution.

When almost forty years of the Great Division had passed by, a man appeared who said: Enough. That man was the Luxemburger Sigismund, Roman Emperor and King of Hungary. It was he who would suture the split in the Church—that is, in the Western world.

The Popes had tried and failed, after them the Cardinals had tried and failed. As Luther would do a century later, men now pinned their hopes to the secular power. Sigismund was the tough, practical man of action whom the threatened and bewildered always await.

There had been many a meeting among scholars and princes over the years, many a secret pourparler. The need for a truly ecumenical council was clearly known, but not till Sigismund was anyone strong and decisive enough to implement that hope. (Perhaps, too, the hour has to strike before the man of the hour can appear.)

In 1414 Sigismund was forty-six years old, a big man, burly, with floating yellow hair, a wide forehead, red cheeks, and a big yellow beard. He laughed a lot, drank a lot, and was in and out of an astonishing number of beds. "Never," says one of the earliest reports of him, "was man less wont to keep his marriage vows." He was staunchly orthodox, however, and death on heretics such as the followers of Wycliffe and Huss. He once sent his butler down into Saint Patrick's Hole in Ireland, where the future could be seen in dreams, and the butler there observed a crowd of young women in Purgatory, waiting for Sigismund with a bed of fire. Informed of it, Sigismund said, "We must shift that bed to Heaven"—and, selling thirteen towns to the King of Poland to raise the money, he built a church. Not unschooled, he read books and knew several languages. Whether all the witticisms allocated to him by history were his cannot be known, but he may well have made the comment that a donkey is better off than a prince, because at least they leave the donkey alone while he eats.

When, in 1396, the Muslims had reached the Danube, it was Sigismund who led Christendom against them, with nobles under him in their thousands—crusaders all, urged on by Boniface IX, the Pope of Rome. It was Sigismund who, that September, was badly beaten by the Sultan at Nicopolis, and who never afterward forgot the clear and present danger. There had been a time in 1401 when he was deposed by Hungary and imprisoned, but he survived to remain King. Later he had nearly died of a fever and the only way they managed to save him was to hang him up by the heels for twenty-four hours to let the fever trickle out of his mouth.

He had a wife, Barbara of Styria, whom he married in 1408. She was tall and graceful, with freckles and long, fair hair. Barbara was the talk of Europe; but Sigismund, although he often found her in the wrong arms, never permanently repudiated her, and people commented that "those who make the horns must not refuse to wear them." Perhaps he loved her; she was his second wife, and a proverb still current in Austria says, "The second wife has a golden behind." Barbara was an unbeliever who mocked at Christianity and called the life to come a foolish dream. She would gather her maids of honor together and laugh with them about fasts and penances and stories of virgins martyred for the Faith. Pleasure was all there was to life, she told them. In after years, when Sigismund had finally died, a priest exhorted her to live in chastity for a while, like a turtledove mourning· its mate. Barbara replied that she thought doves were stupid, and that she much preferred sparrows.

Sigismund saw that with three Popes coexisting, only secular power could be of any immediate avail, and he determined to impose his will on Europe by allying himself with the Kings of England and France, and then inviting everyone concerned—Pope Benedict XIII, Pope Gregory XII, Pope John XXIII, Jan Huss, the Universities, everybody—to one big, crowning, Ecumenical Council at Constance where all, at long last, should be set to rights.

The King of France might be double and the Church in three, but Sigismund was all of a piece. Inwardly unified himself, he would make over the Western world in his image. He was able to lie in wait for years, then to be serpent-swift and deadly; he had no scruples to thwart him, and he was sure that God was on his side.

The only valid Pope was either Benedict XIII, the Clementine, or Gregory XII, the Urbanist. The Pisan Pope was illegal, because the Council of Pisa was illegal, not having been convoked by a Pope; and John XXIII was the second in the Pisan line. Yet it was nonvalid John XXIII whom Sigismund obliged to summon the Council of Constance. John was under severe pressure at the time or he would never have convoked that great assemblage, because he was too clever a man to think of an Ecumenical Council as a place where he could be safe.

As John had feared, Ladislas of Naples had attacked him at Rome and driven him out. In June, 1413, while John fled, Ladislas sacked the city; he had stalled his horses in Saint Peter's, his soldiers had robbed the sacristy, broken open monstrances, thrown out relics, trampled the Host. John had just managed to escape and had been compelled to join forces with Sigismund. Thus he was Sigismund's Pope.

To finance his obligatory visit to Constance, in other words to buy up the Council, John stopped at Bologna that November and did a brisk business: ". . . his chapmen sold prospective archbishoprics, bishoprics, prebends and parish cures, some of the many times over, so that those who before had been top on the list of expectants now found themselves near the bottom, while the tail was getting very near to hell." Benefices were "weighed out by the pound." People said that when Pope John left for the Council he took a million ducats with him.

John and Sigismund met for the first time in person at Lodi, near Milan. The story goes that Sigismund asked an old man there which ruler he thought was the sadder, John or himself. The old man answered that he thought John was, "because the hair is off the top of his head." This made Sigismund laugh; he himself was hairy and not tonsured, of course, but he was graying.

Crossing the Tyrolean Alps, John was jolted into awareness of his present danger by an ominous event. On the Arlberg, either his horse slipped or the Pope's low-wheeled, covered cart broke down and he was tossed into the snow. His attendants ran to his side, asking if he was hurt.

"No, I am all right," he answered, "but this fall is a sinister warning that I should have done better to remain at Bologna."

Later, as his eyes swept the city of Constance, John said: "Here is the pit where they catch the foxes."

24 CONSTANCE BY THE LAKE

A BENEDICTINE, Gabriel Buceli, has related that the city of Constance was built by Noah's grandchildren. Its more recent founding has been assigned to the fourth century, and its name to Emperor Constantius Chlorus (father of Constantine the Great), who died in 306 at York.

In the summer of 1413, a flock of chaffinches one mile long and half a mile wide flew over the Constance area. They were interpreted as a happy omen: they meant that visitors would soon be coming to this place in great numbers, bringing gulden.

The quiet German city in the midst of low hills, on the edge of a vast and peaceful lake with its mountain ring —up to that time known mostly for its linens—was about to become, temporarily at least, the capital of the Western Christian world.

It was Sigismund who had chosen this spot, and as so often, wrested his way. There were the usual delays—creaking carts and shifting saddles over endless miles, boats rowed or sailed, ponderous speeches, exchanges of empty but necessary compliments—but finally Sigismund got his choice of Constance, gave a full year's notice of the Council to be convened, and promised his protection to all comers, stayers and returners home. One of the many leaders specially invited was the ailing King of France; Sigismund urged his mad fellow ruler to be present, and gave as the

Council's purpose "that the one Bride might be brought   221
back to her Lord's divided house. . . ."

*Constance
by the
Lake*

Citizen Ulrich Richental not only attended the Council
but passed it along to the future. Knowing news when he
saw it, Richental hired draftsmen, asked questions, and
twenty years later produced, in text and color, his famed
Konzilschronik, a panorama of the council and of early
fifteenth-century life.

Here is a mounted knight holding an enormous, conical,
striped umbrella, with an angel on top; Pope John on a
cushion with tassels; Pope John crossing the Arlberg, his
cart overturned. To depict long processions through Constance, colored strips of illustrations continue on from
page to page: the clean-shaven John—in green, with loose
white gloves, rings on his right thumb and forefinger—riding a horse, passes under a tentlike cloth-of-gold canopy
held by bearers on foot; Cardinals in red inverted-dishpan
hats follow on mules, two by two, and somebody throws out
missilia to the crowds. Rows of monks; long tapers, red-
tipped to show they are lit; Sigismund in a long gray beard,
kneeling to receive the Golden Rose (a miniature gold
tree) from Pope John; Empress Barbara in a long train and
a snood; choirboys with sheets of written music; donkeys
laden with necessaries; horses, trumpets, banners; many
daggers and swords; a glimpse of the still-preserved Kauf-
haus on the quay (generally the council met at the
Cathedral).

Under a portable canopy walk Jews, in the yellow pointed
hats which they had been obliged to wear ever since the
Fourth Lateran Council of 1215. A Greek Archbishop says
Mass. A man in spectacles reads a paper to Sigismund.
(This reader appears on two successive pages but does not
represent a first—the oldest known picture of a bespectacled
person dates from 1352.) There are such details as bottle-

glass windows; a cleaver; scales; markets straight from life, selling deers' heads, boars, snails, fish, while dogs lurk expectantly under the big trestle tables; an ambulating baker hawks his wares.

Some say that Western Christendom had never seen a more imposing assemblage. This may be true, although in fact more ecclesiastics had been present at Innocent III's Fourth Lateran two centuries before. The peak crowds were there at Constance during the seven months from Christmas, 1414, to the mid-July following, when Sigismund was first in residence. During that period thirty thousand horses were stalled, sixteen thousand (at least) beds were let, seventy thousand to eighty thousand strangers were quartered in town and nearby; and even the great ones lay in the open air, or slept in wine vats or alongside grooms in the stables.

Trying to collect actual attendance figures, Richental went from house to house, copied coats of arms affixed to inns, talked with heralds. But the problem could never accurately be solved. He lists, besides in-and-outers, 72,460 as present. The usual figures are anywhere from 40,000 to 150,000. So far as attendance was concerned, the chaffinches had certainly been right.

According to Dacher's list, there were present 2,300 princes, deputies, knights, and the like; 18,000 prelates, priests and theologians; and 80,000 laymen, including 45 goldsmiths and silversmiths, 330 retail merchants, 242 bankers, 70 shoemakers, 48 furriers, 44 apothecaries, 92 blacksmiths, 75 confectioners, 250 bakers, 83 tavernkeepers dispensing Italian wines, 43 sutlers, 48 moneychangers, 228 tailors, 65 heralds at arms or public criers, 346 buffoons, jugglers and tumblers, 306 barbers, 700 prostitutes.

Dacher's list includes only those prostitutes whose place of residence could be determined. Another list mentions 1,500. There must have been many more; times were good and some saved up enough to retire. One economy-minded citizen sold his wife to the employees of Sigismund's chancellery; she brought 500 ducats and he purchased a house with the proceeds.

The bedazzled Benedict de Pileo wrote paganistically that Venus herself reigned at Constance, "so great is the host of most dainty dames and damsels who surpass the snow in the delicacy of their coloring." (His comparison was five hundred and fifty years fresher then.) An equally ecstatic comment by the one poet of stature who attended, Oswald von Wolkenstein, someone has translated thus:

> *Women here, like angels wooing . . .*
> *They have been my heart's undoing,*
> *They possess my dreams at night . . .*
> > *jewels rare*
> *In their auburn tresses . . .*
> > *their blushing faces*
> *Whence sorrow trips and leaves no traces.*

Oswald also laments that the moneygrubbers at Constance emptied his pockets and left him dry as an empty bottle.

That the Council was truly ecumenical no one could doubt. Even Ethiopians came, but no one knew their language and for this reason they received no official recognition. It is thought that in addition to Latin, French, German and Italian, the basic tongues in use, twenty-seven others were spoken at Constance. Confessionals listed the languages which the penitencer could understand. For debating purposes, those attending were organized into "nations" like the student unions of the same name at the universities; there were four "nations" and each had its own meeting place. The Italians included the Greeks; the Germans included Huns, Poles, Letts, Turks, Bohemians, Moravians, Russians, Flemings and Scandinavians; the French included nobody, and were no strangers to hissing, hooting, quarreling and mutual threats; the English also had some Irish and a few Asiatics and other outlandish persons from over the sea. The real debates and decision-making went on in such gatherings as these of the Nations, and the big meetings in the Cathedral were only "parade days for officially publishing predetermined issues."

Life went on, even during the Council of Constance, and much current clerical and lay business overlapped here: the King of Poland and the Teutonic Knights submitted their quarrel to Sigismund, Sweden wanted Bridget recognized as a saint (since she had been canonized during the Schism), Counts wanted to be made Dukes, a Burgrave wanted to be made a Margrave, there was so much bad money around that a currency reform was called for, the Julian calendar didn't work—the equinoxes now coming thirteen days too soon, throwing Easter out of kilter; imperial towns such as Frankfurt were suffering under exorbitant tolls. Wars went on, too: during the Council, on October 25, 1415, the English destroyed the French at Agincourt.

Famine prices obtained until Sigismund remonstrated with the burgomaster, after which the town council checked extortion. From then on, a bed for two with sheets, pillows and cushions—linen to be washed every fortnight—cost legally not more than one and a half Rhenish gulden per month. An ordinary worker earned ten pfennigs a day, and eighteen if he fed himself; an ordinary fowl cost three pfennigs. Horses, Huss reported, were sold very cheap, as fodder was scarce. Incidentally, among the moneychangers (forty-nine of them Florentines), was twenty-five-year-old Cosimo de' Medici, representing his father, the moneylender who "enjoyed most of the Pope's wealth."

Old women washed and mended; there were 150 vintners in shanties; a small army of bakers trundled their round ovens from street to street on wheelbarrows, hawking pas-

ties, flatcakes, ringpuffs, made of fish, meat and chicken
"well spiced and seasoned." Certainly there was enough to
eat; provender for sale in open markets included badgers,
otters, beavers, eels, birds, fish, snails, frogs and venison.
The poultry, no doubt, presented the usual difficulty; not
long afterward, the lord mayor of London upbraided the
poulterers of his city for causing "grete and noyous and
grevous hurt," keeping poultry "wherof the ordure and
standyng of hem is of grete stenche and so evel savour that
it causeth grete and parlous inffectyng of the people and
long hath done."

Although the international riffraff was there in force,
an underlying order prevailed; known troublemakers were
ousted and the town stayed remarkably peaceful throughout; only two men were murdered in street brawls. (True,
263 extra bodies were fished up out of the lake, the occasion
having offered a tempting opportunity for removing those
with whom one was annoyed.) There was a curfew, and
people had to be quiet at night, carry a light, and neither
ride nor shout. Chains were stretched across streets at some
points to shut out traffic.

The streets rang with music: each great lord had brought
his minstrels: fifes, trumpets, bagpipes, viols filled the air;
English singers won special applause. There were actors—
plays included the Birth of Jesus, the Three Kings and the
Slaughter of the Innocents. There were jugglers, feastings,
dances, processions, tilting, riding. There was love. Among
other generous donors, the Archbishop of Salzburg gave a
halfpenny loaf a day, and soup or a bit of meat, to any
poor man who asked.

The Council was further delayed by an outbreak of *noli
me tangere*, an ulceration of the face and especially the
nose. The grand opening was then postponed till November 3, and on that day everyone was robed and in place
when Pope John, in full pontificals, fell ill and had to be

put to bed. Finally, on November 5, 1414, the Council of Constance officially opened, but it did not really get under way until Christmas dawn, with the advent of Emperor Sigismund and his Queen.

Although Richental's *Konzilschronik* shows Pedro de Luna, Pope Benedict of Avignon, kneeling, as a penitent, Pope Benedict was not there, and sent ambassadors only to Sigismund himself. He wanted no truck with the Council —he said there could be no peace unless it struck down "that idol that had been set up at Pisa." He was sure Sigismund would disavow Pisa—i.e., would disavow Pope John XXIII—and indeed prorogued a Council of his own at Perpignan till Easter, 1415, at which time he believed all Christendom would acknowledge him as true pope. But Sigismund roared at Benedict's envoys, "I don't know who you are!" Then the envoys made the mistake of praising Benedict's holy way of life, his knowledge, his plans to drive back the Muslims and reform the Empire. To see such a jewel as Benedict, they said, it would be worth the journey from farthest East to farthest West; and they suggested that Sigismund come to meet Pope Benedict and Benedict's King, Ferdinand of Aragon, at Nice in the following June. Meanwhile Pope Gregory, he of Rome, the Urbanist, directed all Catholics to eschew the Council. He loathed the Council as much as he did co-Pope John. He also sent envoys direct to Sigismund, and even planned a coalition with Pope Benedict to oust Pope John, their mutual foe.

After all, Constance began as a continuation of Pisa, adjourned in 1409, and many noted that Pisa had not been canonically called and had resulted in a cursed trinity of Popes. To this the pro-Pisans answered that God had been there even if the two Popes had not, and that those who thought otherwise were simply fathers of lies and dogs with vipers' tongues.

As for Pope John, he of Pisa, he had hoped till the last,
what with one delay and another, that he could avoid convening the council. That August, 1414, King Ladislas had
died at Naples. Some say he rotted away with sores, was
poisoned by his mistress, and died shouting: "Devils!"
But Benedict XIII said he "passed to God." Either way,
with Ladislas gone, John had tried to reassert his independence and thwart the council by not attending, but it was too
late. As a great Frenchman would write one day: "Nothing
in this world is so powerful as an idea whose time has
come."

25 THE RUIN OF THE CHURCH

T HE POPE, once the wonder of the world, has fallen," wrote the monk Dietrich Vrie in a Latin poem. "Now is the time of Simon Magus [who tried to buy from the Apostles the power of conferring the Holy Ghost]. . . . Golden was the first age of the Papal Court; then came the baser age of silver; next the iron age long set its yoke on the stubborn neck. Then came the age of clay. Could aught be worse? Aye, dung, and in dung sits the Papal Court."

Corruption in high places was the basic problem at Constance. No whitewash can ever disguise this fact. In all estates some good was present, but the virtuous, a contemporary wrote, was "mocked and made the butt of them all as a freak."

Saint Bernard had commented long before: "The priests of our day are worse than the people." Chaucer deplored "a shiten shepherde and a clene sheep." Monstrelet quotes a poem which he calls "the complaining of the poor commonalty of France," expressing the sorrows and threats of the preyed-on and destitute. A few lines follow:

> Ah, princes, prelates, valiant lords,
> Lawyers and tradesfolk, small and great!
> Burghers, and warriors girt with swords,
> Who fatten on our daily sweat! . . .
> Repent ye will, or late or soon,
> If from our plaints ye turn away;
> For your tall towers will tumble down,

Your gorgeous palaces decay:
Sith true it is, ye lordly great,
We are the pillars of your state.
Ah, welladay! Ye bishops grave,
Lords of the faith of Christian folk,
Naked and bare, your help we crave,
The wretched outcasts of your flock.

Although the Protestants in later years would use it as
a weapon, *The Ruin of the Church*, by Catholic Nicolas
de Clémanges, was no more an attack on his religion than
a doctor's diagnosis is an attack on his patient. The symp-
toms were obvious, and Clémanges, rector of the University of Paris and archdeacon of Bayonne, set them forth
that the Church might heal herself. As the self-appointed
responsible body, Constance should have responded to the
challenge of the reformers, should have known that systems
and civilizations stand or fall according to the character of
their peoples.

Affirming that wantonness, pride and avarice "engendered all the other evils in the Church," Clémanges says
of the priests: ". . . and being softened by an effeminate
excess, they then had to satisfy three masters . . . Wantonness, which required the delights of wine, of meat, of sleep,
of splendid games, of whores and panders. Pride, which desired tall houses, towers and castles, costly garments, horses
bred for speed. Avarice, which had carefully amassed great
treasure to pay for these things."

Of the continual treasure hunt of that age when "every
stroke of the pen had its price," he says the clergy "would
rather suffer the loss of ten thousand souls than of ten *sols*."
And if Luke 10:9 should be quoted to them, *Freely have
you received, freely give*—"They have their answer ready:
that they have not received it for nothing, and for this reason are not obliged to hand it over for nothing."

He describes the ignorance of those who obtained benefices: "People who know as much Latin as they do Arabic;
who do not know how to tell an A from a B. . . . [And]
almost all priests are unable to read, unless . . . counting
the syllables. . . . What fruit then will they pluck from
their prayers . . . when they know not what they are saying nor what they are praying?

"And why is it," he asks, "that of those who petition for
benefices, so few can obtain them without first going to
court against some antagonist?" Life was an endless law-
suit. As for the lack of judicial calm at the Papal Court,
"they consider their court to flourish if it roars with many a
suit, many a brangle, if it explodes on all sides with enraged
cries."

If the mendicant friars are so Christlike, he asks, "how is
it that they magnify it so, out of their own mouths?" And
as for the nuns, "What are the convents of girls today if not
execrable houses of Venus?"

"Let us weep then over the ruin of the Universal
Church . . . for who ignores the fact that this cruelest of
beasts . . . devouring and destroying all things, namely
the abominable plague of the Schismatic split, has been
brought on . . . and made broad by the wickedness of
the bosom of the Church."

On a tender note, Clémanges ends with this prayer:

*Now in conclusion we humbly beg one thing of Thee,
most gentle Jesus. Whatever judgments Thou must visit on
Thy Church, and they will no doubt be heavy, requite her
not with vengeance according to her evil deeds, but according to the mildness of Thy mercy which passeth understanding; punishing her, use Thou the pity of which she
is unworthy; and striking off the wicked and superfluous
things, cut not away the few not wholly vain. Press then in
such a way as not to crush. Break in such wise as not to*

shatter all. Chastise, not to extinguish all. And that the Church may not be likened to Sodom and Gomorrah, leave her at least some seedlings, remembering Thine own most sacred Word, when Thou didst promise to stay by her always, even unto the end of the age.

26 THREE ARE ONE AGAIN

C ONSTANCE INTENDED that it and a succession of Ecumenical Councils should govern Western Christianity through the medium of a Papacy answerable to the Council; its basic purposes were to name a subservient Pope, permanently remove the three rival claimants, stamp out heresy, and reform the Church "in its Head and in its members."

Analyzing this new attitude toward the Papacy, which he traces to the influence of Parisian theologians as already seen at Pisa, Creighton writes: "The foundation of the Council's authority was the theory that the plenitude of ecclesiastical power was vested in the universal Church, whose head was Christ, and of which the Pope was the chief minister . . . but a Council had concurrent jurisdiction in all important matters, a corrective power in case of abuses, and a power of removing the Pope in case of necessity . . ." There was, moreover, a German school to be reckoned with, "who had a more ideal system before their eyes, who aimed at diminishing the plenitude of the Papal primacy, and making it depend on the recognition of the Church."

In the words of Dietrich of Niem, who was also the biographer of John XXIII:

The Catholic Church consists of all who believe in Christ, who is its only Head, and it can never err: the Apostolic Church is a particular and private Church, consisting of *Pope, Cardinals, and prelates; its head is supposed to be*

*the Pope, and it can err—the Pope is a man, born of man,
subject to sin, a few days ago a peasant's son; how is he to
become impeccable and infallible? He is bound to resign
or even to die if the common good should require it. . . .
Union with a particular Pope is no part of the faith of the
Catholic Church, nor is it necessary for salvation; rather,
Popes contending for their private good are in mortal sin,
and have no claim on the allegiance of Christians.*

*A General Council represents the universal Church; and
when the question to be settled is the resignation of a Pope,
it does not belong to the Pope to summon the Council, but
to prelates and princes who represent the community. The
Pope is bound to obey such a Council, which can make new
laws and rescind old ones.*

Finally, Dietrich asks that all three Popes resign and that
the new Pope be not chosen from amongst the Cardinals,
for these were parties to whatever had transpired.

Niem had known many a Pope at first hand, having served
as apostolic secretary to the Urbanist and Pisan Pontiffs
all the way from Urban VI to John XXIII. His question
as to papal infallibility would never be answered. Official
pronouncements by different Popes were contradictory; to
which did infallibility adhere? Not long before, Avignon's
John XXII had issued a Bull saying that the doctrine of the
poverty of Christ was heresy. This automatically made him
a heretic if one believed Nicholas II, whose previous Bull
declared that the doctrine of the poverty of Christ was true.
In a later age, Pius IX would make a dogma of papal infallibility—but perhaps he was misled by his nightly com-
munings with Saint Philomena, who was, he reported, his
spiritual guide: the modern John XXIII would formally
establish, in April, 1961, that Saint Philomena had never
existed at all.

Meanwhile, John's bags of gold were doing him no good. Bribery, threats, maneuvers—nothing availed. Society was closing in.

In a secret meeting, the Council considered an indictment of the Pope's entire life, an exposure of his vices, his outrages, his crimes—in short, of his utter unfitness to sit on the papal throne. John was to have been confronted with this indictment at an open session, but the more farseeing realized the damage which would be inflicted on the office if these scandals were published. The Sacred College, too, would suffer, for after all it was the Cardinals who had elected John.

Pope John, discovering what was in the wind, sensed his peril. He called the Cardinals to a meeting. Here he admitted the truth of some of the accusations, but fiercely denied many of them. Then he made a rather surprising proposal: he would go before the Council and confess his misdeeds, but would insist that no charge except that of heresy could depose a Pope. The Cardinals warned against this move.

Next, John was given more to worry about than public exposure—now tabled—of his sins. A delegation came, asking him to abdicate. To its amazement, his answer was yes. Full of good will after the unexpectedly easy victory, the envoys left the wording of John's statement to the Pope himself.

On February 16, 1415, John submitted an offer which he had drawn up, in regard to ceding the Papacy. His offer was vague, to say the least. Criticized for ambiguity, he drew up a second offer, also unacceptable. At this point the Pope's opponents decided to produce their own version. John turned it down. Their second paper was handed to him by Sigismund in a sign-or-else fashion. John tried in every way to reject it. But Sigismund was not to be waved off, and at last John agreed to go before a general session of the Council and read out the repellent words.

He presented himself, therefore, to the delegates of all the Nations and here the Patriarch of Antioch handed him the declaration forced on him by Sigismund. The Pope read it over to himself as if for the first time and then paused in thought for long moments, but when he began to read aloud his voice was steady:

I, Pope John XXIII, [he read out clearly so that every syllable sounded through the cathedral] for the repose of Christendom, I profess, engage, promise, swear, and vow to God, the Church, and this Holy Council, willingly, freely, to give peace to the Church, by the way of my simple cession of the Papacy; to do and to fulfill this effectually, according to the determination of this present Council, when and so soon as Pedro de Luna and Angelo Corario, called in their respective obediences Benedict XIII and Gregory XII, shall in like manner cede the Papacy, to which they pretend, by themselves or by their lawful Proctors: and even in any case of vacancy by disease or otherwise, in which by my cession unity can be restored to the Church of God through the extirpation of the present Schism.

John had not yet finished reading when "the whole assembly broke out into a paroxysm of rapture."

On the following day, at the second public session, the Pope read his statement again. When he reached the words "I swear and vow . . ." he bent one knee and laid a finger on his breast.

At the end Emperor Sigismund, hastily putting aside his crown, threw himself down and kissed John's feet. The Patriarch of Antioch as the Council's representative, with equal fervor did the same. But even with his feet kissed by

King and Council, even with the words "profess, engage, promise, swear and vow," it was still obvious that John had left himself an escape clause: his cession was to be simultaneous with that of Pope Benedict and Pope Gregory. In twenty years, neither King, Cardinals, Council nor war had brought Pedro de Luna even to the brink of cession—and although now eighty-seven, he was blooming. As long as Pope John's contract to resign was conditioned on mutual cession, John had practically a lifetime lease on his share of the Papacy.

He was not without defenders. It was argued that if Pisa was canonical, then so was John. The Italians said that if Sigismund went down to Nice to see Pope Benedict, leaving Pope John out, as was now urged, they would desert the Council. Outward respect was still maintained. Behind the scenes, however, John spoke of Sigismund as a beggar, drunkard, savage and fool. Sigismund said to John: "You Italians seem to think that you lead the world in knowledge and power, but I call you the dregs of the earth." John said to Sigismund: "And do you imagine that you sit on the same bench with me because you are a Luxemburger? . . . If you were not . . . King of the *Romans* you would be sitting at my feet, and I only grant you this honor as an Italian, not as a barbarian." But the amenities were observed: John was humble enough in public, knowing the Council was in no mood for an assertive Pope; meekness and delay were all he had left. In his new image, he graciously bestowed on Sigismund the Golden Rose.

But the next day the Council moved to elect a new Pontiff, someone who, obviously, would not be John. When his supporters protested, they only goaded his opponents into mentioning the unmentionable: the Pope's way of life. Upon hearing the charges against John, now brought into the open, Robert Hallum, Bishop of Salisbury, spoke for the vast majority when he exclaimed that the Pope "ought to be burned at the stake."

It was after vespers on March 19, 1415, and the Pope was lying down. The Emperor came in. To Sigismund's question as to his health, John answered that he was not entirely well. He did not think that Constance was good for him; he found the air oppressive; a change was indicated. To this the Emperor objected. The Pope ought not to leave Constance, he said, while the Council was still in session.

John promised to stay on. He said he couldn't leave anyway, that he was lame in one foot. To prove it he seized a cane, got himself off his couch and hobbled about the room. He still clung to the Way of Cession as the best way of remaining Pope, but he knew this was no time to dicker. The men of Constance were saying, in effect, "A plague on all three of your houses." As for his courtesy to Sigismund, John had clearly wasted one Golden Rose.

The next afternoon while Duke Frederick of Austria was tilting for fifty gold rings against Queen Barbara's brother out on the flat land between the town wall and the river bank, and almost all of Constance was watching the show, a gray-clad citizen aboard an aged nag clopped out through one of the city gates. Dressed as a groom, with a scarf tied over his mouth, and on the pommel of his saddle a crossbow, Pope John was making good his escape. With three Popes in the world, he was leaving Constance Popeless. At Ermatingen on the Rhine he stepped into a waiting boat and the current hurried him away to Schaffhausen.

Except for Sigismund, Constance might then have split wide open. The streets filled with armed men, shops were hastily battened down, people, hearing that the Pope was about to return and attack, streamed out through the gates. But Sigismund rode through the streets and, statesmanlike, quieted the populace down. And the Council was saved.

Letters arrived from Pope John at Schaffhausen with palpable untruths: he had not broken his promise; the jousting Duke Frederick (his arch-ally) had known nothing of his escape—and one truth: that he was now enjoying a better climate. The Pope, soon deserted even by Otto Colonna, his last remaining Cardinal, sailed on down the Rhine with Duke Frederick. It was not long before they hunted John from Schaffhausen to Freiburg, from Freiburg to Breisach, and ran him to ground.

On March 23, four days after the Pope's escape, Gerson of the University of Paris addressed the French Nation and told them that the Council was above a Pope. His address, delivered as the representative of France's King, made him, except for Pierre d'Ailly, the leading mind there. At the third public session, on March 26, the Council declared itself canonical and stated it must not be dissolved until it had ended the Schism.

At the Council's fourth session occurred what has been called "the most interesting event in the whole dogmatic history of the Christian Church": under the guiding hand of Cardinal Zabarella it was proposed, following the Gerson line, "that the Council should declare itself to be supreme above the Pope." Such a careful historian as Lea observes that the Council's "mere convocation was a recognition of its supremacy over the successor of Peter." Gerson's view, and that of the University of Paris, was that a Council could judge, correct, even depose a Pope, "as you might pluck a sword from a madman."

As the days passed, Pope John was escaping, being caught, assuming new disguises, resigning, retracting his resignation. He was still valuable; an Italian moneylender offered 300,000 florins for him, "as is." Meanwhile Sigismund frightened off any future supporters of John by punishing Duke Frederick, so effectively attacking his lands that ever afterward the Austrian Duke was known as Frederick Empty-Purse. When informed of John's latest escape Sigismund cried: "Let him go! and if he gets to Avignon I'll drag him back by the hood with my own hand even from that Palace on the hill!"

Peremptorily summoned to reappear at Constance, John replied that he wanted nothing better. On May 13, at the Council's ninth session, the big argument within the Cathedral was about who should go to the door to see if John was there. In the end England's Bishop Bubwith proceeded to the western door, flung it wide and called out the Pontiff's name three times.

May 14 was the day of the "fateful tenth session," when the president in the Council's name read off the crimes of John XXIII. "Never probably," comments Milman, "were seventy more awful accusations brought against man than against the Vicar of Christ. . . . Before the final decree, sixteen of those of the most indescribable depravity were dropped, out of respect not for the Pope, but for public decency." The list of dark evils, even abbreviated to fifty-four, went on, on, on. Pope John was ". . . untruthful, addicted to every vice, had led Pope Boniface IX astray, bought his way into the College of Cardinals, cruelly misgoverned Bologna, poisoned Pope Alexander V, believed neither in a resurrection nor in a life to come, was given over to animal pleasures, was a mirror of infamy, a Devil incarnate, fouled the whole Church with simony . . ." wherefore the commissioners there assembled pronounced him "suspended from his papal office as a murderer, a sodomite, a simoniac and a heretic"—and ordered all Christian folk to withdraw their obedience. The Council deposed him on May 29.

Pope John formally abdicated shortly thereafter at Radolfzell, yielding up the Papal Seal and the Fisherman's Ring. The Emperor held him prisoner here and there—at

Gottlieben where Huss was; at Heidelberg Castle where he spent three years of captivity above the Neckar, at Mannheim—until at last he managed to buy himself free. In 1419, perhaps on the theory that one is innocent until proved insolvent, his successor was to make him Cardinal Tusculanus. Enjoying this rank, and living in Florence with his friend and banker Cosimo de' Medici, John died on December 22, 1419, and was buried in the Baptistry at Florence in a magnificent Renaissance tomb under a bronze figure reclining on its side. So much for the world and its evaluations and its tributes: for Huss's ashes, there would be the wind and the river.

After John XXIII was done away with by the Council of Constance, two Popes remained: Gregory the Urbanist, Benedict the Clementine. The latter enjoyed the more prestige; but there was hope of a successful bargain with the former. Both men were in their eighties. Benedict had the King of Aragon as his supporter; and Queen Joanna II, who followed the late Ladislas on the throne of Naples, acknowledged him in secret, or said she did. Gregory had no comparable allies.

The Council of Constance invited Gregory to reconvene it as Pope, and then to abdicate. In exchange, Gregory would be made Cardinal Bishop of Porto and permanent Legate of the Holy See at Ancona: less imposing titles than Pope, but in the circumstances reassuring. Gregory, tired of it all, accepted. He was, however, too wise to go to Constance in the flesh; never enthusiastic about co-abdication, he cared even less for co-imprisonment or perhaps co-death. He worried, even though he was at all times protected by a relic he kept by him, his tooth of Saint Catherine of Siena. The Council was reconvened in his name by his legate Giovanni Dominici, but the Pope himself remained at a safe distance. On July 4, 1415, he abdicated.

Richly provided for, Gregory went his way and died, presumably in the course of nature, on October 18, 1417. The last thing he said was: "I have not understood the world, and the world has not understood me."

It is obvious that the Council of Constance was determined to insure papal cooperation; punctilious at first about being convened by John XXIII—for a Council, to be valid, must be convened by a Pope—it had now called upon Gregory to convene it again. We see here one illegality being added to another: initially, the Council had been called by an unlawful Pope, as John's legitimacy depended on that of his predecessor, Alexander V, elected by the Council of Pisa, itself not convened by a Pope and hence illegal. The reconvened Council of Constance was also uncanonical, in the non-Urbanist view; Gregory was the Urbanist Pope, succeeding Innocent VII, who succeeded Boniface IX, who succeeded mob-elected Urban VI the Impossible. Furthermore, if Pisa was a valid Council (which it was not), then Gregory was not a valid Pope anyhow, since the Council of Pisa had deposed him. It was with all these factors in mind that, after John had celebrated the first Mass in the Cathedral, Cardinal Zabarella rose and inaugurated Constance as a continuation of the Council of Pisa.

Pastor states that Gregory's convoking the Council meant that he, Gregory, should be recognized as lawful Pope, and that this was his price for abdication; that it also meant that the Council rejected the rivals of himself and his Urbanist line (i.e., rejected the Clementine Popes and the Pisan), and repudiated all the Council's previous activities. But how, one must ask, could an illegal body legalize a Pope? And if the mere act of convoking the Council legitimized the Pontiff, then of course John XXIII, who convoked it first, had the prior claim.

In effect the men of Constance bestowed—out of a hat—

on each of the two convening Popes, John and Gregory, a kind of spurious legality of which it then deprived them.

At all events, there was now only one single Pope. For the first time in thirty-seven years, except for lightning intervals following papal deaths, Western Christendom had but one ruler: the Clementine, Pedro de Luna, Pope Benedict XIII.

27   THEY CAUGHT THE WHITE GOOSE BY THE LEG

T HE MEN OF Constance now ground their knives to perform a human sacrifice.

It happened that some decades before, the Englishman John Wycliffe had observed that the churches were "dunnus of thefis and habitacionis of fendis." Starting out to reorganize the Church, he wrote that the King was God's Vicar and had sacred power even over the wealth of the clergy. It was sinful for the clergy to hold property, but not for laymen. Each Christian, too, had "dominion" from God, he said, thus bypassing the priests. This was the braver of him, in that ancient forgeries like the False Decretals, greatly enhancing the power and possessions of Pope and hierarchy, were still believed in, and would not be exposed till the Reformation.

Affirming that Scripture alone was the ground of faith, Wycliffe, a priest himself and Master of Balliol, translated the Bible into English. He took his case to the people through his organization of simple preachers dressed in long russet gowns. "Lollards," sneered the hostile ecclesiastics at these men—by which they meant babblers, and mumblers of prayers.

"I believe that in the end truth will conquer," was Wycliffe's reply. He denounced Indulgences for money or to "crusaders" sent to kill other Christians. (The doctrine that the Pope disposes of these Indulgences from the "Treasury of the Church" or from leftover merits of holy Beings had been sanctioned by Pope Clement VI at Avignon in 1343.)

Wycliffe was against war; against simony, confession, pilgrimages, vows of celibacy, papal excommunications, saint worship, image worship: "Certis, these ymages of hemselfe may do nouther gode nor yvel to mennis soules, but thai myghtten warme a man's body in colde if thai were sette upon a fire." In 1381 he formally denied the "Miracle of the Mass," transubstantiation, which set the priest over the rest of men because he could "make God."

Wycliffe's last advice, "a simple counsel of my own," shortly before he was stricken in December, 1384, while hearing Mass in his parish church at Lutterworth, was that Pope and clergy "should surrender all temporal authority to the civil power." He thus echoed in his death year a book that was completed in 1324, the probable year of his birth— Marsilius of Padua's *Defensor Pacis*, which placed Ecumenical Councils above Popes, said papal primacy was not in the Bible and that Paul not Peter was Bishop of Rome.

For great conversions, they say, there must be three factors present: a devout lady at the Court, a crisis and a monk. Wycliffe's Lollardry reached Bohemia by way of Richard of England's first wife, good Queen Anne: and waiting to receive it was a peasant's son, Jan Huss.

Huss—"Goose"—was the darling of Prague. Priest, university rector, he preached righteousness, using the Czech language, and denounced the immorality of the clergy. He thus raised up a host of enemies. But the people were with him, and against the hierarchs—so much so that in 1411 all Prague was on his account placed under an interdict by John XXIII: the newborn lay unbaptized, the dead unburied.

Summoned to Constance, Huss accepted with a full heart. He and some friends left Prague October 11, 1414, under escort of thirty horse, themselves jouncing along in two carts. Huss was bareheaded, in priest's dress, and sat with his books packed around him, one of them Wycliffe's *De sufficientia legis Christi*, with which he hoped to win over those he was going to meet, the leading minds of his time. On October 18, at Spires, Sigismund confirmed his promise of a safe conduct for Huss; by this document Sigismund took Huss under the protection of the Holy Roman Empire in his going to Constance, his staying there, and his returning. But as Huss set out, a Polish cobbler had grasped his hand and warned him that he would never come back, and that he should look for his reward not to the King of Hungary but the King of Heaven.

Everywhere along the way, crowds gathered to see Huss, especially because a hostile bishop had come through ahead of him and told them all to stay away. In each town, Huss cried out his name to the people, and posted up a notice in Latin and German on the church door—the public bulletin board of the day—telling who he was and that he was going to the council to defend his faith. On November 2nd or 3rd, twelve thousand turned out to see him as he arrived in Constance. He rented a room in the house of a widow named Fida who kept a bakery, and stayed quietly in his lodgings. On November 4th he wrote friends that he had been privately approached and asked to settle everything as it were out of court, but that for his part he expected to win Constance over, adding that the greater the fight, the greater the victory. Later he again wrote, somewhat surprised at being neglected. In any case, the Emperor had not yet arrived, and Huss pinned his faith to Sigismund.

It was a recognized principle of the Church that faith and oaths pledged to heretics were void. Gratian's twelfth-century *Decretum* held that it was lawful to torture and kill heretics and confiscate their property. From the start, Huss was treated as a heretic awaiting trial, and as if what the men of Constance were going to do to him was legal, right and proper. On November 28, they surrounded the widow

Fida's house and took him away; this happened after Pope John had assured Huss's friends that with such a document as Sigismund had issued him, Huss would be safe in Constance even if he had murdered John's own brother.

They held him a few days, then chained him in a cell, freezing cold, beside the outlet of a sewer. At Christmas, Sigismund landed nearby in all his magnificence. Months passed, during which the subtlest of theologians, who had judged him already—fifty or sixty of them at least—having looked for heresies to condemn him out of his writings, came to examine him and reported all he said and did.

He got sick and ran a temperature. Constance needed him alive, however: the Pope's physicians were sent to him, and saved him with clysters. By January 19 he was a little better, and asked for pens, ink and another shirt. Without reference books he framed replies to the list of accusations as to what he believed, and wrote all night sometimes, on subjects like the Body of Christ, Repentance, and the love of God.

His ideas were not dusty answers but matters of great moment to unnumbered human beings. Out of them would come defenestrations at Prague, the fatal apoplectic stroke of Wenceslaus in 1419, the Hussite Wars for generations still unconceived. A hundred years from this time Luther, "the Saxon Huss," would exclaim: "We are all Hussites without knowing it." In doctrine, except for the Eucharist, the prisoner mostly followed John Wycliffe.

One evening, fourteen hundred years before the Council of Constance, a Being different from other men, in this world a carpenter's son, was sitting at table with the few friends He had. The best of these was about to deny Him; the worst, in exchange for a few coins, was going to sell Him to the state. After they had shared a meal, the meal of the poor and homeless, He being with them for the last time

passed around some bread and told them to eat it—it was
His body; then gave them a cup of red wine and told them
to drink it, it was His blood. They knew He meant this as a
symbol, for they could see Him with them, in no way
changed. It was a sort of keepsake He was giving them: a
something eternal to remember Him by.

That tenderest gesture was in a short while perverted to
the uses of power; rivers of blood flowed out of that cup.
But for twenty centuries that act of love would engage the
mind. 'Abdu'l-Bahá of Persia affirms today: ". . . the heavenly bread did not signify this material bread, but rather
. . . the divine graces and heavenly perfections of which
His disciples partook. . . . He was with them in person.
. . . He was not transformed into bread and wine." The
Fourth Lateran Council of 1215 said that the inner reality—
"substance"—of the bread and wine was turned by the priest
into Christ's body and blood. Coptic Christians would not
mix their wine with water; that would be dualism, and they
were Monophysites. The Eastern Orthodox would use un-
leavened bread and "intinction," certainly a finer word than
"dunking." In Gaul, the bread on the altar was shaped like
a man. Erigena, who died in 875, was a stercorist, or dung-
ist, believing that part of the elements were voided. Huss
did not deny transubstantiation, but he and his followers
were cup people: they wanted not only bread for the laity
but wine too, and were called Utraquists ("in both kinds")
or Calixtins (from *calix*, cup). Small wonder that the common man, long wearied of it all, has made the words "hocus-
pocus" and "hoax" from *hoc est corpus*.

When the examiners offered Huss twelve theologians to
present his case for him to the council, he said he had
chosen as his advocate the Lord Jesus Christ. Finally they
chained him and rowed him away to the Castle of Gottlieben ("God love") on the Rhine, to a tower room where
he could walk, always chained. At night he was fastened to

the wall. He kept hoping for permission to address the Council, to answer the "bagful of lies" that were being spread against him. He began to spit blood and to suffer from dysentery in this castle; a sign of God's love, he said, being addicted to puns.

At the beginning of June, Huss was brought back in chains as usual to Constance and on June 5, in the Gray Friars' refectory, the Council assembled, the reports of witnesses were read and also excerpts from Huss's book *On the Church*. And so Huss had his way, and did manage to appear before the quintessential people of his world. But it seems that on this day the uproar was such that he could not be heard.

He was now a pale thin man in shabby clothes. About forty-five or forty-six years old. Smelling of prison, come from a prison cell, not the brilliant social events of the Council. For him there had been no banquets, no dances and joustings, no beautiful women.

This was the gathering he had thought he could persuade, the ones he had thought by his eloquence to move and so bring about reform. He seems to have appeared before them three times in all, but we doubt if they saw him even once.

"I came hither of my own free will," he told them. "Had I refused to come, neither the King nor the Emperor could have forced me, so numerous are the Bohemian lords who love me and who would have afforded me protection."

Cardinal Pierre d'Ailly (he had been elevated to that rank by John XXIII), indignant, cried out: "See the impudence of the man!"

There were loud calls and stirrings and then John of Chlum calmly stood up and said: "He speaks truth, for though I have little power compared with others in Bohemia, I could easily defend him for a year against the whole strength of both monarchs. Judge, then, how much more could they whose forces are stronger than mine!"

Told to recant his "errors," Huss refused to unless they were proved to be errors, and spoke up to praise Wycliffe, damned by the Council a month before. They led him off, and Sigismund exulted: "When I was a boy, I remember the first start of this sect, and see what it is now! But we shall make an end of the master in a single day . . . when I get back we will take up with that other man—his pupil—what's his name?" And they cried, "Jerome!" and Sigismund answered, "Yes! Jerome!"

Huss had left a letter at home in Bohemia with a disciple, Master Martin, to be opened in the event of his death. He told there of the persecution he suffered because he had opposed the bad lives of the clergy, and willed his gray robe to Martin (unless Martin didn't like the color) and his white robe and what few other things he owned, and also said he was sorry that in the days before being ordained he had wasted his time playing chess, to the loss of his own temper and that of others.

Now he wrote his last letters, praying he would be able to face with joy and patience whatever was ahead. His books had been ordered burned, but he asked his friends in Prague not to give them up, for the Council members would die and scatter "like the storks and butterflies," and their doings would last no more than a spider's web. After him, God would raise up others stronger than he, who would lay bare the simony and wickedness on every hand. The Council was "the scarlet woman of the Apocalypse," he said. He never retracted a word.

July 5 was the last entire day of his life, and they were still trying to get him to recant. Cardinals d'Ailly and Zabarella, the Patriarch of Antioch, five bishops including England's Bubwith and Hallum—all questioned him again. Sigismund also sent Louis of Bavaria and some of Huss's friends; in vain.

July 6, 1415, Saturday, Sigismund being present, the whole Council assembled in the Cathedral. Huss was kept waiting outside the doors till after Mass. Then they led him in to the center of the church where they had set up a table with sacramental vestments on it. He was told to stand on this table. The Cardinal of Santa Pudenziana preached a sermon in which he dwelt on rotten flesh and scabbed sheep and on how Sigismund was about to win, this day, an eternal crown.

Now in his dying hour, Huss fixed his gaze on Sigismund and said: "I came freely to this Council, under the public faith, promised by the Emperor, here present, that I should be free from all constraint, to bear witness to my innocence." Sigismund answered nothing: but he blushed.

Before representatives of the Nations read out the sentence from the rostrum, a warning was given that any noise, handclapping, foot stamping, would be punished with excommunication and two months in prison. Some of Huss's "heresies" were read, the others taken as read: Huss had dared to attack tithes, endowments, priests being in mortal sin, and the Pope as antichrist. They then put on him alb, stole, chasuble, and set a chalice in his hand and afterward ritually took all of his priestly regalia away. Bidden again to recant Huss cried in a loud voice that he was afraid to, because he was afraid to offend God, to perjure himself, or to harm those he had taught. After that they quarreled among themselves how to spoil his tonsure—shave it or clip it off. Huss turned to Sigismund and said, "The bishops cannot even agree over such blasphemy as this!" His hair was finally cropped in the shape of a cross. They crowned him then with a tall white headdress that had three clawing black Demons on it and the word: "Heresiarch."

An early picture shows the cavorting Devil on Huss's absurd hat, and beside Huss the executioner, a showman enjoying his hour, hurrying Huss along with the same jaunty, lewd brutality as the Devil on the hat. All of Constance was in the streets to watch.

Huss was led past a bonfire of his own books. They took him out where the marshes were, to fields along the south side of the Zurich road. Here were three carts piled with faggots and straw. Huss knelt on the ground, wept, prayed. His crown fell off. Someone put it on again—wrong way up —and he was seen to smile. Over the chosen place, the new grave of a Cardinal's mule, they fastened his hands to a stake at his back, and the crowds made them turn his head away from the east. The future chronicler, Ulrich Richental, called up a priest who offered to confess him but Huss said, "There is no need. I have no mortal sin." To Duke Louis, asking yet once again would he recant, Huss said, "I have but preached and written to restrain men from sin, and in the truth of that gospel I will gladly die."

They piled straw and wood to his chin, and all the while, at the end there, he sang, "Have pity on me, Christ, Son of the Living God!"

The flames went up, he shrieked, writhed, and "died in the Lord."

It was not enough for his life to be put out. The shoes and jacket, normally for the executioner, were thrown to the blaze, augmented now because the earth had cracked and the dead mule was smoking too. No relics must be left behind. The charred bones were carefully poked, the skull smashed, a stake was driven through the heart. What little was still there afterward, went into the Rhine.

Pope John, Pope Gregory (by proxy), Huss, Jerome—all these made the mistake of attending the Council of Constance. Only Pope Benedict was too wary to attend. In the end, Constance went to him. In mid-July, 1415, the Emperor was prayed off on his mission, and at once a letter appeared, posted on the church doors, directing the Council to take care of itself as best it could, for the writer now had important business elsewhere. It was signed: The Holy Ghost.

Sigismund thus took on a task which the King of France, the Roman Popes, the Dukes of Bourbon, Burgundy and Berry, the University of Paris, the Councils of Pisa and Perpignan and Constance, and the pressure of four-fifths of the Roman Catholic world had attempted and at which they had failed: he would, so he hoped and believed, induce Benedict XIII to stop being Pope.

Benedict had now worn the tiara twenty-one years. He had lived to see France desert him and then rally to obedience again; to see his renegade Cardinals bombard him, then come back and fall at his feet; to see his rival Popes eliminated one by one: Boniface IX, Innocent VII, Alexander V, all taken by death; John XXIII and Gregory XII struck away by the Council of Constance. Was not the hand of God in all this? Could not Benedict enjoy the private dream of every rival claimant, that he would as a gesture remove his tiara and the Council would set it on his head again? With something like this in mind, late in 1415 he would still propose to convoke an Ecumenical Council in such a place as Avignon, Lyons or Marseilles, at which he would be confirmed as Pope and then would abdicate.

But Constance wanted a pliable Pope and Benedict would be sure to rule. Constance wanted someone everybody could agree on, and Benedict in two decades of struggle had alienated many blocs of partisans. Benedict must go. Sigismund the all-conquering, with him fourteen delegates elected by the Council (none being Cardinals), would solve this Benedict problem too. The irresistible would destroy the immovable.

How great the stature of the eighty-seven-year-old Pope still was, is proved by the fact that the leading temporal ruler of the day came wooing him. Sigismund was to meet Benedict at Nice. He crossed Switzerland and Savoy and reached Nice to find this rendezvous, in the good old way, changed to Perpignan. Sigismund was on his way there when King Ferdinand of Aragon, Benedict's man who would also attend the meetings, wrote the Emperor for a postponement till August, pleading illness. (Apparently Ferdinand really was ill: someone had told him that henbane would be good for his kidney stones; it was not.)

Meanwhile Benedict had gone to Perpignan, remained at the meeting place all through June, and left, publicly declaring Sigismund contumacious for not arriving. For one thing, Benedict was disturbed at the thought of Sigismund's bodyguard of four thousand men—he himself had only his nephew, Rodrigo de Luna, with three hundred. Besides, everyone knew what had happened to Huss. Foxlike, Benedict zigzagged here and there as Sigismund relentlessly came on. At least, Ferdinand of Aragon would surely be present if he could—he owed his throne to Benedict's help, and that of the Pope's personal saint, Vincent Ferrer, who would also attend, with his Flagellants.

On September 19, 1415 they set up on a dais outside the

walls of Perpignan a sumptuous brocade-covered armchair on which it was customary for a visiting monarch to sit and receive the inhabitants' homage prior to entering their city. Sigismund then rode in on a dancing Castilian horse, passing along between the housefronts hung with precious tapestries and rugs. According to custom, the Emperor as he rode held his sword with its point straight up, to show he was not in his own domains. There was the usual feasting, the jousts and tourneys, the ceremonies at the Cathedral.

In the great audience hall of the palace of the Kings of Majorca, Pope Benedict received Sigismund. The venerable Pontiff was seated on his throne. He wore a red robe, and a red hood bordered with ermine. About him stood his Cardinals and court. Sigismund, followed by his own lords and prelates and his fourteen delegates from Constance, was escorted to the foot of the throne. Benedict rose, saluted briefly by touching the ermine border of his hood, and sat again to hear the Emperor's greeting.

"Most Holy Father," was the substance of the visitor's words, "I am not ignorant of the fact that you and you alone can reunite the Christian world . . . I beg, I exhort, I ask and I implore you to grant with all good will this long-desired union to the Church."

Benedict smiled. In a clear, decisive voice, he answered, "I have toiled, never resting, for this long-wished-for union. For this I have crossed provinces, for this I have sailed the seas, ignoring the dangers, braving the perils, yet accomplishing nothing. With your aid, with your efforts, it is now my hope that we shall have union at last. To this end, I know, God has chosen you."

Sigismund knelt and kissed Benedict's two hands, and the Pope took the Emperor in his arms and kissed him on the lips.

In their subsequent official conversations, Sigismund informed Benedict he had come to obtain the Pope's renun-

ciation of the tiara—on which abdication, he said, the union
of Christendom depended. And he showed him the documents drawn up at Constance. Benedict answered that he
would follow that way which would lead the soonest to
union. He said he would renounce, he would concede. But
his conditions were that all that had been done against him
at Pisa (the deposing of him and so on) was to be annulled
and disavowed; he was to be acknowledged true Pope by all
the rulers and all the faithful; the elevation of the next
Pontiff was to be according to canon law.

Sigismund, and King Ferdinand—who was now having second thoughts as to which side he was on—saw at once that
what Benedict meant by giving up the tiara was that all
Christendom should recognize him as Pope.

At the Perpignan Palace came a critical day in Benedict's
life, a day when he would state his case for all time. He was
old, haggard, his motions had slowed, but his eye was piercing, his voice confident. He knew exactly what he wanted,
what he had always wanted, every day, every long hour,
through twenty-one years of hunger and blood and the terror by night and the perils of escape and the dangers as he
rocked on the sea: he wanted to be what he had been
elected to be—Christendom's Pope.

That day, toward September's end, Benedict talked in
Latin to Sigismund. He said that he, Benedict, was one of
the remaining few above ground who knew, from the inside
and from the beginning, the whole story of the Great
Schism of the West: he had been one of the Cardinals
who elected Urban VI, and one of the same Cardinals
who, shortly thereafter and in effect simultaneously, elected
Clement VII. Since then men had been born, had lived out
their days and died, it was all so long ago. Seven hours the
story took in the telling, when the Two Swords, the spiritual
authority and the temporal authority, confronted one another in the Palace of the Kings of Majorca.

"You say my title is clouded," Benedict told the Emperor and his silent assemblage. "So be it. But before I was Pope I was Cardinal, made Cardinal before there ever was a Schism. I am the only Cardinal left alive from before the Schism of the West. If, as you say, all the Popes since that day are in doubt, then so are all their Cardinals. And since it is the Cardinals who elect the Pontiffs, I who am the only veritable Cardinal, I alone can elect a veritable Pope.

"I am as well the only living man who can pronounce as to who is and who is not valid since the beginning of the Schism. I am the only living man who was present that day at that Conclave in 1378 when the Schism began.

"Say I am not the valid Pope: still, I am the only valid Cardinal and there is nothing on earth to prevent me from electing myself. Say you do not want me for Pope, you still have to accept me for Cardinal, and no man on earth can wear the tiara without my vote."

As he finished, there was silence in the vast hall. Here, and they knew it, much that was admirable had spoken: virtue in an age of vice; piety; idealism of purpose—qualities all too rare at the Council from which they had come. But they could not listen to yesterday forever. Times had changed in these forty years, and Benedict had not. The Council had declared itself above all Popes, let alone all Cardinals; his great quarrel was no longer in vogue. They filed slowly out of the Palace, unpersuaded.

The meetings at Perpignan tapered off. Sigismund sent a prince or so to beg Benedict yet another time to renounce the papal throne, *pro forma* only, knowing it was hardly to be expected that the Pope would grant to lesser men what he had refused to Sigismund.

About this time Saint Vincent Ferrer, almost the last great ally of the aging Pontiff, made his public speech. It was in the chapel of the Palace and everybody was there from Benedict on down, the crowds in their thousands spilling into the streets. Facing the pulpit, the beleaguered old Pope sat back to hear again, from his champion, as he had heard so many years, words of courage and hope.

Up there above them all, the Saint opened his mouth in the breathless silence. "Dry bones," he cried, stretching wide his quivering arms, "hear ye the words of the Lord!" Then he crashed down his fists on the pulpit, and there poured from his lips his repudiation of Benedict XIII. As Benedict listened in astonishment and pain, and the murmurs of the crowd swelled to a roar, the Pope saw not only Aragon leaving his camp, but Navarre as well, Castile as well, and the Comtat of Foix, and faraway Scotland, and multitudes upon multitudes throughout the Western world. With those uncounted thousands of miracles to his credit, Saint Vincent had proved unable to perform the greatest miracle of all: keeping a loyal heart.

This was almost the end. Benedict did agree, yet once more, to the Way of Cession, if the Council of Constance would transfer its deliberations to Marseilles, Avignon, Lyons, Nîmes, Montpellier, Béziers, or Toulouse; and indeed, the French party seemed briefly to support him. Then all collapsed, Sigismund left, and Benedict decided he must once again take to the sea.

At Collioure, in mid-November, the King of Aragon's men caught up with the Pontiff. They found him not far from the tall, cylindrical tower the vanished Templars had left behind; he was seated in an armchair on the sand, his Cardinals and courtiers about him, watching the loading of his galleys, soon to be off. The King of Aragon's ambassadors knelt down in the sand and their spokesman delivered Ferdinand's message: it was one final imploration to renounce the tiara. Benedict gazed past the envoys, out to sea; they might have been thin air. The Pontiff uttered no word.

It was high noon. Benedict rose, and leaning on an attendant's obedient arm, walked slowly to the water's edge and boarded his galley. They set up his armchair on the roofed-over afterdeck and there—the ambassadors waiting— he had his usual meal: fruits and preserves, his goblet of old wine, and ended up with prayers, after which his doctor served him a cup of herb tea. Already, the wind was right, the sails were filling, the pilot asking to be off. And then, only then, Benedict gave his reply to the envoys of Ferdinand:

"Tell your King this from me," he answered them. "You send me into the wasteland, and I made you King."

29 BUSINESS AS USUAL

POGGIO BRACCIOLINI, a papal secretary, was not interested in religion. For all of him the Schoolmen might never have tried (like the Muslim theologians before them, from Baghdad to Spain) to reconcile reason and faith. Albertus Magnus, wearing Arab dress and expounding Aristotle from Muslim works, might never have given lessons, in Paris, to Thomas Aquinas. That Huss was a Realist and the men of Constance mostly Nominalists was of no moment. Poggio was a new man, a Humanist. He preferred, during his stay at Constance, to hunt for classical manuscripts that the monks in neighboring monasteries had stowed away as rubbish in places where "you would not have thrown criminals sentenced to death." The monks let him take away these manuscripts by the cartload.

At other times he liked to frequent the baths at Baden, and from an observation post over the water, toss coins and floral crowns to the prettiest of the lady bathers.

It was Poggio, however, caring nothing about heresy, who has left—in a letter to his friend Leonardo Aretino—the best eyewitness account of how the Council of Constance burned Huss's disciple, Jerome of Prague.

"When I consider," wrote Poggio, "what his choice of words was, what his reasoning, what his countenance, his voice, his action, I must affirm, however much we admire the ancients, that in such a cause no one could have approached nearer to the model of their eloquence."

He summarizes thus Jerome's cries to the council: "What an injustice is this, that after being kept in the strictest confinement for three hundred and forty days, in dirt, squalor, and filth, in fetters, with the lack of everything, while you were listening to my calumniators, you will not hear me for a single hour. . . . Where shall I turn me now, conscript fathers? Whose help shall I implore?"

Poggio, a noted wit himself, writes that the victim even jested. "Being asked what he held as to the Sacrament, he answered that before consecration there was bread, but after consecration there remained only the true body of Christ, and no one but a baker would think there was bread."

Allowed, far too late, to speak, Jerome had dared to praise Huss, freshly burned. He shouted his interrupters down. He talked himself into the flames. At the stake, when they tried to build up the wood behind him, where he could not see, he cried, "Come, light the fire in front. Had I feared it, I would not be here now!"

"A man," wrote Poggio, "worthy of being forever remembered."

Terrified, Leonardo wrote back to warn Poggio against expressing such sentiments. Rightly so, for Constance was formidable and had tasted blood.

Constance never again reached the brilliance of those seven months—from Christmas, 1414, to August, 1415—when Sigismund and Queen Barbara first visited the council city. And after his defeat by Benedict XIII, for it was no less than that, the Emperor's own mighty grip on the Council was loosened too.

As its third main achievement, the first two being oustings and burnings, the Council of Constance, on November 11, 1417, elected a new Pope, Martin V—and it was the Council, rather than the so-called Conclave, because the electors included thirty representatives of the Council as against only twenty-three Cardinals. This election was, of course, uncanonical; the Third Lateran Council (1179) and a decree of Pope Alexander III had ordained that only Cardinals, shut up in Conclave, should elect a Pope. By this time, 1417, the Council's own precarious validity hinged on the legitimacy of Urbanist Pope Gregory XII, who reconvened it after John's abdication; and none could say for sure that the Urbanist was the rightful line. Pope Martin himself was dubious as to his election, since he took pains to have Benedict's three apostate Cardinals, who joined him at Mantua, form a little Conclave of their own and elect him again.

The choosing of Martin V came as a great relief to Christendom, for many had prophesied that out of this Council would appear yet a fourth simultaneous Pope, and now there were only two. The new Pontiff was Otto Colonna. Pope Boniface VIII, who a century before had cast out the Colonnas root and branch to the fifth generation—that same Boniface who was the author of the Bull *Unam sanctam*, perhaps the strongest of all statements on the universal supremacy of the Pope ("every human being is subject to the Pope of Rome")—would have been aghast at their return to power. But the twelfth-century Saint Malachy had foreseen the new Pope as *"Columna veli aurei"*; a Colonna and thus a pillar. Martin had also been Cardinal of Saint George of the Golden Sail. Urbanist and Pisan, he was one of the Cardinals who, at Pisa, had elected Alexander V. He was also one of those Cardinals who, at Bologna, had seen in pirate Baldassare Cossa the qualities requisite for a Pope, and helped to elect him John XXIII. He had followed John when the latter escaped to Schaffhausen, and had been the last Cardinal to return from him to the Council of Constance. On good terms with everyone, Martin was no friend of reform. The street urchins of Florence sang a song about him, to the effect that he was not worth a penny:

Papa Martino
Non vale un quattrino.

After the enthronement there actually were some stormy debates over reforming the Church, but nothing much came of them. Indeed, Martin's first act as Pope was to approve the rules of the papal Chancery, thus making reform impossible. For these rules "organized and protected" the most crying abuse of the age, the selling by the Pope of offices and dispensations, judgments and Indulgences. They "set forth the system by which the Papacy had managed to divert to itself the revenues of the Church." They were the "code" on which depended for their existence those very ills which the Council had met to do away with. The long line of Catholic reformers, the countless publicizers of what was wrong, had wrung their hands in vain: the merchants would open for business as usual.

The great failure at Constance, perhaps the inevitable failure, was the Council's inability to deal with the problem of moral conduct—not of simple believers but of those who were supposed to guide them and set the example. Had the Council addressed itself to the evils lamented by such as Clémanges as energetically as it attacked supposed heretics and the current surplus of Popes, the Protestant Reformation might never have happened. But once the moralists had taken Constance as a world forum where the immorality of all ranks of the clergy could be exposed, the Council either had to deal effectively with the problem of morals or place the Church in the position of admitting its impotence to change men's lives.

Sigismund, tired now, washed his own hands of it all, saying to those who came to him for help: "When we insisted on taking up the reform of the Church before the election of a Pope, you . . . would have a Pope first. Now you have got him, go to him and ask for reform."

On April 22, 1418, Martin closed the Council, feeling that it had already lasted far too long. On May 16, with pomp and circumstance, the new Pope left Constance, taking its *Business* glory with him. Sigismund followed soon after. The great *as Usual* assemblage had gone on for three years and six months.

It has been said of Constance that the Council defeated Pope John XXIII, but Pope Martin V defeated the Council.

We are usually told that the Council of Constance ended the Great Schism by reestablishing over Western Christendom one single Pope. This not only is not true, it is an affront to the memory of Benedict XIII.

Virtuous, orthodox, elected so far as anyone on earth could tell by canon law, Benedict lived on until 1423, and he never abdicated, never sold out, never set aside the tiara nor stepped down from the papal throne.

On March 8, 1417, after a trial lasting from the previous October, Constance had declared Benedict "contumacious." After still more delays, he was, four months later, on July 26, "deposed."

If Pisa, try as it might, could not depose Urbanist Gregory XII, so that Constance was obliged to buy that Pope off; if Pisa could not, either, depose the Clementine Benedict, so that Sigismund, Holy Roman Emperor, had himself to journey to Benedict and address him as Pontiff—then neither could Constance depose the same Benedict now. A Council cannot depose a Pope. This has obtained since the days of Diocletian the Roman, whose reign ended in 305. When Pope Marcellinus offered incense to Apollo, a Council which included three hundred Bishops assembled at Sinuessa, and declared that man has no power to depose a Pope, stating also that the Apostles had not cut off Peter for denying Jesus Christ.

Meanwhile Benedict XIII had the last word on the men of Constance by excommunicating the whole lot of them.

PART FIVE

THE LION
OF THE ROCK

30 JOURNEY TO THE OTHER ROCK

THE PALE autumn sky was turquoise but the wind changed to piercing cold as Benedict, Pope of the Sea, bore westward from Collioure. Darkness was seeping over the farther reaches of the water. A black tempest wall rose up against the fleet of galleys and Benedict's pilot waited for the Pope's order to turn back. But with Benedict there was no turning back. He had faced many a storm in his time; he would sail on against the dark. More, he would use the storm: he would read the tempest. In the storm would be written his answer to the great enigma of his life.

He spoke to those who huddled about him where he sat in the castle on the raised afterdeck. "If I am *not* Christ's Vicar," he told them, "let the storm pull me and my galleys down to the bottom of the sea. Thus will the Church find peace and rest. But if God saves me from the tempest, that will be a sign. That will show I am Christ's Vicar, and I will know how to do what do I must."

He knelt down then, his robes blowing in the stiff wind. All those about him, sailors as well as Cardinals, knelt too, facing, with Benedict, death and the judgment hour. All lifted their eyes to the roiling sky, and Benedict prayed.

Suddenly, the darkness was no more. The sea quieted, a crescent moon floated at peace in the evening sky. Up there in the deep green of the sky rode Pedro de Luna's heraldic emblem, his token and sign, the crescent moon.

Benedict came up from his knees and shouted in triumph: "I am the Pope!"

And his galleys glided on south and west toward Peñiscola.

Without further incident, once the miracle was over, Benedict's fleet slipped along the east coast of Spain away from Collioure. At regular intervals, the Pope was served his light meals, his preserved fruit and honey, and the faithful doctor brought him teas of mint or manna or tamarind as his health seemed to require. This Doctor Jerónimo de Santa Fe, was the scholarly Jew who had been converted to Christianity when his spiritual leader, Salomon ha-Levi, under the magic of Saint Vincent, had turned into Pablo de Santa Maria. There had also been prayers; and on the lighter side a monk played the bowed and pear-shaped rebeck.

All along, wherever people heard the Pope was coming, crowds gathered, jamming the shore.

Like any voyager, Benedict kept his mind on the journey's end. As he surely did not know, the Rock he was heading for, Peñiscola, far south along the coast from Barcelona, had been owned by the Phoenicians, long gone. After them, Greeks; after them, men of Carthage. The Arabs, with no *p* in their alphabet, apparently took the name, Peninsula, to be Baniskala—*bani* meaning "sons of." Nobody came there for the harbor, small and as if scooped out, ·with a difficult, rocky approach. It was the invulnerability that brought them. Finally—just before they were cut down as purported servants of the Devil by King Philip the Fair and Clement V, first of the Avignon popes—the Templars were in this place. This, Benedict may well have known: across the entrance portal to the castle proper was the coat of arms with three flowers repeated in a horizontal band, said to be that of Fray Berenguer Cardona, who headed that doomed Order at the height of its glory. When those proud tenants were gone, the castle was turned over to the Order of Montesa, formed by the Kings of Aragon to war on the Muslims

of Andalusia. A Master of that body had ceded the Rock to
Pope Benedict.

There was fresh water here, yielded by springs. There was
also, for sightseeing, the Bellower or Bufador of Papa de
Luna, a blowhole carved into the heart of the Rock by aeons
of storms, and through which, if the waves were high,
trapped water geysered upward with a demonic roar.

Now the island Rock rose black before him in the sky,
against a calm gold sea that changed to green as it rippled
to the shore. Benedict could smell the land through the salt
air, breathe wood smoke and the scent of orange trees. He
saw the low, bare hills in the foreground, and the far, opal-
escent mountains; saw people massed about the landing,
and, at the water's edge, foam piled like lace on a papal
gown. Too old not to feel eternal, he did not muse on
death. His head was full of plans. As if triumphant, his galleys sailed in through the guarding rocks of the harbor.

Once his ship was made fast, two Cardinals took the
Pope by the arms and helped him ashore down the slanting
gangway, and the crowds of townspeople, fishermen, farm-
ers, soldiers knelt on the sand. The Pope's entourage formed
a slow procession, through the low archway that still bears
his coat of arms: his tiara between crossed keys, and beneath the triple crown the horseshoe of his upside-down
new moon.

Up the side of the Rock they went, up the long slanting
way to the castle, the Pope perhaps not walking but on a
palfrey or in a cart, and as they moved along the clerics sang
Benedictus qui venit. Here and there the chant was picked
up in the multitude following until at last, like scattered
candles lit from one taper and all aflame together, the whole
long line from castle walls to shore was singing. What did
they know of the distant forces at work beyond the blond
sea? Intricate shifts of nations emerging from feudal chaos;

decline of the papal power; legacy of disillusion piled up by a worldly Church, which had not left Caesar's things to Caesar, had sought its kingdom in the present instead of hereafter, had divided because there were spoils to be divided. These people had never heard of John Wycliffe or Jan Huss. They had come to welcome their Pope.

Those who were closest to Benedict could only grieve that day. They were aware that King Ferdinand, sick in body, weak in will, had written Benedict off. Once the other monarchs of Spain deserted him as well, Benedict would have only Scotland—a faraway place in the northern mists, somewhere beside Ultima Thule—and after that only this Rock. Others who were near him in body, far in heart, wondered if they were following him into a snare. Some, the observant and detached, must have asked themselves if the old man climbing up this long hillside would ever climb down again.

Long years, Benedict sat on this summit or paced this Rock, so far away in space and time from his days on Avignon's Rock of the Lords. He was eighty-seven when he withdrew to this place to make his stand. History had passed him by. Yet Benedict could not change. Was it only the thickening and hardening of the artery walls in an old man's brain? No, surely it was the essence of de Luna himself. His stubbornness was such that it has passed into the Spanish language: the phrase *estarse en sus treces* (*trece* meaning thirteen or thirteenth) to persist in your opinion, goes back to Pope Benedict XIII.

Did he see the context in which his life unfolded? The Pope had become a monarch among monarchs, but more, for he claimed his sword was over all the rest. His envoys were in every Court, his spies knew all, his will was broadcast from a thousand pulpits, his coffers held more treasure than the storehouses of individual kings. In reaction to this, the theory had developed that a Pope must be offset. A

Council must serve as countervail, otherwise the doubly ruling papal sovereign was too strong.

After a month here on his Rock, Benedict was told of the *Journey*
Capitulation of Narbonne. At Narbonne, December 13, *to the*
1415, Aragon, Castile, Navarre and the Comtat of Foix— *Other Rock*
their purpose being to end the estrangement of Spain from
the Council of Constance—agreed to close the Schism either
by the Way of Cession or by deposition from the throne.
They answered for Benedict's safety, should he present himself before the Council of Constance, in his going, staying
and coming back. After this Capitulation King Ferdinand
sent to the Rock yet again and had his answer again: anathema and deposition for Ferdinand.

This Capitulation of Narbonne was the real collapse of
Benedict's temporal power, and it had been brought on by
the traitor of Aragon. Finally only Scotland was left—comfort as cold as that country itself. Even on the Rock, Ferdinand's soldiers blockaded Benedict, keeping out news and
food. The Pope's people drifted away. One Cardinal (later
none; still later he named more) and some twenty officers
of his Curia, were left; and always the faithful nephew,
Rodrigo de Luna. At one moment, readying his galleys to
escape, Benedict made as if he were going overland, to give
in to King Ferdinand. For a while, the blockade eased.

The ailing Ferdinand then set out for Castile, where various prelates loyal to Benedict had delayed the conciliatory
delegation to Constance. Ferdinand worsened on the way
and suddenly could go no farther; nine days passed and on
April 2, 1416, he was dead. Yet another of Benedict's be-
trayers and foes struck down. Ferdinand had withdrawn his
obedience, and had died. Benedict had seen many such
proofs, in his nine decades of life, that Heaven was with
him. He forgot that his friends had died as well.

The Council of Constance went on, session after momentous session, and Benedict paced the summit of the Rock.

All that time, two years and four months from when Constance had got rid of his two rivals in 1415 till the day it elected Martin V, he, Benedict, had been the only Pope. But Constance had proved unable to settle the Urbanist-Clementine question, the nub of the Great Schism of the West. Also, Benedict was Spain, his rulers were Spain, and Constance would not vote for Spain. Benedict often remembered the time in Perpignan when Sigismund had come wooing him as Pope; begging him to abdicate—and you cannot abdicate what you do not possess.

By now it was early spring, 1417. Benedict was eighty-nine years old. The castle lookout brought him instant notice of two envoys from Constance who had appeared at the base of the Rock: two Benedictine monks. They were confronted by Rodrigo de Luna at the head of two hundred knights.

On the following day, Benedict received the two monks. The Pope sat in his audience hall on the upthrust peak of the Rock. About him were at this time three Cardinals, some Bishops, and other officers, besides some hundreds of persons, both men and women, crowding the hall. As a way was cleared for the black-robed envoys and they were approaching the throne, Benedict joked with the prelates beside him:

"Two ravens," he inquired, "flying back to the Ark?"

The monks read off their message from the Council of Constance. Benedict listened at first, but anger boiled within him and he struck the arm of his chair.

"No!" he shouted. "The Church is not at Constance! It is here at Peñiscola! They call me heretic. They say I prevent union because I will not deliver the Church into their hands! Tell them they are heretics, not I. Tell them for me, I will never deliver up the Church!"

Although eligible for punishment since they brought bad news, the monks were not too concerned about getting

safely back to Constance: this Pope was not known as
cruel, or a torturer. Stolidly, and having expected nothing
different, they asked if that was Benedict's official reply. He
let them wait a day or so and gave them their answer again,
in substance thus: he did not recognize the Council of Constance; it was not ecumenical; he annulled all it had done,
since it had no authority to act; Constance was in schism.
He acknowledged only the Council he himself had convoked
at Perpignan.

It was after the two monks had returned with this answer
that Constance tried Benedict *in absentia* and "deposed"
him on July 26, 1417.

Constance declared Pedro de Luna among other things
"a man rejected of God," forbade him "to represent himself
as Pope," absolved all Christians of oaths sworn to him
before, and cut off any man, ecclesiastic or lay, who should
support him or give him asylum, "on pain of being deprived
of their benefices . . ."

With this, Constance tried to close the books on the
Great Schism of the West. And yet, even in our times,
Catholic doctrine refers to Benedict XIII as "Pope in his
obedience."

31 THE QUINCE-AND-HONEY PASTY

NEW KING ALFONSO V of Aragon was allied with the Orsinis over in Rome, whereas Pope Martin's family, being Colonnas, were against the Orsinis. Alfonso, therefore, did what he could to help his fellow Aragonese, Pope Benedict, who was against the man who was against the Orsinis. For example he delayed a public proclamation of Benedict's condemnation by the Council of Constance.

Meanwhile like so many others before him, Pope Martin V tried and tried again to do away with Benedict XIII. He sent a legate, Cardinal Adimari, to Alfonso, and the two having conferred they appointed yet another of those eternal commissions to betake themselves to Benedict and prevail upon him to renounce his tiara.

The chosen envoy this time was Leonardo de la Caballería. On the same throne, in the same great Gothic hall where he had received the Ravens from Constance, frail, weary, scarred with the years, but Pope, Benedict awaited him, and as Leonardo knelt, extended his arms in welcome.

Leonardo brought with him promises of both noble rank and fortune: welcome to the Church's bosom, fifty thousand florins a year, peace and the secure enjoyment of his collection of over a thousand books (housed there at Peñiscola), freedom to live wherever he wished in Aragon, and the same benefices they already enjoyed for those of his Court. A magnanimous Pope Martin, a generous King Alfonso, thus approached the nonagenarian holed up on his Rock.

Silent, Benedict heard them out. Then the old man rose
carefully from his throne and was helped from the audience
chamber. He went away into a separate room, the room
called his study, with its rounded ceiling, its long window
giving on the sea. The thudding waves were sometimes
quite loud in this study in the sky. He could look way down
over huddled roofs and see headlands to the south. Muffled
human sounds rose up to him; the Rock was on occasion a
sort of beehive humming with voices. One might hear a
guard laugh or a rooster crowing.

After his meditation and prayer, he stood for a moment
in his summit courtyard. Over the wall, down the side of the
rock, he had a way out: steps leading almost vertically into
the waves. Below him, in the air, a hawk was fixed.

He had olive trees and cypresses and other plantings here,
against the warm ivory of walls that partially enclosed this
court. What stately, mournful grandeur in this place. There
was a point of windless quiet here, in the center of the court
itself, but always from without, this peak was buffeted by
winds, winds that could never wear away such walls. How
wide the gap between the man who lived on such a peak
and the ones who crawled over the flatlands down below.
How impregnable a man felt up here, how right his cause.

Standing in his courtyard, Pope Benedict answered the
delegation from the Pope of Constance and the King:

"This that you ask," he told Leonardo, "this is a thing we
cannot do. For we, and we alone, are the true and valid
Pope."

And so it came about that the enemies of Pedro de Luna,
men of their times, confronted with immovable eternity
on a dual papal throne, were left with only one way to
unriddle it all.

In his summit room, Pope Benedict had a small table on
which Domingo Álava, once canon of Saragossa, now his

steward, would put out his simple meals, together with the preserves, jellies and sweets which the Pontiff loved. Once Benedict had done, Álava would take away the boxes of confections and also what food could still be kept, and place these things under lock and key.

On a certain noonday, as he read, Benedict reached for his box of sweets, chose a pasty with a filling of quince and honey, put away his book, exchanged a few words with the hovering steward who was a long-time companion, and lay down on the couch for his usual nap. It was July, 1418.

Álava took away the remains of the meal. In a little while Pope Benedict was jolted awake. Dazed, not knowing where he was, he found himself racked by violent spasms. Somehow he got off his couch and staggered to the door, where he collapsed in a servant's arms. A crowd of familiars rushed to him, among them Álava, raising his eyes to heaven and making gestures of astonishment. They laid the Pontiff back on his couch. From the now crowded room, Álava hurried for the doctor. Basins were brought. Over a period of hours, Benedict retched and vomited. Between spasms he would lie back on his pillows, half conscious, once gone so limp and still they thought him dead. His faithful Doctor Jerónimo forced emetics down the Pontiff's throat. Had it not been for Jerónimo, the Great Schism of the West might have ended then, on that hot and endless July afternoon. Had it not been for Jerónimo, and for one other thing that the strange malady left untouched: Benedict's iron will.

A few days passed, and the Pope seemed himself again, despite his now thin diet of broth and milk. But it had been a terrible ordeal for a man ninety years old; the cure itself, which may well have included certain purges—laurel, centaury, fumitory, hellebore, catapuce, buckthorn berries, herb ivy were of the day—and a strong diuretic and the rubbing of the Pope's skin with counter-irritants, was drastic enough.

Benedict, obviously, was getting no younger, and after

nine decades, illness is often a man's lot. It was Rodrigo de
Luna who first suspected the truth, and his suspicions were
immediately confirmed when two men disappeared from
Peñiscola: one was the Pope's steward, Domingo Álava, the
other his associate, a Benedictine monk from the Monastery
of Bañolas, a certain Brother Palacio Calvet.

The agents of Rodrigo soon apprehended the fugitives
and dragged them back to the dungeon at Peñiscola to be
"questioned." Questioned first, Álava confessed that he had
been seduced by Brother Palacio—who came offering two
Church offices, twenty thousand florins in cash, promises
from Cardinal Adimari, legate of Pope Martin, and the
argument that Pope Benedict was prolonging the Great
Schism—to tamper with the Pontiff's food. The monk had
then given over to Álava a quantity of poisonous material
extracted from herbs, which he said he had obtained from
Adimari, and showed Álava how to disguise its taste in a
filling of quince and honey, of which Benedict was known
to be particularly fond. Only the fact that Álava, in his
clumsiness, had mixed too heavy a dose, thus inducing almost immediate vomiting which quickly rid the Pope's system of the poison, had saved Benedict's life.

As for Brother Palacio, the mere threat of being questioned secured a confession from him, and the link with
Adimari was established.

This scandal rocked Aragon. Everyone knew that Pope
Benedict had refused Cardinal Adimari's overtures, made
on behalf of Pope Martin, to renounce the Papacy. They
knew as well that Aragon's clergy (whom Adimari had assembled at Lerida to repudiate Benedict) had turned Adimari down. A letter from the Archbishop of Crete now
reached the Synod of Lerida, openly charging Pope Martin
with attempted murder of the Clementine Pope. From
Benedict's Court went a detailed account of the poisoning,
addressed to the Bishop of Valencia (and now in the crown

records of Aragon). Pope Benedict himself pointed at Pope Martin in a Bull which he sent out on November 13, 1418. "Like a page of classical Latin literature it read," said one admirer of its Ciceronian heights.

Cardinal Adimari did not improve matters by calling the delegates at Lerida "barbarians, infidels, and Devils." The Synod responded with an indignant committee of twenty-four, demanding an explanation of these terms, whereupon the Cardinal denied having used them: he had been misquoted, or his words had been taken out of context. Because the Synod was rapidly leaking away, Adimari declared it over, but not before he had his secretary read out to them the sentence of Constance, declaring Benedict heretic, schismatic and deposed. As an extra, Adimari levied on the Aragonian clergy a tax of sixty thousand florins to defray the expenses of persecuting their beleaguered Pontiff and anyone else who should reject Martin V. The Synod only moved to condemn Martin's Legate to Martin himself, and disbanded.

With justice or not, Martin's Legate, Cardinal Adimari, was believed a murderer, and there was yet another pendulum swing toward Benedict. If Benedict was such an obstacle that he had to be put out of the way at any cost, even by murder, then there must be something to what the old man said and kept on saying about being the rightful Pope. Besides, the poison had not worked. Did that not prove that God was on the side of Benedict XIII?

Cardinal Adimari fled for his life. He went to the King of Aragon in Barcelona and babbled about false charges, but found Alfonso a poor listener, for the King cried out: "You could hardly bring peace to the Church by such a crime!"

Adimari, terrified of Rodrigo de Luna, hurried out of the country. As for the poisoning, a trial was held in Saragossa the year following, after which a pyre was raised on the narrow strip of land joining Peñiscola to the shore. And on this, for his role in the attempted murder of the Pope, Palacio Calvet was burned to death.

Álava the steward was spared, because he told them of a circumstance which satisfactorily explained all the facts: Brother Palacio had worked on his mind with necromancy and had put him under a spell.

To POPE MARTIN's dismay, Pope Benedict, there on his Rock, continued to function as head of the Church. Aragon had come back to him *de facto*, and he still had Scotland till October, 1418. Armagnac and other pockets maintained allegiance. On April 20, 1419, it was Pope Benedict who granted the Count of Armagnac, Jean IV, a dispensation so that he could marry his cousin, Isabelle of Navarre, without committing incest. When their baby son was christened, it was Pope Benedict who provided the consecrated oil. A Bull of Martin's, dated September 14, 1419, admitted that Benedict had most of Languedoc and Guyenne.

They say that Alfonso V, the new King of Aragon, dickered at one time with Martin to hand over Benedict—Popes being legal tender then—for such amenities as the cession in perpetuity by Martin of all the benefices of Sicily and Sardinia. Negotiations having broken down, Alfonso turned loyal to the Pope of the Rock. In any case he was now more than ever Benedict's man.

Pope Martin then preached a crusade against Pope Benedict, offering all who should attack their fellow Catholics at Peñiscola the same Indulgences once extended to those attempting to wrest the Holy Land from the Muslims. No one responded and the crusade collapsed.

As for Benedict's Armagnac connection, it would have a curious outcome. In 1420 his Vicar General there was Jean Carrier, collector of a huge pile of records on the Great

Schism of the West and historian of that complicated disaster. When Pope Martin declared Jean contumacious, Jean felt the time was ripe to look for a more martyrdom-proof abode. He chose the unsubduable Castle of Tourène, founded on rocks that rise up sheer over the steep, narrow gorge of the Viaur. After Jean took refuge there and Pope Martin's Nuncio laid siege to him, people dubbed the place Peñiscolette (Little Peñiscola). Like Benedict's Rock of Peñiscola, this castle too was a factor in lengthening out the Great Schism of the West. Meanwhile the Count of Armagnac, Jean IV, hardly bothered to open Pope Martin's letters, much less answer them.

Martin kept right on issuing commands to Jean Carrier, the beleaguered Vicar General of Benedict XIII. On November 28, 1422, Carrier was given ninety days to appear out of his impregnable fortress and be declared a heretic.

Meanwhile in 1420, as Spain was laughing at Martin and satires flew from mouth to mouth with the all too familiar charge of simony, it looked as if Pope Benedict would find a champion in King Alfonso, who put out to sea with twenty-five galleys to conquer Sardinia. The King of Aragon indeed "pacified" Sardinia and sailed on. We next find Joanna II of Naples adopting this King as her son and heir. Unfortunately, instead of marching on Rome to benefit Pope Benedict, Alfonso determined to inherit Naples right away. He was bundling the attractive Queen off somewhere when the populace, commanded by one of Joanna's innumerable lovers, a man named Sforza, trounced six thousand of Alfonso's men. Whereupon Alfonso burned Naples, which lost him his new mother. Joanna not only went over to Pope Martin but adopted Louis III of Anjou in Alfonso's place. Seeing how the wind blew, Alfonso then took to his galleys and pointed them due west. When Pope Benedict heard of it, he knew that his own road to Rome was closed forever.

And not only his road to Rome. News of the returning galleys darkened what were to be Benedict's last days up there on the peak of his wave-jarred, sun-battered Rock. Ever since 1378, his life pattern had been an astonishing succession of ups and downs. He had never had a logical reason to give up hope: in what looked like the depths, he had always been succored, perhaps by a new ally, or some reversing event, or even—and not to be laughed at—a favorable omen. Always, before, there had been hope.

Benedict was ninety-five years old. He was, in himself, a book, a chronicle of almost a full hundred years. If one imagines that some of those who trained him had been sixty in 1328, the year he was born, and some who had trained his trainers had been, perhaps, seventy in 1268, one can see his immediate experience reaching as far back as the twelfth century, and him still lasting on, well into the fifteenth. Such arithmetic, of course, can be true of anyone, but Benedict was not anyone; his was a predestinating life.

These days, probably his depression was physical (he did not recover rapidly, as he used to, and he had never felt right since the poisoning), Pedro de Luna took to remaining indoors. He did not pace his summit any more, or look eastward or westward over the empty sea: the vacant blue water that he could, at will, people with victorious sails, coming to throne him again, coming to exalt him before all mankind, so that all might know what he himself knew, and all might acknowledge what they assured him when they set the tiara on his brows so long ago: "Receive this tiara adorned with the three crowns and know that you are Father of Princes and Kings, Ruler of the world and Vicar on earth of Jesus Christ . . ." That blue infinity stayed empty now, slow day after slow day.

In the body's strange journey, his emaciated, bowed-over form was coming close to its wished-for reunion with the ground. Days on end, he would not leave his bed. If he did

stir and try to rise, two of his companions held him under
the arms to be crutches for him, as his legs had gone very
weak. Against the pillow, they watched his waiting face, the
face of a traveler in some vehicle that slowly approaches a
goal. The fierce, eagle-like nose jutted from hollowed cheeks;
the bony jaw held firm; if an eyelid opened, a ray pierced
out.

For a period, Pope Benedict had no Cardinals at all.
Three of his renegades had voted separately for Pope Martin, at Martin's direction. It was a gesture of dubious worth:
if Martin was valid, their votes added nothing; if invalid,
he had no right to summon them to a conclave. A fourth
joined Martin, and soon after died; then two of the others
died—three dead out of four. Benedict's people saw in this
either the hand of God or of Martin V.

A long time passed. Benedict may quite reasonably have
turned against Cardinals in general, for he named nobody;
at worst they might betray him, at best might wish to be
consulted. Not till 1422 in the autumn did he appoint
four new ones, and then only because at long last he was
matched with a power as patient, as implacable as he was
himself.

Two of his Cardinals were by him, up there on the Rock.
As they stood at his bedside, they swore an oath: once their
Ruler had left them, they would hold a Conclave and elect
his successor, the third Clementine Pope. Those two he had
now elevated were Juliano de Loba and Xímeno Dahe, both
of Aragon; the others were two absent Frenchmen. Benedict
sent off trusted messengers to one of these, Dominique de
Bonnefoi, telling of his elevation; and to the Count of
Armagnac he addressed a letter announcing the Cardinalate
of the other, Jean Carrier, and asking that Jean Carrier proceed at once to Peñiscola. This the new Cardinal Carrier
was unable to do, besieged as he then was by Pope Martin's
legate at Peñiscolette; and when he ultimately did appear

at Peñiscola his coming served only to extend the Great Schism.

Some say the naming of the Cardinals took place in November, 1422, but others say it was May of the following year. The problem arises because no one knows exactly when Benedict died: November 29, 1422 (the date accepted by Valois) or May 23, 1423. Benedict named the Cardinals, historians say, two days before his death; and according to his register, they were appointed November 27, 1422.

It finally happened toward evening, on that lonely summit that thrusts into the sky. It was a day like other days: like the waves following one another down there, it was one of an endless series, repeated forever. It had been exactly the same before Benedict came to this place and made it his lair, exactly the same before the Phoenicians came. And so it would dawn again after Benedict died, a week after, or five and a half centuries after.

He lay, thin and light, his old bones hardly raising the bedclothes. He recognized the people watching beside him and spoke their names. Whether it was autumn or spring down there on the flatlands we cannot say; up here the sun was declining in the vacant circle of heaven; below, the waves slammed against the rocks under the castle walls. He must, as the dark came on, have looked at his two new Cardinals who were to perpetuate his line, and held fast to the hand of Francisco de Aranda, who had stood by him through many a long year.

For years, Benedict's old bones slept in the crypt of his sky-high chapel that gives onto the terrace courtyard of Peñiscola. In 1430, Rodrigo and Juan de Luna got permission from King Alfonso to take the body away. There was the usual rumor at the unsealing of the crypt, of a fragrance seeping out and down into the town; then the tomb was

opened and Pope Benedict lay in the light, looking exactly
as he had looked the day they buried him. His vestments,
however, crumbled away in the air, as did a parchment that
had been placed beneath his head.

By night, they moved the immovable. They took him
away inland, over the barren mountains. They passed walls
built up with stones, and olive trees and huddled settle-
ments. They came alongside the fortress of Morella, tilting
blackly over them, hewn from its mountain top: here he
had been, to meet King Ferdinand. Donkeys passed, bundles of olive branches with legs and ears. In places the soil
was yellowish, and lumpy sheep looked like yellow rocks.
The de Lunas climbed to a peak, sank to lesser hills, passed
by harsh boulders, reached orchard slopes. Alive, he too had
jolted along these weary miles; now he was turning home.

They came to the River Jalón, and high up there on its
shelf, giving on mile upon mile of bare mountain and sky,
they could see, fronting over the plain, a giant rectangle of
a castle, the austere and noble palace of Illueca, where
Pedro de Luna was born.

They came to a network of dusty lanes. From the little
square, with its village fountain, a lane led steeply to their
journey's end. Up they rode, their mounts' hoofs slipping,
the cart with the coffin eased carefully up; dismounted;
ushered him back, through the massive Romanesque portal,
the same one he had left, had walked out of erect and strong
so long ago, with that row of carved faces above it—a human
face, openmouthed, and some lion faces—passed inside, and
slowly, carefully, up the dark stone steps. They carried him
to the very room where he was born and lit a lamp there,
to be kept burning day and night.

Not for Pedro de Luna, condemned as a heretic, to be
buried in holy ground.

In 1537 an Italian prelate named Porro visited that room,
and saw how people even from far away climbed the steep

lanes to the palace and paid their respects to the mummi-
fied body under its glass. Porro raised his heavy walking stick
and smashed it down on the crystal coffin, then had to run
for his life. After that the room was closed by the Archbishop of Saragossa, and visits forbidden. In the eighteenth
century, though, a Father Lamberto saw lights burning
there.

In 1811 a good many de Lunas were massacred trying,
typically against all odds, to defend their castle during the
War of the Succession. The French attackers then looted
Illueca, shattered the coffin with their rifle butts, hacked up
the remains and hurled the lot over the Castle wall. Old
bone and bits of leathery skin vanished in the dry bushes
of the ravine below; but peasants found and saved the head.

This head survived. Then it had to be buried during the
Spanish Civil War in 1936—and was tucked away so hastily
that it became a casualty of the war: it still exists, they say,
in the palace of the Counts of Argillo y Morata at Sabiñan;
exists only as a dull red skull, with the right eye still in the
socket.

Ignored, desecrated, blotted out, Benedict XIII still chal-
lenges the world through that one eye. He has never really
been forgotten. Friends of his, the university faculties and
students of Saragossa, in 1923 commemorated his passing
five centuries before: in the high chapel on the Rock, where
his bones had lain, they placed a tablet of gray marble
which bears, besides floral designs and his arms (his tiara,
his keys, his inverted moon), words including these: *El*
gran Aragones . . . de vida limpia . . . austera . . . gene-
rosa . . . sacrificada por una idea del deber. And his friends
added, significantly to some, that the secrets of history
would be disclosed on Judgment Day.

Visitors to that chapel in the sky could hear, not long
ago, an angry tapping there. A high window stands at the

end of the chapel, opposite the Cross; something loose was
banging out there in the wind, surely it was that, not the
angry tapping of an old man's cane. As the sound monotonously went on, the harsh, insistent tapping demanding to
be heard, the visitors noticed that the Cross, which had
been straight before, was leaning to one side. Vaguely un-
comfortable, one of them straightened the Cross, and they
went out to the courtyard of the summit, and looked, as
Pedro de Luna had looked, questing a thousand times, far
out and down across the empty water—green that day like
folds of Kashan velvet, brought by merchants from over the
sea.

PART SIX

THE LINGERING ECHOES

33   ONE IS THREE AGAIN

O FF THE TERRACE of the Castle summit at
Peñiscola, down a flight of stairs, is a long room with a
barrel-shaped ceiling where you hear the wind buffeting
very strong above the sea. Here in the center of the floor
a ladder sinks through a narrow opening to yet another,
deeper room—a prison, a treasury, who knows? The Castle
is full of surprises—deep holes, high ledges, mysterious steps,
some so narrow you would have to go up them sideways,
walls many feet thick, chambers dark and bare.

On June 20, 1423, there in that long narrow room below
the terrace, faithful to their promise, three of Benedict's
Cardinals entered into Conclave: specifically, met and wran-
gled, each with a different vote in his mind. Arguments
were giving way to insults when the gallant (and practical)
Rodrigo de Luna stepped to the door. He reminded the
Cardinals that Gil Muñoz, whom they had been considering because he dated back to the election of Urban VI, was
a long-time Clementine and had transmitted messages from
the King of Aragon to themselves—and that this Gil was
possessed of twenty thousand or perhaps even thirty thousand florins.

Promptly thereafter, Muñoz was elected and began to
reign as third Clementine Pope, Clement VIII, although
he put off his coronation for three years, until May 19, 1426.

And then there was the "Hidden Pope."
On December 12, 1423, Benedict's fourth Cardinal, Jean   291

Carrier, having finally extricated himself from the Castle of Tourène (Peñiscolette), arrived at Peñiscola. Before climbing that summit he made his way to a notary and wrote out a legal protest to the effect that his visit in no sense constituted recognition by him of Pope Clement VIII.

He came, saw, and declared the election of Clement VIII invalid. The three other Cardinals, he said, were guilty of simony and of yielding to pressure; this automatically deprived them of their right to engage in another election, which fact left him, Jean Carrier, the only person who could legally elect the successor to Benedict XIII.

He claimed the three Cardinals had concealed the death of Benedict for six months, had used his papal seal for their own purposes, and enriched themselves from the treasury. He affirmed that Gil Muñoz, otherwise Clement VIII, was the vilest of sinners; that at the moment he was chosen Pope, a fetid odor had spread throughout the Conclave; also that a goat had been seen by night on the terrace of the castle, a certain proof—if more were needed—that the Devil was at work.

Clement VIII, he said, was invalid for the same reason Urban VI had been invalid: pressure brought to bear on the Conclave. Martin V could not be Pope either, because he was an excommunicated person, and also because his election had been uncanonical: for the Conclave that elected Martin was adulterated—composed not of Cardinals alone but also of representatives of the Council of Constance. This meant, Carrier said, that there was no Pope at all and only one man on earth to elect the next one: Jean Carrier.

On November 12, 1425, the Cardinal entered into a one-man Conclave. Why he delayed action two years, during which time Pope Martin and Pope Clement reigned on, is not known. At any event, he now conferred with himself, presumably burned no ballots, reached his decision, and directed his chaplain to say a Mass of the Holy Ghost. Wit-

nesses and a notary were called in, and the election of the
new Pope was duly recorded. A man is no less right because
millions think otherwise, and Jean Carrier believed that his
act was just. If it be claimed that all this was illegal, so was
the Council of Constance.

Cardinal Jean Carrier had reached outside the Conclave
for his choice. The Pope he named, Bernard Garnier, who
became Benedict XIV, was a Frenchman, a native of
Guyenne; little else is known of him, for he served out his
ministry in secret, as the "Hidden Pope."

After the election, Cardinal Carrier says that he emulated
Paul at Damascus (Acts 9:25) which would indicate that
he was lowered over the walls of Peñiscola in a basket. He
disappeared by night, and hurried to France, where he
sought refuge with the Count of Armagnac.

After the coronation of Clement VIII in 1426, Alfonso V
of Aragon, who had forbidden his realms to any envoy of
Pope Martin of Constance, reluctantly embarked on negotiations with him. Barbed words had been exchanged
between the King and Pope Martin for some years, but
enough was enough; and one day, just before King Alfonso
rode off at the head of an army to make war in Castile, and
while his horse pawed impatiently under him, he agreed to
the abdication of the Clementine.

On July 26, 1429, the now defenseless Clement VIII,
with all dignity, mounted his throne at Peñiscola. He revoked all the decrees passed either by himself or by Pope
Benedict against Otto Colonna, Pope Martin of Constance.
He said that he had accepted to succeed Benedict XIII only
in the hope of securing peace for the Church, and that had
the opportunity been offered earlier, he would have accomplished his purpose sooner. To these words he added, with
probably equivalent respect for the truth, that he was abdi-
cating of his own free will and at the solicitation of none.

One condition, however, he laid down: that he would abdicate provided the Church recognized Benedict XIII as a
valid Pope. This Clement VIII was obliged to do—otherwise, Benedict's Cardinals would be invalid, he himself
would be invalid, and his abdication quite meaningless.
Thereupon, Clement abdicated, and when next seen, was
wearing the dress of a lay doctor.

Meanwhile he had asked his Cardinals to proceed with
a new election, and with no difficulty these had found themselves agreed on Otto Colonna, already known for a dozen
previous years as Martin V. Thus, for all practical purposes,
ended the Great Schism of the West.

The former Clement VIII lived out his life obscurely,
dying at a very advanced age in 1447.

In any event, almost twelve years after the election of
Martin V at Constance, there were still three Popes—Martin himself, Clement VIII and Benedict XIV. And following Clement's abdication in 1429 there were still two, as
Martin and the "Hidden Pope" divided the tiara.

M Y DEAREST LADY,'' wrote the Count of
Armagnac to Joan of Arc, "there are three contenders for
the Papacy: one lives at Rome, who calls himself Martin V,
to whom all the Christian Kings obey; a second lives at
Peñiscola who calls himself Pope Clement VIII; for the
third, no one knows where he lives except the Cardinal of
Saint-Étienne [Jean Carrier] and a few other persons with
him; he names himself Pope Benedict XIV. . . . May you
implore our Lord Jesus Christ that through His infinite
mercy He may declare to us through you, who among these
three is the true Pope and which . . . we ought to believe
in, either secretly, or by some dissimulation, or a public
declaration. For we all stand ready to do the will and pleasure of our Lord . . ."

Joan, eighteen years old, tall and lithe, all in white armor,
her great white banner spangled with fleur-de-lys, was about
to march on English-occupied Paris. As the letter was
handed over they were calling for her to mount her battle
horse. Her men were ten thousand thieves, eager to be off.
Joan, to keep her soldiers from throwing the messenger into
the river, made only a brief comment and then hurriedly
dictated a reply, her note being dated August 22, 1429 (by
which time Clement VIII had abdicated, reducing the
choice of Popes to two).

"Of this matter," she wrote, "I cannot well make known
to you the truth at present, until I shall be in Paris or elsewhere at peace. For I am at present too much prevented by

295

the business of war. But when you learn that I am at Paris, send me a message and I shall make you to know in truth which one you should believe in, and you will have knowledge of it through the advice of my rightful, sovereign Lord, the King of all the world."

The Council of Constance might never have met. Joan did not say with the Council: the true Pope is Martin V. Not the Council but the Voices of the Maid would know who was Pope. Could this be why Martin let them destroy her? He was reigning Pontiff as she marched on Paris, for he lived on till February 20, 1431, three months before "the English" sent her up in flames: and he was the best-informed ruler of his time.

An English historian, sickened by that age, writes of its clergy in "curled hair and hanging sleeves," diverting the greed of the nobles away from the Church to war, which meant to brigandage and slaughter; of the high-minded Lollards stamped out; of the Parliaments "like armed camps," their meetings mere sittings of the nobles' retainers (at the "Club Parliament" in 1426, these retainers shouldered clubs); of belief reduced to sorcery and magic. He finds only "one pure figure . . . Joan of Arc." And he adds that everybody in England held her for a witch.

France's Charles VII, the son, he hoped, of mad King Charles—dead since 1422—was weeping at Chinon. He was scornfully called the King of Bourges. North France was a desert; the ravaging English with their upright longbow, that Welsh "crooked stick with the gray goose wing," and its rapid discharge, each archer behind his own sharp palisade, were victorious now as they had so often been since Crécy in 1346. Eleven thousand Frenchmen, a hundred of them princes and lords, had died in 1415 on the field at Agincourt. Peasants, jamming into famished towns, were thrust outside and became either corpses or brigands; at

Rouen, then the largest and richest city of France, twelve
thousand had been thus pushed out, to agonize between the
trenches and the walls; when the moribund women gave
birth down there, the newborn were "drawn up in baskets
to receive baptism, then lowered again to die at their
mothers' breasts. . . . Misery and disease killed a hundred
thousand in Paris alone."

It was at such a time that the Archangel Michael appeared to Jeannette d'Arc in a blaze of light, and commanded her to seek out King Charles VII and give him
back his throne.

Joan's father threatened to drown her, and the priest was
deaf. "I must go to the King if I wear off my legs to the
knees," Joan told them. "This is no work of my choosing,
but my Lord wills it."

"And who is your Lord?" they asked her.

She answered: "He is God."

Somehow she got to Chinon, and picked Charles out of
a crowd, when they had put another man on the throne
to trick her. For another sign, she exposed to Charles his
secret doubt—which was that, knowing his mother, he was
not sure he knew his father. She told him from her Voices
that he was lawful heir to France.

Charles thereupon gave her armor, a horse and men and
she rode toward Orléans, and unopposed, passed into the
city through the English lines. The English battled, gave
up and retreated.

She returned to Charles, by then amusing himself at
Tours. He must come to Reims, the Maid told him. Every
French King must be crowned where Clovis was baptized;
without the crowning by the Archbishop at Reims, France
did not hold a man as King.

The enemy, Charles well knew, stood between him and
Reims, but in the days of her mission men did as Joan said
they must. On the road, near Patay, the English blocked

them. "We will fight," Joan said. "We will have the god-
dams, though they hang from the clouds!" She fought and
won.

Incredibly, impossibly, she had Charles crowned at
Reims; holding her banner she stood by in the Cathedral
and watched it done. When she was blamed, later on, for
bringing her flag into church, the Maid had an answer: "It
bore witness to the battle," she told them; "it is only right
it should bear witness to the glory."

Her Divine work now finished, Joan longed to ride against
Islam. But she turned and fought the English again, got
her second wound before Paris, went on to defend Com-
piègne. Outside these walls, shepherding the rear guard,
Joan was unhorsed. She could not remount. Her people
saved themselves and shut the city gates.

The Duke of Burgundy sold his prize to the English, the
Bishop of Beauvais (Pierre Cauchon), buying her on his
own behalf and that of the King of England for ten thousand francs. In Rouen, English territory then, she was tried
as heretic and witch, and where Pope Martin was during her
long ordeal—he lived till February, 1431—we do not know.
We do know that his messengers were everywhere, cease-
lessly coming and going.

"What say you of the Pope?" her judges asked her, on
March 1. "Which of them do you hold for true?"

Joan answered: "Are there two?"

And they thrust before her the letter she had written to
the Count of Armagnac.

It was not all of her own dictation, Joan swiftly countered. It should be read in the context of her oral statement
to the messenger. Under oath, she accepted Martin V as
Pope, having received no revelation otherwise. But this was
not enough, in fact it was too much, for her accusers were
not looking to try her, but were compiling legal reasons for
burning her alive—one of many good reasons being this, that

Joan had dared to promise at some future time to receive, direct from God, and make known the truth, about the Great Schism of the West.

Joan was at last handed over, as humanity will never forget, to the "secular arm," that arm at Rouen being the English. Yet Joan knew who had killed her. As her eyes fell on the Bishop in those final minutes, she called out in a terrible voice: "*Évêque, je meurs par vous!* Bishop, at your hands I die!"

Long after, it was only to still the taunts of the English, who cried that Charles owed his throne to her spells, that King Charles cleared the name of Joan of Arc; so explained the Archbishop of Reims, in his letter to Jean d'Aulon, Joan's old companion at arms.

The year Joan was destroyed, all except her heart, because it would not burn, a poet was born in France. Villon grew up to write a "Ballad of the Ladies of Long Ago," and in this Ballad, which time has kept, Joan was neither heretic, harlot nor witch. France was as guiltless of her death as the Church. It was the English who killed her. These are among the lines Villon wrote, when he was looking into the past for ladies who had disappeared:

> *Where is that wise Héloïse*
> *For whose love Abélard once yearned,*
> *Till, castrate, to a monk he turned?* . . .
> *Where Archippa, where Thaïs,*
> *She to Archippa close akin?*
> *Or Queen Blanche, white like fleur-de-lys,*
> *Whose siren singing drew men on;*
> *And good Jehanne, out of Lorraine,*
> *That in Rouen the English burned?*
> *Where are they now, O Heaven's Queen?*
> *Where are the snows of long-dead winters gone?*

35 AND STILL MORE BLOOD

ND WHAT OF Cardinal Jean Carrier, he of the one-man Conclave, and Benedict XIV, his Hidden Pope? The Cardinal was captured in 1433 and held prisoner by its noble Lord in the Castle of Foix. He never abjured his faith in Benedict XIV as the only Pope in the true Succession; to him, the fact that Benedict had only a few followers was irrelevant.

Then Benedict XIV died, but not before naming Jean Farald as Cardinal. And this Jean Farald, feeling obliged in his turn to fill all by himself the vacancy in the Holy See, elected Cardinal Jean Carrier as Pope.

Cardinal Carrier thereafter assumed the style of his predecessor, and reigned on in his cell as Pope Benedict XIV the Second. Dying excommunicate, he was refused Church services and his body was shoveled into a grave at the foot of a rock.

A document made public by Valois shows that even this death did not close the books on the Great Schism of the West.

In the village of Coulet, parish of Montou (Canton of Rodez), not far from the Château of Tourène which had been the haunt of Jean Carrier, there lived a blacksmith called Jean Trahinier. About the year 1431, the village people began to notice that the blacksmith and his family avoided the parish church of Montou, and to receive the Sacraments would go over to the neighboring hamlets of

Cadoulette or Murat. The reason for this, it later became
known, was that the curé of Montou acknowledged Martin V as Pope, while in the other two villages the Trahinier
family could find priests of their own belief. These were
Jean Moysset, Guillaume Noalhac, de Jouqueviel and Jean
Farald—the same who was named Cardinal by the Hidden
Pope.

The Trahiniers believed that once Benedict XIII was
dead, the legitimate Pope had become the hidden Benedict XIV, otherwise Bernard Garnier, former Sacristan of
Rodez. As for Martin V, they considered him merely one
more antipope in the series produced by the Schism. In
speaking of Martin the Trahiniers would use the term *"Arri,
Marti!"* (Gee-hup, Martin!)—in their case occupationally
apt, and indeed a well-known medieval appellation for a
donkey.

Then, around 1446, Pierre Trahinier, the blacksmith's
son, found himself on the wrong side of the Inquisition. He
was jailed, promised to obey the Pope of Rome and was
released. No doubt this episode determined the family's
future for the next twenty years, because Father Jean, his
sons Pierre and Baptiste, and the daughter Jeanne, left
home to wander here and there for over two decades. The
gorges of the Viaur are full of caves, and the family lived
sometimes in these holes, sometimes in the woods. They
went out only at night, avoiding the roads. Friends helped
to feed them, and now and then one of the sons would get
a day's work. On occasion they would all hold a meeting
with the priests of their persuasion, and only at such times
approached the Sacraments. It was thus that one night,
about 1465, they took Communion in a wood at the hands
of Cardinal Jean Farald; he had brought along two consecrated Hosts between the pages of a book, and the Trahinier
family supplied fire, candles and a cloth.

But the Trahiniers grew careless and after living fifteen

months in the mill at La Solairie, early in 1467 they were all arrested, except for Baptiste, and thrown into the prison of Rodez. On April 17 of that year they were brought to trial.

These poor people stood firm in the presence of their judges. They said they had heard tell of the Ecumenical Council at Constance, but to them the Council's censure of Benedict XIII was of no significance. The only Pope they now recognized was Jean Carrier, Pope Benedict XIV the Second, and they were certain that he was still alive.

Rather than compromise their salvation by entering "the Wicked Church," the Trahiniers stated that they would give up whatever they possessed. It was Easter but they refused the Sacraments unless administered by one of their own priests. They believed in every point of Catholic doctrine, and thus were not heretics, like many who had flourished in that region. Nor did they say they had any direct revelation; the father, blacksmith Jean, indeed let the others call him "Prophet Elias," but his children did not claim he was really a Prophet.

As the trial went on, the blacksmith died. He did not recant. Then the ecclesiastical judges "paternally" exhorted the children until finally the daughter gave up and renounced her faith. The son, however, made an appeal to the King of France. On May 25, 1467, the brother and sister, dressed in smocks on which was depicted the story of their crime, stood up in New Market Square at Rodez to hear their sentence read out in the name of the Inquisitor and the Bishop.

The dead blacksmith was declared guilty of schism and heresy; his memory was therefore condemned and his remains, which had already been thrown into a garbage and excrement pit, were to be turned over, unhygienically enough, to the secular arm—no doubt for dismemberment and burning.

The daughter, Jeanne, was to be treated mercifully, because after all she had recanted: she was sentenced merely to life imprisonment on bread and water. She was not excommunicated and the Bishop and Inquisitor reserved the right to mitigate her punishment if they saw any reason to.

The son, Pierre, being schismatic, heretic, and a lapsed member of the Church, was, like his father's dead body, delivered over to the secular arm.

Thus closes the last faint and bloodstained trail of the Great Schism of the West; closes fittingly enough with the screams of yet one more human being, killed for his beliefs. And for all the world knows, or ever may know, the true papal line broke that day or night when Jean Carrier, Benedict XIV the Second, last of the Clementine Popes, died without a successor and they bundled him away, and shoveled him under a rock, in a secret grave.

CHRONOLOGY

1328   Birth of Pedro de Luna. (See note on page 306.)

1368   Pope Gregory XI calls de Luna to Avignon.

1375   De Luna made Cardinal.

1376   Gregory XI leaves Avignon for Rome. Florence raises the Papal States against Pope Gregory XI.

1377   Gregory XI condemns the teachings of Wycliffe. Richard II becomes King of England.

1378   Gregory XI dies. In April, Bartolomeo Prignano, Archbishop of Bari, elected Pope Urban VI in Rome by a Conclave under duress. On September 20, the same Cardinals who elected Urban, elect Clement VII at Fondi. The Great Schism of the West begins.

1379   Pedro de Luna goes to Spain as Cardinal Legate to present the Clementine case.

1380   Saint Catherine of Siena dies. Charles V of France dies. His son becomes Charles VI.

1381   The Peasants' Revolt in England. Charles III of Durazzo crowns himself King of Naples.

1382   Queen Joanna I of Naples murdered.

1384   Wycliffe dies. Louis I, Duke of Anjou, dies.

1386   Pope Urban VI kills his dissident Cardinals. Ladislas becomes King of Naples.

1389   Urban VI dies. His Cardinals elect Boniface IX.

1391   The Jews are massacred in Spain.

1392   Charles VI suffers first attack of insanity.

1393   Pedro de Luna returns to France. England restricts papal power through "great" Statute of Praemunire.

1394   Clement VII dies. His Cardinals elect Pedro de Luna as Pope Benedict XIII.

1395   Dukes of Berry, Burgundy and Orléans arrive in Avignon; Benedict XIII is asked to take the Way of Cession.

1396   Truce in Hundred Years' War continued. Muslims defeat Sigismund and allied army at Nicopolis. Richard II of England marries seven-year-old Isabella of France.

1398   French withdraw obedience from Benedict XIII. He is besieged in Palace of the Popes at Avignon.

1399   Richard II deposed. Henry IV becomes King of England.

1402   Jan Huss placed in charge of Bethlehem Chapel, Prague.

1403	French restore obedience to Benedict XIII.
1404	Boniface IX dies at Rome. Innocent VII elected Urbanist Pope.
1405	Benedict XIII at Genoa.
1406	Innocent VII dies. Gregory XII elected Urbanist Pope.
1407	Louis, Duke of Orléans, supporter of Benedict XIII, murdered.
1408	Benedict XIII sails to Porto Venere. Gregory XII refuses to meet him. France declares herself neutral as between the two rival Popes.
1409	Benedict XIII holds Council of Perpignan. Council of Pisa "deposes" Gregory XII and Benedict XIII, elects Alexander V as Pisan pope. Western Christianity now divided among three Popes.
1410	Alexander V dies. John XXIII becomes Pisan Pope. Sigismund elected King of the Romans.
1413	Henry IV dies. Henry V becomes King of England.
1414	Council of Constance opened by Pope John XXIII.
1415	Council of Constance "deposes" John XXIII May 29. He then abdicates. Gregory XII abdicates. Benedict XIII sole remaining Pope. Council burns Jan Huss July 6. English defeat French at Agincourt October 25. Sigismund meets with Benedict XIII at Perpignan. Benedict XIII flees to Peñiscola.
1417	Council of Constance "deposes" Benedict XIII. On November 11, elects Cardinal Otto Colonna as Martin V. Gregory XII dies October 18.
1418	Attempt on Benedict XIII's life.
1419	Pope John XXIII (Cardinal Tusculanus) dies in Florence December 22.
1420	Treaty of Troyes. Henry V of England becomes Regent of France.
1422	November 29, possible date of Benedict XIII's death. Charles VI of France and Henry V of England die, succeeded by Charles VII and Henry VI.
1423	May 23, possible date of Benedict's death. Three of his Cardinals elect Clement VIII.
1425	Cardinal Jean Carrier elects Benedict XIV, the Hidden Pope.
1429	Clement VIII abdicates. His Cardinals elect Martin V. Joan of Arc asked by the Count of Armagnac to pronounce on the Great Schism.
1431	Joan of Arc burned alive at Rouen.
1433	Jean Carrier taken prisoner. Later becomes Pope Benedict XIV the Second and dies in prison. Exact dates uncertain.
1467	Pierre Trahinier burned at Rodez for continued adherence to the line of Benedict XIII.

NOTE: For over five centuries, 1328 was the accepted date for Pedro de Luna's birth. Then, in 1933, M. Seidlmayer published evidence in favor of 1342. This places the writer on de Luna in a difficult position: if he accepts this later date, he goes against the weight of history. He also has to compress the early career of Pedro de Luna into a very small compass. Because of the tender age at which benefices could be secured in the fourteenth century it is theoretically possible for de Luna to have held the following ecclesiastical offices successively: Canon at Vich, at Tarragona, at Huesca and at Majorca; Archdeacon at Tarazona, at Huesca, and at Saragossa; Provost at Valencia; Sacristan at Tortosa—besides studying at the University of Montpellier and making a big enough name as professor of civil and canon law to be called to the Papal court at Avignon in 1368. Yet all this would represent a considerable career for a young man of only twenty-six, especially one whose university work was interrupted by war in Aragon.

I have chosen to use 1328 as the date of Pedro de Luna's birth because it accords better with the known facts of his life. From the date of his becoming a cardinal, 1375, he appears not a relatively young man of thirty-three but rather as one of maturer years. When he speaks in 1378 at the time of Urban VI's election and again at the Spanish inquiries into the Great Schism a few years later, his words have the gravity of an older man. Also, before the election he builds a tomb, not the usual act of a man only thirty-five. Those who would make his appearance when he left Avignon in 1403 jibe with the 1342 birth date, must always portray him as aged beyond his supposed years. The testimony of his later life also belies the later birth date. Moreover he addressed his rival Pope, Gregory XII (born about 1326 and hence about eighty at the time), as one of equal longevity: "Delay not, consider our age . . ."

In any case, either birth date, 1328 or 1342, can be used without a real distortion of history. Certainly it is characteristic of the man—who lived in controversy during most of his years (whether they were eighty-one or ninety-five)—that both his birth date and the year and day of his death are disputed.

BIBLIOGRAPHY

'Abdu'l-Bahá, *Some Answered Questions*, translated from the Persian by Laura Clifford Barney. Chicago, 1918.

Altamira, Rafael, *A History of Spain*. London, 1949.

Ameer Ali, *A Short History of the Saracens*. London, 1924.

André, J. F., *Histoire de la papauté à Avignon*. Avignon, 1887.

Arnold, T. W., *The Preaching of Islam*. London, 1935.

Baddeley, St. Clair, *Charles III of Naples and Urban VI*. London, 1894.

————, *Joanna I of Naples*. London, 1893.

Bainton, Roland H., *Here I Stand: A Life of Martin Luther*. New York, 1956.

Bédier, Joseph, *Littérature française*, 2 vols. Paris, 1961.

Bemont, C., and Doucet, R., *Histoire de l'Europe au Moyen Age*. Paris, 1931.

Bonnechose, Émile de, *Réformateurs avant la réforme, XVè siècle*, 2 vols. Paris, 1860.

Bourilly, V. L., and Busquet, R., *Histoire de Provence*. Paris, 1944.

Brewer, E. Cobham, *A Dictionary of Miracles*. Philadelphia, 1884.

Bridget of Sweden, Saint, *Revelations*. London, 1873.

Browne, E. G., *A Literary History of Persia*, Vols. 1 and 2. London, 1906.

Browne, Lewis, *Since Calvary*. New York, 1931.

Cambridge Medieval History, Vols. 7 and 8. Cambridge, 1932.

Casas, Augusto, *El Papa Luna*. Barcelona, 1944.

Catherine of Siena, Saint, *Lettres*, translated by E. Cartier. Paris, 1858.

Champion, Pierre, *Vie de Charles d'Orléans*. Paris, 1911.

Christophe, J. B., *Histoire de la papauté pendant le XIVè siècle*, 2 vols. Paris, 1853.

Clamanges (Clémanges), Nicolas de, *Le Traité de la ruine de l'Église et la traduction française de 1564*, edited by A. Coville. Paris, 1936.

Copleston, F. C., *Medieval Philosophy*. New York, 1961.

Creighton, Mandell, *A History of the Papacy during the Period of the Reformation*, Vol. 1. London, 1882.

————, *Epochs of the Papacy*, 16 vols. London, 1886–1898.

Croake, James (pseud. for James Paterson), *Curiosities of Christian History Prior to the Reformation*. London, 1892.

308

Cummings, C. P., *The Revelations of Saint Birgitta*. London, 1929.

Darwin, Francis D. S., *Louis d'Orléans* (1372–1407). London, 1936.

Draper, J. W., *History of the Conflict between Religion and Science*. New York, 1898.

————, *The Intellectual Development of Europe*, 2 vols. New York, 1876.

Evans, Joan, *Life in Medieval France*. London, 1957.

Ferguson, Wallace K., *Europe in Transition*, 1300–1520. Boston, 1962.

Froissart, Jean, *Chronicles*, 2 vols., translated by Thomas Johnes. New York, 1901.

Gallotti, Jean, *Le Palais des papes*. Paris, 1949.

Gardner, Edmund G., *Saint Catherine of Siena*. London, 1907.

Gayet, Louis, *Le Grand Schisme d'Occident*, 2 vols. Florence, Berlin, 1889.

Gheon, Henri, *St. Vincent Ferrer*, translated by F. V. Sheed. London, 1939.

Gibbon, Edward, *The Decline and Fall of the Roman Empire*, 3 vols. New York: Modern Library, n.d.

Gill, Joseph, S. J., *Histoire des conciles oecuméniques*, 12 vols. Paris, 1965.

Girard, Joseph, *Évocation du vieil Avignon*. Paris, 1958.

Glasfurd, Alec, *The Antipope* (Peter de Luna, 1342–1423). New York, 1966.

Gotor, Anselmo Gascón, *Pedro de Luna, el pontífice que no cedio*. Madrid, 1956.

Green, J. R., *History of the English People*. New York, 1884.

Gregorovius, Ferdinand, *History of the City of Rome in the Middle Ages*, 10 vols., translated by A. Hamilton. London, 1894–98.

Grunebaum, G. E., *Medieval Islam*. London, 1953.

Hansen, H. H., *Die Kostümgeschichte aller Zeiten* (Knaurs Kostümbuch). Zurich, 1957.

Hartlaub, G. F., *Der Stein der Weisen*. Munich, 1959.

Hassall, W. O., *How They Lived*. Oxford, 1962.

Heim, Maurice, *La Passion d'un roi, Charles VI le fol* (1368–1422). Paris, 1955.

Huizinga, Johan, *The Waning of the Middle Ages*. London, 1963.

Hutchison, Harold F., *The Hollow Crown*. New York, 1961.

Jameson, A. B., *Legends of the Monastic Orders*. London, 1852.

Jarry, E., *Vie Politique de Louis de France, duc d'Orléans 1372–1407*. Paris, 1889.

Joergensen, Johannes, *Sainte Catherine de Sienne*. Paris, 1920.

Joudou, J. B., *Histoire des souverains pontifes qui ont siégé à Avignon*, 2 vols. Avignon, 1855.

Juvénal des Ursins, *Histoire de Charles VI, roi de France*. Paris, 1836.

Kitts, E. J., *Pope John the Twenty-third and Master John Hus of Bohemia*. London, 1910.

Labande, L. H., *Le Palais des papes*, 2 vols. Avignon, 1925.

Langlois, C. V., *La Vie en France au moyen age*, 4 vols. Paris, 1924–28.

Lavisse, Ernest, *Histoire de France* . . . 1328–1422. Tome 4e. Paris, 1902.

Lea, Henry C., *A History of the Inquisition of the Middle Ages*. New York, 1888.

Lecky, W. E., *History of European Morals*. 2 vols. New York, 1898.

Lenfant, Jacques, *Histoire du concile de Constance*. Amsterdam, 1727.

Loomis, L. R., *The Council of Constance* (translator). New York and London, 1961.

Luce, Siméon, *La France pendant la Guerre de cent ans*. Paris, 1890.

Luna, Manuel, *Don Pedro de Luna (Benedicto XIII)*. Madrid, 1903.

Maimbourg, Louis, *Histoire du Grand Schisme d'Occident*. Paris, 1686.

Mérimée, Prosper, *Notes d'un voyage dans le Midi*. Paris, 1835.

Michaud and Poujoulat, *Mémoires pour servir à l'histoire de France*. Paris, 1836.

Milman, Henry H., *History of Latin Christianity*. 9 vols. London, 1864.

Mollat, G., *Les Papes d'Avignon*, Paris, 1949. (Also English, translated by J. Love, London, 1963).

Monk of Saint-Denis, The, *Chronique*. Translated by M. L. Bellaguet. 6 vols. Paris, 1839-52.

Monstrelet, Enguerrand de, *Chronicles*. Translated by Thomas Johnes. 5 vols. Hafod Press. 1809.

Nabíl, *The Dawn-Breakers*. Translated from the Persian and edited by Shoghi Effendi. New York, 1932.

Pastor, Ludwig, *The History of the Popes*. Edited by F. I. Antrobus. London, 1891.

Pennington, A. R., *Epochs of the Papacy*. London, 1881.

Perroy, Edouard, *L'Angleterre et le Grand Schisme d'Occident*. Paris, 1933.

Pillement, Georges, *Pedro de Luna, le dernier pape d'Avignon*. Paris, 1955.

Poole, R. L., *Wycliffe and Movements for Reform*. London, New York, 1896.

Powers, George C., *Nationalism at the Council of Constance*. Washington, 1927.

Puig y Puig, Sebastían, *Pedro de Luna, Ultimo Papa de Aviñon*. Barcelona, 1920.

Quicherat, Jules. *Procès de condamnation et de réhabilitation de Jeanne d'Arc* . . . 5 vols. Paris, 1841–49.

Richental, Ulrich, *Das Konzil zu Konstanz*. Bearb. von Otto Feger. 2 vols. 1964.

310

Rocal, G., *Châteaux et manoirs*. Paris, 1938.

Rocquain, Félix, *La Cour de Rome et l'esprit de réforme avant Luther*, Vol. 3. Paris, 1897.

Roth, Cecil, A *History of the Marranos*. New York, 1959.

Rúmí, Jalálu'd-Dín, *The Mathnawí*. Translated and edited by R. A. Nicholson. Vol. 8. London, 1934.

Sa'dí, *The Gulistán*. Translated by F. Gladwin. London, 1808.

Salembier, L., *Le Grand Schisme d'Occident*. Paris, 1902.

Salles-Dabadie, J. M. A., *Les conciles oecuméniques dans l'histoire*. Paris, Geneva, 1962.

Shepherd, William, *The Life of Poggio Bracciolini*. London, 1837.

Spinka, Matthew, *Advocates of Reform*. Library of Christian Classics, Vol. XIV. London, 1953.

——, *John Hus' Concept of the Church*. Princeton, 1966.

Thibault, Marcel, *Isabeau de Bavière*. Paris, 1903.

Tilley, Arthur, *Medieval France*. Cambridge, 1922.

Trollope, T. A., A *History of the Commonwealth of Florence*. 4 vols. London, 1865.

Vallet de Viriville, *Procès de condamnation de Jeanne d'Arc*. Paris, 1867.

Valois, Noël, *La France et la Grand Schisme d'Occident*. 4 vols. Paris, 1896–1902.

Watt, W. Montgomery and Cachia, Pierre, A *History of Islamic Spain*. Garden City, N. Y., 1967.

Wylie, James H. *The Council of Constance to the Death of Hus*. London, New York, 1900.

INDEX

AL